Empowering
YOUTH
with ADHD

Your Guide to Coaching Adolescents and Young Adults
for Coaches, Parents, and Professionals

Jodi Sleeper-Triplett, MCC, SCAC

Specialty Press, Inc.
300 N.W. 70th Ave., Suite 102
Plantation, Florida 33317

Book Design and Layout: Babs Kall, Kall Graphics

Specialty Press, Inc.
300 Northwest 70th Avenue, Suite 102
Plantation, Florida 33317
(954) 792-8100 • (800) 233-9273
www.addwarehouse.com

Printed in the United States of America

ISBN 978-1-886941-96-0

Library of Congress Cataloging-in-Publication Data

Sleeper-Triplett, Jodi.
Empowering youth with ADHD : your guide to coaching adolescents and young adults for coaches, parents, and professionals / Jodi Sleeper-Triplett.
   p. cm.
Includes bibliographical references.
ISBN 978-1-886941-96-0
1. Attention-deficit disorder in adolescence–Counseling. I. Title.

RJ506.H9S57 2010

616.85'8900835–dc22

2010019995

What the Experts are saying...

With *Empowering Youth With ADHD*, Sleeper-Triplett has provided an essential, groundbreaking resource for parents, coaches, and professionals! Practical, insightful, and clearly written, this book outlines the best practices for coaching to improve attention and executive functioning in individuals with ADHD and explains the vital role of this intervention. As a professional working with children and adults with ADHD and associated conditions, I am so pleased to be able to recommend this book to the many parents and professionals struggling to help youth reach their potential and learn to manage organizational and other weaknesses. Sleeper-Triplett is a true pioneer in the coaching field and provides tremendous guidance that is both research based and clinically validated.
Laurie Dietzel, Ph.D.
Coauthor, "Late, Lost, and Unprepared: A Parents' Guide to Helping Children with Executive Functioning"

Sleeper-Triplett's wealth of experience will benefit anyone in the position of helping youth with ADHD to become empowered and overcome obstacles presented by ADHD. She presents coaching as the missing link in the current treatment models to help anyone working with youth struggling with this disorder overcome challenges. Her years of experience as a coach outline proven techniques for both professionals and parents to use to empower and promote independence in teens to live independent, fulfilling lives.
Nancy A. Ratey, Ed.M., MCC, SCAC
Author, "The Disorganized Mind: Coaching Your ADHD Brain to Take Control of Your Time, Tasks, and Talents"

In addition to supplying the essential background information, this step-by-step guide provides all of the necessary skills for establishing a successful coaching relationship with adolescents and young adults. By calling upon real-life examples and offering practical solutions, Sleeper-Triplett establishes herself as the expert in this arena of coaching.
Patricia Quinn, M.D.
Developmental pediatrician, Washington DC
Director, Center for Girls and Women With ADHD

Sleeper-Triplett has that elusive combination of heart, intelligence, energy, and spirit that have made her the pre-eminent coach and coach trainer for youth with ADHD. *With Empowering Youth With ADHD*, Sleeper-Triplett's tireless commitment to meeting the needs of this underserved population takes on a new and inspiring trajectory!
Susan Sussman, M.Ed., MCC, SCAC

This is one inspiring, informative, and impactful book, clearly and vividly written. It pierced into my soul so that I know when I follow the wisdom contained within, I will be creating a better, happier world because the youth of today become the leaders of tomorrow. After 23 years in the field, I can honestly say this book contains the clearest 360-degree description of coaching I have ever read, including my own publications. If you are curious about the where, when, how, what, why, and who of coaching adolescents and young adults with ADHD, buy it, read it, read it again, use it as a resource, and share it with everyone you know, whether or not they have ADHD.

Teri-E Belf, the world's first MCC
Director, Success Unlimited Network, LLC
Partner, Wrinkle Wisdom
Author, "Coaching With Spirit"

Empowering Youth With ADHD is a valuable resource guide for anyone seeking to learn more about coaching young people with ADHD. Whether the reader is a parent or professional who is new to coaching or an experienced coach wanting to develop more knowledge and skills to work with this population, Sleeper-Triplett's book is chock full of information and ideas to understand more about how to use coaching so adolescents and young adults with ADHD can become more self-determined.

Theresa E. Laurie Maitland Ph.D., CPCC
Coordinator, Academic Success Program for Students With LD and ADHD
University of North Carolina, Chapel Hill

Written in a clear and straightforward way by one of the true pioneers of the coaching field, this book demystifies coaching and explains in great detail everything you need to know about the coaching process. Whether you are a professional coach that wants to learn more, a parent, or a young person considering coaching, this book will be of enormous benefit to you.

Kevin Murphy, Ph.D.
The Adult ADHD Clinic of Central Massachusetts
Coauthor, "ADHD in Adults: What the Science Says"

Empowering Youth With ADHD is a must read for any educational, medical, or mental health professional committed to helping teens and young adults with ADHD.

Empowering Youth With ADHD is an exceptionally well-written, diverse volume. It is a must for all professionals.

Sleeper-Triplett's approach to coaching is reasoned and reasonable. The strategies offered in this volume can make an immense, positive difference in the lives of youth and young adults with ADHD.

Sam Goldstein, Ph.D.
Editor-in-Chief, Journal of Attention Disorders

This book will be invaluable for those wanting to learn the art of coaching teens and young adults with ADHD and for their parents. It presents a clear and compelling case for coaching as a unique and valuable bridge between the adolescent's urge toward independence and his or her ongoing need for structure and support.

Kathleen Nadeau, Ph.D.
Director, Chesapeake ADHD Center of Maryland

This book is a comprehensive resource and practical guide for coaches. It provides an in-depth focus on coaching individuals with ADHD who have deficits in executive functioning and life skills. It is a must read.

Equally valuable is that this book provides information for parents as they decide if their son or daughter needs a coach, and it informs professionals on the important role a coach can play in helping an individual with ADHD achieve success.

Larry B. Silver, M.D.
Clinical Professor of Psychiatry
Georgetown University Medical Center

Empowering Youth With ADHD provides a user friendly, practical guide to coaching for adolescents with ADHD. Sleeper-Triplett's passion for coaching as a resource to help youth with attention challenges is contagious. She describes a coaching approach that is centered on empowering youth to work from their strengths, and her approach is both respectful and warm. The book is well-organized and its conversational style makes it a pleasure to read.

Sharon Field Hoffman, Ph.D.
Professor (Clinical), Educational Leadership
Wayne State University

Empowering Youth With ADHD is an insightful look at often misunderstood challenges that our children experience. Sleeper-Triplett provides the reader with a critical and practical understanding of what a youth with ADHD lives with and how you can make a tangible difference in their lives. We don't need more theories on this subject; we need practical tools and skills—and that's what Sleeper-Triplett has successfully provided.

D. Luke Iorio
President and CEO, Institute for Professional Excellence in Coaching (iPEC)

Empowering Youth With ADHD is a book that is a must for anyone interested in the field of ADHD coaching. This book is clear, easy to read, and full of practical advice for an ADHD coach, anyone considering being an ADHD coach, a parent of a youth with ADHD who is thinking about coaching, and any professional who works with youth with ADHD. Sleeper-Triplett has always been a consummate professional in the field of ADHD coaching, doing excellent work, and this book is no exception. She says it best: "If you are inspired to enrich the lives of young people with ADHD through coaching, I hope you will join me in this movement to make a difference in the lives of many!" This book is a good first step.

Sheryl K. Pruitt, M.Ed., ET/P
Clinical director of Parkaire Consultants, educational consultant,
educational therapist, speaker
Coauthor, "Tigers, Too: Impact of Executive Functions/Speed of
Processing/Memory on Academic, Behavioral, and Social Function of
Students With ADHD, Tourette Syndrome, and OCD: Modifications and
Interventions" and "Challenging Kids, Challenged Teachers: Teaching
Students With Tourette's, Bipolar Disorder, Executive Dysfunction, OCD,
ADHD, and More"

This book undertakes the enormous task of educating a wide constituency (coaches, parents, and professionals) about coaching. Laying the foundation with a discussion of the basics of both ADHD and coaching, this book then details the steps to establishing a relationship and providing the support that is such an essential part of coaching. Sleeper-Triplett manages to give enough basic information to the parent while providing the necessary details essential to the serious professional.

The personal coaching agreement is an invaluable tool. If everyone knew how to use it, both the home and the academic fronts would benefit.

Sharon K. Weiss, M.Ed
Behavioral Consultant

Dedication

To all of my clients—past, present, and future:

Your willingness to open your hearts and minds to new possibilities, in spite of life's challenges, is an inspiration to me every day.

To my father, Alfred Sleeper (1917-1970):

Your love, generosity, and kindness live on in my heart.

Table of Contents

Acknowledgments

To all of my friends, colleagues, and clients who supported me on this journey, thank you for your encouragement, support, and positive energy.

To Nancy Ratey and Susan Sussman, your pioneering work in ADHD coaching opened the door to a career path through which I have been able to pursue my dreams. I am grateful for your guidance and friendship over the years. You are shining examples of professionalism, integrity, and excellence in our field.

To my amazing friends and cotrainers Loretta Spindel, Russell Colver, and Harriet Steinberg, who supported me both personally and professionally through the ups and downs of my creative process: I appreciate that even in the age of caller ID, you still choose to take my calls.

From book proposal to final chapters, Suzanne and Bob Murray of StyleMatters Writing Services were the perfect partners. Suzanne, your heart is as much a part of this book as mine. And many thanks to Stefanie Lazer, my copy editor, for your expert eye and fast turnaround of the final manuscript.

Certain sections of the book needed the expertise of others. David Parker, Myra Bridgforth, Rebecca Fleischer, Elisa Nebolsine, and Dee Casio, thank you for giving of your time and expertise in reviewing the section on coaching versus therapy in Chapter 1. Rick Steinberg, M.D., I owe you a huge debt of gratitude for volunteering your medical expertise in Chapter 3 and for supporting my work in ADHD coaching for youth.

To my publisher, Harvey Parker, of Specialty Press, thank you for believing in my work and stepping up to take on this project without hesitation. Thanks, too, to Babs Kall of Kall Graphics, whose attention to detail and creative designs brought my book to life. You were both a joy to work with on this project from start to finish.

Fred Glave, my brilliant advisor and mentor from SCORE DC: Your support of my work and belief in my ideas gave me the much-needed nudge to move forward.

Dana Kunzelman and Mike Johnsen, Support Teams East and West, respectively: Thank you for your willingness to go with the flow and take on tasks, large and small, to keep JST Coaching up and running.

Margo Wolcott of MW Studio designed my website and was instrumental in creating my brand. The past two years have been a roller coaster of growth and change for my company and my website, and you are always there to creatively support my endeavors. Thank you.

To my longtime friend and favorite photographer, Dale Blank, thank you for providing a second opinion and a fresh perspective as Babs and I worked on the cover art and final layout. Your eye for color and detail were of great help, and your photos of amazing sunrises, sunsets, and seascapes continue to put a smile on my face each morning.

To my mother, Barbara R. Woodward: Your love, strength, determination, and youthful heart are an inspiration to us all. I thank my sisters, Lynn Colby and Debra Olthouse, and my niece, Amy Chapin, for cheering me on during this process.

To my son, Andrew: More than once you have praised me for all that I have accomplished in my career. By far, you are my finest accomplishment. Thank you for your love and support and for sharing your creative ideas and expertise over the years. You are the best.

I give special thanks to my husband, David Triplett, for his love and support throughout my coaching career and especially during the writing process. You gave me the space to pursue my passion.

Introduction

When my son was in elementary school, I set aside one day a week to volunteer in his classroom. In the third and fourth grades, children are told that they need to learn to pay attention, stay in their seats, behave appropriately, and follow instructions. It is considered grade appropriate and age appropriate to do so. Well, anyone who understands attention deficit hyperactivity disorder (ADHD) in children knows that this is not easily accomplished and that grade and age don't equate to capability. Many times, when I arrived at my son's school to help out, certain students were identified for me to work with one-on-one outside the confines of the classroom. In effect, I was coaching the students with ADHD, learning disabilities, behavioral problems, and the like, while supporting their learning. I found myself making a connection with those students who did not get the attention needed in the classroom to achieve at the level of their peers.

One situation, in particular, stands out for me as the defining moment when I knew I wanted to become a coach for youth. Yes, it was one of those huge "aha" moments in my life and my career, and it occurred, of all times, during Thanksgiving lunch.

The iconic holiday repast was being provided in the cafeteria for students and parents. The place was a flurry of activity—groups coming in and going out; some cleaning up; and others waiting in line with their green plastic trays for the annual feast of turkey, mashed potatoes, stuffing, green beans, cranberry sauce, and gravy. Once our group got through the line, we sat at a round table: three families and one lone child, Kyle, whose parents were not able to attend. Kyle was one of my students on volunteer days, so he felt comfortable at the table.

We proceeded to dig into our meals while talking around the table. At one point, I turned to Kyle and noticed that his meal was untouched. "Kyle, aren't you hungry?" I asked, to which he responded, "Mrs. Triplett, I am starving, but there is so much to choose from and so much going on today with everyone here visiting that I don't know where to begin." At that point, I "walked" around the plate with Kyle.

"Do you like the roll?" I asked.

"Yes," he replied.

"Okay, how about a Thanksgiving sandwich?" I inquired.

"Wow," he said, "how do I make that?"

Together, we identified all of the things on the plate that Kyle liked: turkey, stuffing, potatoes, and cranberries. Kyle piled them all on the roll and inhaled his Thanksgiving sandwich.

Imagine how many Kyle's missed out on lunch that day. What else were these children missing every day at school, at home, or with peers? At that moment, I knew that I wanted to help youth with ADHD and decided to focus my coaching on this population. Through coaching, I have seen many children, adolescents, and young adults move forward in their lives with greater confidence, increased self-esteem, and a skill set to support them now and in the future. This is one of the reasons I believe so strongly in coaching and have dedicated my time to bringing coaching youth with ADHD into the mainstream.

I am driven as well by the fact that I have seen how powerful coaching can be in my own life. I truly believe that everyone can benefit from coaching, and, in fact, I would not have written this book if it were not for the support of a life coach. I had thought about writing a book, weighing my decision, or lack thereof, in a cocoon. Through coaching, I had the opportunity to share my ideas in a safe space, voice my trepidations and my excitement, and garner the energy to move forward. Receiving unconditional support from a coach truly made a difference.

Although the success I've been fortunate to experience over the years sometimes looks like it came easily, I have not accomplished it in a bubble. Every time I find myself wanting to try something new or different in my life, I hire a coach. In the process, I secure invaluable support, discover new perspectives, and find fresh motivation and courage to go for the goals that are important to me. Having seen what a huge driver of success coaching can be in my own life, I can't help but want to spend my time sharing this empowering process with other people. When the timing is right, coaching can and will change your life or the life of someone you care about!

Slowly but surely, general knowledge and awareness of the merits of coaching are starting to move into the mainstream. First, executive coaching arrived on the scene to help corporate leaders maximize their success in the business arena. Then, as it became clear that coaching had the capacity to help people reach goals in all areas of their lives, not just the professional domain, life coaching emerged—and not just for executives, but for all adults who had an interest in seeking a new or different life for themselves. Over time, coaching for youth started to trickle into the world of possibilities, along with coaching for young people with ADHD. This is where we find ourselves today, in a time period with an ever-increasing awareness that coaching can be added to the care plan for young people with ADHD and that coaching can help all young people get off to a strong start in the world.

Although much is left to be done in terms of spreading the word regarding the power of coaching for young people, including those with ADHD, I have seen great strides being taken toward public awareness since the time I first began knocking on doors 14 years ago to let people know about the possibilities inherent in ADHD coaching. In the years that have followed since I first pioneered my work in this field, ADHD coaching for young people has been made available throughout the United States and Canada and is gaining attention in many countries around the world. It is my great hope that this book will make another positive contribution to the movement to bring ADHD coaching to more young people who could benefit.

Why Is the World Abuzz With Talk of Coaching?

Many times each year, I have the opportunity to speak locally and nationally to parents and professionals and to provide informational interviews for radio, TV, and print media focused on ADHD coaching for youth. It is not uncommon afterward for an overwhelmed parent to rush up to me or contact me with a story about his or her own child, inquiring as to how the young person could benefit from coaching and how to find a good coach.

Parents get excited about the possibility of something new to help their children with ADHD because parents are often tired, frustrated, or heartbroken at watching their children suffer and feel hopeless. Although coaching is a relatively new field, it is not a passing fad or an alluring but empty solution. Coaching is special and different. Built on solid principles, coaching is also very real and effective.

One of the things that makes coaching so appealing is the sense of partnership and equality that occurs between the coach and the client. Unlike doctor–patient or therapist–client relationships, which tend to have a sense of hierarchy to them, even when the doctor or therapist has a wonderful manner and treats the patient or client with great respect, the coaching relationship is meant to be balanced and without hierarchy. The coach does not wear a mantle of power; the power is in the coaching process and in the partnership built on mutual trust and respect. Whereas someone wouldn't likely go out for a cup of coffee with one's doctor or therapist, the collaborative nature of coaching makes it altogether possible for coach and client to connect at the café.

From this reality, another characteristic that makes coaching appealing emerges. Clients can meet their coaches out for coffee, in public view—or can comfortably say to a friend, "I'm going to meet with my coach tomorrow"—because the field of coaching does not tend to carry a stigma with it. Right or wrong, desirable or undesirable, people are oftentimes more willing to disclose that they are working with a coach than that they are working with a therapist or a psychiatrist. As I share later in the book, coaching is not at all a replacement for therapy and should not be billed as such by coaches, nor should it be a false label through which therapists can try to attract clients. Coaching serves a different need and purpose than therapy, as discussed in depth in Chapter 1; nonetheless, the fact that coaching tends not to carry a stigma with it is a reality that can be used to some advantage by coaches and clients.

Coaching is also incredibly flexible, which makes it an exciting option for many people. The sky is the limit in terms of what people can focus on in coaching: losing weight, planning a trip around the world, turning a hobby into a career, or creating a home environment that's organized. All a person needs is a realistic goal and a willingness to work toward that goal, and a coach can be there to support the individual. And for all of the goals that people have that they've been unable to accomplish —getting a new job or starting to exercise, for example—coaching can offer the jump start that people crave. In coaching, individuals get to do things their own way—on the basis of their own skills, strengths, and comfort zone—but with the support of a qualified coach to help along the way.

As the coaching field has evolved, those of us working with young people with ADHD have discovered that there are some really good ways to adjust coaching methods to work effectively with this population. Now, in addition to medication, tutoring, and therapy, coaching can be added to the treatment possibilities of young people with ADHD. When all of the pieces of the ADHD puzzle are addressed—from adjustment of brain chemistry to strengthening of skills and acquisition of strategies—young people with ADHD can begin to see light in their lives and to unlock their ability to go after their dreams.

Who Should Read This Book?

When I first started writing this book, I spent a good deal of time considering whom to include in the book's audience. Certainly, I wanted the book to be of assistance to anyone interested in becoming an ADHD coach for young people, whether that someone was transitioning from a different line of work into coaching or adding this niche to his or her already existent coaching practice. But I also wanted to reach out to any individual who wanted to learn more about ADHD coaching for young people, whether that be a family member who was searching for ways to help a young person with ADHD live a better life or a professional who sees clients with ADHD from time to time and would like to know a little more about coaching.

As a result, I did my very best to design a book that speaks to the full range of readers interested in learning more about ADHD coaching: coaches (new, experienced, or in transition), parents, teachers, medical professionals, psychologists, school counselors, and more. If you work with or support young people with ADHD in some capacity in your work or life, this book has the potential to be a powerful resource for you.

Young people, too, can read this book to learn more about how the coaching process can be helpful to them and to consider whether coaching is right for them. Coaching promises a collaborative process in which the young person is in control of his or her choices and future. For those young people interested in pursuing coaching, this book can provide a better idea of what to expect before engaging in coaching.

Because the focus of this book is coaching, the text focuses in large part on— you guessed it— coaching! As a result, coaches and anyone who hopes to become a coach will likely find that the text speaks to them, line by line, from start to finish. Parents who want to know more about coaching as a treatment option available to their sons or daughters with ADHD or hoping to learn more about what coaching is as they enter into this new process with their child can also find useful information packed into the entirety of the book.

Professionals who have the time to read this book from cover to cover can also benefit from a complete reading. In particular, such readers are likely to gain a clear picture of what a qualified coach looks like and how he or she practices, as the book covers everything from the definition of coaching to coaching ethics to the typical stages of the coaching process. For those professionals or noncoaches who would like to simply get an overview of coaching, I've included a section at the end of every major chapter called A Note for Everyone. This section summarizes the material from the given chapter and highlights issues relevant to the wider reading audience.

These same readers may also enjoy selecting certain chapters to read on the basis of their particular interests.

- *Those new to coaching* might appreciate Chapter 1, which defines coaching, youth coaching, and ADHD youth coaching and explores the differences between coaching and therapy, along with Chapter 2, which fleshes out the role of the coach.

- *Those interested in understanding more about why coaching works* might enjoy reading Chapter 6 on motivation, Chapter 7 on support and structure, and Chapter 8 on skills and strategies, as these chapters give insight into how things like incentives, accountability, support, structure, and skill building work together in coaching to help a young person make progress toward goal completion.

- *Those familiar with ADHD coaching in a general sense* but who want to be better prepared to tell clients what to expect when they get referred to a coach might be interested in reading some of the more practical chapters, such as Chapter 4 on prescreening; Chapter 5 on the intake session; and Chapter 7, which covers the personal coaching agreement in addition to the previously mentioned support and structure. If you are interested in learning more about ADHD coaching for young people, there is likely something in this book for you. If you are a coach or a professional, you may also want to keep a copy of the book on hand to share with the families who inquire about coaching.

This Book Can Help You...

Coaches

- Assess whether you'd like to work with youth with ADHD
- Learn the basics of ADHD coaching for youth
- Discover the skills and techniques to build a successful coaching business
- Become better able to make referrals when your adult coaching clients start talking about their children

Parents

- Gain a better understanding of the coaching process: what to expect and how it works
- Identify your potential role in the coaching process
- Learn more about what makes a coach qualified
- Reduce your concerns and skepticism about coaching

Professionals

- Find out what coaching can provide to your clients
- Discover how you can partner with coaches in support of young people with ADHD
- Learn more about what makes a coach qualified
- Gain information on the coaching process to share with your curious clients

As you will discover while reading this book, I believe that young people with ADHD have all of the potential they need inside of them. Coaches, parents, and allied professionals are in a position to help young people realize that potential—not by doing things for them but by empowering them to draw on their strengths and gifts and develop into their best selves!

Helping Adolescents Versus Young Adults

As noted in this book's title, the guidance provided over the course of this book applies to supporting adolescents with ADHD as well as young adults with ADHD. By *adolescents*, I am referring to young people aged 13–18 years, who are typically in their middle school, junior high, or high school years. By *young adults,* I am referring to young people aged 18–25 years, some of whom may be attending college, others of whom may be working, post–high school or without having completed high school.

Although we as a society tend to see these two age groups as being distinctly different (think of your mental image of a 16-year-old teenager versus a 20-year-old college student), the maturity we see in young people is not necessarily pegged to chronological age or age group. This is particularly true in young people with ADHD, who may have missed out on important socialization opportunities or emotional development over the years because of their challenges related to ADHD. It is incredibly important when supporting these young people that we remember to meet each individual where he or she is and not to make assumptions about how mature, advanced, or skilled the individual should be given his or her particular chronological age.

To put this into practical terms, I'll share that I've had young adults come to me for coaching who have successfully graduated college but who have had far fewer social skills than some adolescents. On the flip side, I've worked with some adolescents who are socially on par or even more socially adept than their peers while they still struggle with executive functioning challenges in organization and time management that impede their progress in other areas of life. Instead of looking at age, what's most important is for us to assess factors such as emotional intelligence, cognitive ability (or disability), and coexisting conditions. Instead of trying to put one-size-fits-all expectations onto young people or expecting one child to perform exactly as another because they are in the same age bracket, we have to look at the impact of ADHD, learning disabilities, and coexisting conditions on young people to get a clear handle on where they are in their development and what kind of support they really need. As result, the question isn't, When is (or was) the young person's 18th birthday? The question is, What is (and was) going on for the young person now (and in the past)?

As a result of the need for this flexible approach across age ranges, there really aren't any prescriptions that can be made for working with adolescents versus young adults. Each young person needs to be assessed individually. That being said, in cases where the guidance in this book may vary depending on the client's maturity level and abilities, I will make mention of the different considerations to be kept in mind when working with those of lesser or greater maturity level, ability, and readiness.

Vision for This Book

This book is based, in part, on my International Coach Federation-approved training course, Coaching Teens & College Students With ADHD. This training course is the first of its kind worldwide, and I have had the honor of teaching individuals in the United States, Canada, Denmark, Honduras, Israel, Japan, Norway, South Africa, Switzerland, the Netherlands, Tunisia, and United Arab Emirates. I have also had the pleasure of training counselors, teachers, and support staff in public school systems, colleges, and universities around the United States. In writing this book, I hope to share the best of the knowledge I have gained over the years in working with young people with ADHD, listening to what these young people have to say, observing the techniques and strategies they most respond to, talking to parents and professionals who know this group very well, and staying abreast of the leading research being put out by scientists.

My greatest vision for this book is to open the door to the future for young people with ADHD through a coaching model that works. ADHD coaching is a solid option for young people that deserves more attention than it currently receives. In addition, my hopes for this book include the following:

- encourage more people to learn how to coach this population

- explain what coaches can and cannot do for clients

- discuss the boundaries of coaching to promote ethical and professional conduct by all coaches

- bring allied professionals into the multimodal treatment camp; we *can* all work together for the benefit of young people with ADHD through this collaborative process!

Ever since I helped Kyle build his Thanksgiving sandwich in the midst of the noise and craziness of a festive school lunch, I've known I wanted to make a difference in the lives of young people with ADHD. I am honored to be able to share this book with you in hopes of spreading the news about ADHD coaching for youth a little bit farther and a little bit wider. May you and your clients or loved ones have the occasion to experience firsthand the power of coaching and to encounter the ways in which coaching can help young people with ADHD blossom into the successful adults they were meant to be.

O N E

Why Coaching for Adolescents and Young Adults?

When I meet people for the first time and tell them about coaching for adolescents, I sometimes get "the look." The look can consist of a crinkled nose, wide eyes, a furrowed brow, or a tilted head—any combination of facial expressions that convey a person's complete confusion, maybe even bewilderment. Sometimes the look is quickly followed by a "huh?" or the more polite, "That sounds nice. Um, remind me again—what is coaching?" As a relatively new field, coaching is still unknown to a fair number of people. In fact, many of the parents who speak with me say that they have heard of sports coaching but know nothing about this thing called life coaching. Those who do know of life coaching have only heard of it being used with adults. Coaching youth? That's a whole new idea to most people.

Thus, this chapter is dedicated to defining coaching for young people. It describes coaching for youth in a general sense, as well as within a context of supporting young people with ADHD. For readers who are keen on learning more about the coaching process and how it can be helpful to young people, this chapter offers definitions, insight, and clarification. For readers who know of coaching but are skeptical about its value for young people, this chapter reveals why and how coaching can be so useful to adolescents and young adults. For coaches already working with young people, this chapter provides information for self-education as well as for educating readers' current and future clients.

Coaching Young People—What a Concept!

The what, why, and how of coaching have been tossed around, discussed, and debated for many years. As just touched on, parents often know what athletic coaching is and sometimes executive coaching, too—they may have even heard of life coaching for adults—but they often don't know about life coaching for youth. The idea of putting young people in the driver's seats of their own lives—before they are adults—is a foreign concept to many people.

There are also understandably confused professionals, who may have heard of coaching but who often see it as doing the work of therapists and thus hesitate to refer. They may think, Why refer someone to a coach when he or she can be referred to an actual therapist? As discussed in this chapter, coaching is different from therapy. Finally, those parents and professionals who do know about coaching for young people often don't know how to find a qualified coach or are unaware of what "qualified" really means in the field of coaching. The confusion, despite coaching's 20-year history—not even taking into account the years before it was called coaching—still outweighs the understanding of coaching as a valuable tool for effecting positive change in adolescents and young adults.

The coaching of young people is built on the same core principles as the coaching of adults. So let's begin with an exploration of what coaching is, in general. The leading professional association for individuals in the coaching profession, the International Coach Federation, defines coaching as "partnering with clients in a thought-provoking and creative process that inspires them to maximize their personal and professional potential." This definition applies regardless of type of coaching (executive coaching, life coaching, or ADHD coaching) or age (adults, young adults, and adolescents).

Coaching 101

Although the focus of the present book is on coaching youth with ADHD, a clear understanding of the multiple kinds of coaching in existence can be useful because there is some overlap among these types. Under the larger umbrella of *coaching* are *executive coaching* and *life coaching*. Executive coaching typically refers to an engagement between coach and client regarding issues in the work setting or professional domain. Life coaching generally relates to clients who seek support and partnership in achieving goals outside of work or inclusive of all of the life domains: personal, professional, and otherwise. And, of course, there is some overlap between executive and life coaching, because people are rarely able to completely separate work from life.

Distinctions between executive and life coaching are often made to highlight the key focus of the client and coach's work together—largely professional goals versus personal goals—or the context in which the coaching is taking place (e.g., sometimes sponsored by one's workplace vs. initiated on one's own). Although executive coaching is provided only to an adult audience given its relationship to the professional domain, life coaching can be provided to both adults and young people.

In addition to executive and life coaching, there is ADHD coaching, which can be offered to both adults and young people. ADHD coaching is built on the core fundamentals of life coaching but also involves some differences from life coaching, such as a higher level of accountability and a greater focus on building skills and strategies. Figure 1 depicts some of the most common forms of coaching available today.

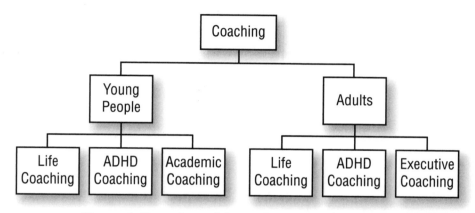

Figure 1. Overview of the major types of coaching.

As shown in Figure 1, coaching can be provided to both young people and adults; applied to the work or the personal context; and used to manage ADHD, academics, or one's holistic life goals.

The Nuts and Bolts of Coaching

Now let's look at the nitty-gritty of what coaching is, regardless of age of client or context, because as I mentioned earlier, there is common ground among all types of coaching. Coaching consists of a collaboration between client and coach to help the client move forward with his or her agenda, whether it be general (e.g., feel more satisfied with life, fit in better at school, enjoy work more, experience less daily stress) or specific (e.g., find more time for family, earn a job promotion, get accepted into college, or develop a healthy lifestyle). Coaching involves a free-flowing, creative process driven by the client and supported by the coach. Ultimately, a trained coach will use his or her skill to evoke thought in the client and encourage the client to identify goals, as well as the actions that need to be taken to reach those goals.

Thus, the coaching process offers a useful time and space for brainstorming options, exploring next steps, and engaging in simple coaching exercises to help the client become more confident and motivated to achieve goals. In addition, coaching may involve accountability check-ins that provide the client with an opportunity to receive support, report progress, and share successes along the way. The sum experience for the client is a supportive environment in which he or she can explore new options and have a partner on the journey toward developing the life he or she wants. Figure 2 below outlines the core phases in coaching and provides a visual overview of the coaching process.

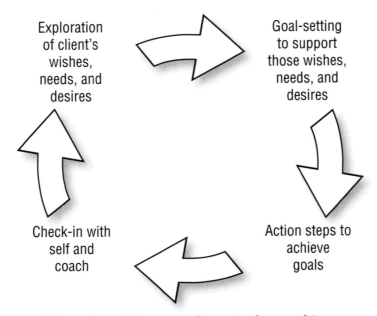

Figure 2. Overview of the core phases in the coaching process.
© 2010 Jodi Sleeper-Triplett

The exploration process that helps a client verbalize his or her agenda and identify supportive goals (i.e., exploration and goal-setting phases) can be done using a variety of coaching tools, such as storytelling, generating a vision, or identifying one's values. For example, in the case of storytelling, the coach might request, "Describe the happiest you've ever been" or "Tell me about your best vacation." In the realm of creating a vision, the coach might ask, "Where do you see yourself in five years?" or the coach might invite the client to "create a vision of yourself being healthy and happy." To engage in values exploration, the coach might ask the client, "What's really important to you?" Regardless of the tool, the coach provides the client with an opportunity to explore his or her wishes for life so that the client can move forward in a way that is truly reflective of his or her unique desires, personality, and needs. This approach applies to the many types of coaching, whether

- in *executive coaching*, where a client might be prompted to identify a vision for the effective leader he or she hopes to become

- in *life coaching*, where a client might discover that he or she wants to explore a new career path

- in *ADHD coaching,* where a client might set a goal of learning skills required to succeed in the workplace.

Regardless of the type of coaching or the age of the client, the coaching process is designed to put the client at the center of his or her own experience: to empower the client to find a path to an agenda reflective of his or her own needs, desires, and interests and then to design a plan for achieving that agenda in a way that feels and works best for the client.

The What, Why, and How of Coaching for Young People

In reality, there is very little difference between coaching young people and coaching adults. In both cases, the coach works with the individual to help him or her make progress toward designing a "picture" of that person's wishes and then developing and achieving goals in support of that picture. An adult in life coaching might discover that she wants to join a women's group, spend more quality time with her spouse, and spend less time in the office. A teenager in life coaching might discover he wants to try out for a sports team, get a part-time job, and make new friends. In each case, the issues differ, but the overall coaching process will be similar, following along the lines described earlier in the chapter.

The "Aha" That Young People Can Lead the Way

The biggest difference between coaching for young people and coaching for adults is that for most young people, the coaching process may represent their first experience making independent life choices. In coaching, the young person really does get to be the one in charge. Parents of clients may have trouble accepting this reality because, as parents, they are used to making decisions for their children and telling them what to do. The young person, too, may find it hard to believe that an adult—the coach—would really let him or her take the lead. It's the job of the coach to help the young person understand that the process isn't about the coach giving advice to the young person or pushing mom or dad's agenda but instead about providing the young person with an opportunity to discern answers to questions like "What do you want to do now and in the future?" and "What are your visions and dreams?"

When I ask questions like these to young clients for the first time, they often look at me with an expression of shock on their faces. "What do you mean I get to decide?" they seem to wonder or outright ask. "I get to choose?" Most young people are so used to their parents or other adults telling them what to do, when to do it, and how to do it—or at least giving plenty of directive support and feedback—that they find it hard to believe an adult would sincerely be leaving decisions up to them.

It takes time, but eventually young people discover that the coaching relationship is different from what they've known until now. The coach is not the parent; the coach is not the teacher, the advisor, or the band director. The coach does not have a predetermined agenda for the client or hidden goals. Instead, the coach is there entirely to support the client in pursuit of whatever unique goals the client selects for him or herself. Here is an example of a conversation between coach and client that reveals how a coach directs the young person to consider his or her own goals, rather than those of the parents.

A Coaching Dialogue: Inviting Clients to Lead the Way

Coach: What career paths have you thought about?

Client: Well, my parents are lawyers, and I know they want me to do that so I should probably go to law school.

Coach: I would like to request that you put your parents' wishes aside for a moment. What is it that you would like to do?

Client: Hmmmm…I never thought about it before.

Coach: As we've discussed, coaching is about you and your choices. What types of careers are you curious about? What might you want to explore?

Client: Well, I really like working outside. I wonder what types of careers let you do that.

Coach: Hmmmm…Are you willing to check out outdoor career opportunities this week and bring your discoveries to our next coaching session?

The coach helps the client ask what the client really wants so he or she can move beyond the "should's" of the adult world toward a life that is reflective of the client's own needs and desires. Over time, the client becomes used to this process of being asked to formulate his or her own ideas and plans and grows comfortable with it. The client's trust in the coach is likely to increase, and the client's own ability to start reflecting on what the client wants for him or herself tends to deepen as well. Meanwhile, parents adjust to their new, less directive role and learn to communicate with their maturing children more effectively.

The Fundamentals of Coaching Young People

Coaches work with young people to help them identify their own goals, dreams, and vision for the future. Counter to some parents' or even young clients' expectations, the coach does not control the coaching plan. Instead, the coach supports and monitors the success of the plan. Coaching is an inquiry-based process such that the coach doesn't decide the agenda or the action items. Whatever agenda emerges from the client's responses, the coach stands behind the client and that agenda.

Most often the coaching process begins with an initial two-hour intake session, which is similar to the intake session in adult coaching with the exception of parents being present. During the intake, the coach asks background questions to learn more about the client and offers powerful, open-ended questions to get to the heart of the client's values, goals, and desires. As the process unfolds, the coach and client create a personal coaching agreement, which contains the client's goal/s and lays out client-generated action steps for success. Oftentimes, young clients want to focus on specific short-term goals during coaching (e.g., get a B in history or sign up for football tryouts). These goals may help the client to become more confident and develop the readiness for loftier, long-term goals that may not have seemed possible at the start of the coaching relationship. As the client progresses, he or she is likely to expand goals, achieve more success, get a feel for independent thinking, and develop a comfortable, trusting relationship with a coach.

As in coaching with adults, the young client sets the agenda for the coaching process, while the coach elicits information to clarify and identify the details of the client's agenda and the plan for how to reach the client's goals. Thus, when working with the young client, the coach is careful not to redirect the coaching toward an agenda that has been predetermined by the parents or one that the coach views as a better alternative for the client.

It is also up to the coach to listen carefully to questions, concerns, and feelings that might get in the way of the client's path toward the agreed-upon goals. For example, the client may set a goal to learn how to ski, only to find out that skiing is cost prohibitive at this time in his or her life. (Note that questions related to the feasibility of the clients' goals are posed during the coaching process.) The client chooses instead to put the goal of learning to ski on the back burner and to find a more affordable option (e.g., taking up tennis or running). In addition, the coach will listen for any hesitation that might be coming from the young client due to lack of skill or knowledge of how to go after the selected goal and then respond by encouraging the client to explore what it might take to increase skill or knowledge in order to accomplish the goal.

Imagine a young person interested in pursuing a career in graphic design. What might that career look like? What type of work does this particular young person envision doing each day? What excites the young person about the field of graphic design? How might he or she move forward toward this goal starting today? What might stop the young person from pursuing this goal? These are the kind of questions that the coaching process will help the client ask and answer.

A useful way for coaches to structure their questioning for clients would be to follow the sequence posed by Sir John Whitmore in *Coaching for Performance*, which he calls the GROW model:

- **G**OAL-setting for the session as well as short and long term
- **R**EALITY checking to explore the current situation
- **O**PTIONS and alternative strategies or courses of action
- **W**HAT is to be done, WHEN, by WHOM, and the WILL to do it.

The GROW model is easy to use and draws upon basic coaching principles in a structured manner that is useful for adolescents and young adults. The goal when using this model in coaching is to provide an opportunity for clients to discuss and consider their options, as well as to explore the risks, the benefits, and the ensuing questions that come up through powerful questioning by the coach and increased learning and self-awareness in the client.

As mentioned previously, most young people are accustomed to being told what to do by adults. The coaching partnership opens up a door to a new kind of relationship that offers support and encouragement without pressure and that, in turn, fosters the growth of the client. When parents and allied professionals understand the core of coaching and allow the coaching process to unfold, these parents and professionals typically report an increased level of communication with and self-satisfaction within the young person. This does not negate the benefits of good parenting or therapeutic intervention when warranted. Rather, it is an opportunity to consider expanding the choices available for an adolescent who has a desire and a readiness to move forward in a manner that is more independent and goal oriented than is currently the case. By engaging a coach, the young person attains a new outlet for self-growth—one that doesn't focus on emotional issues as therapy would do and one that doesn't focus solely on academic issues as would be the case with tutoring.

Instead, the client can work on free-flowing ideas, goals, and dreams within a structure that nonetheless keeps those ideas realistic and intact. Coaches who watch a client write out goals will see the positive impact of goal-setting on motivation. Coaches who conduct a reality check and discuss options with clients provide support to those young clients, many of whom do not yet have a good concept of the benefits that can be realized by setting realistic and attainable goals. Coaches can create a plan for the steps to be taken and notice how easily the plan becomes more realistic for the client when the action steps are small, reasonable, compelling, and personalized. For example, a client wants to run in a marathon. She brainstorms the action steps with the coach, including getting a medical clearance from her doctor, breaking in her new running shoes, and scheduling incrementally aggressive training over the next six months.

Coaching supports young clients by providing structure, skills, and strategies for success. In coaching, the client is being empowered to make decisions, ask questions, and ponder the consequences, both positive and negative, of their choices. The client does, in fact, always have a choice, and the coach works from the premise that changing one's mind and making a different choice is always an option. Consider the college add/drop period available to all students, in which students can change their minds by withdrawing from one class and signing up for another. Young adults need the same freedom to select their goals and then to change their minds. Coaches can thus remind clients frequently that it is okay to make changes and that the coach will be available to brainstorm new ideas, explore new choices, and help the client stay on track with short- and long-term goals.

It's also important to note that not all adolescents and young adults are ready for the coaching process; in addition, roadblocks may pop up for those clients who are struggling with ADHD and related issues. Also of note, there will be a gap in the maturity level from one adolescent to the next. One young person might talk about the pressure of going off to college and how he's not sure that leaving for college is really what he wants to do. Being at home, being with friends, finding a job, and being in a familiar environment might be the things that are most important to him. "Flying the coop" is not the first priority. Now take a look at another young person, who might be the same age but a few years ahead in maturity and who embraces the idea of heading off to college, meeting new people, living independently, and forging a future in a field of interest that has already started to bubble in her head and heart, creating excitement about what lies ahead.

These are two very different adolescents—neither one is better or worse than the other. Their goals are simply different, their levels of independence are different, and their peer groups are likely different. Coaches have the opportunity to work with both types of adolescents to help them go after what they want in life and to assist them in creating a clearer picture of what they hope the future will hold. The goals may be different for each client and the desires may shift during the goal-setting and coaching, but the result will, one hopes, be the same—discovery for the adolescent or young adult of how to pursue a comfortable, successful, and self-directed path.

Why Coach Adolescents and Young Adults?

What is the value of providing coaching services to young people? Can youth really benefit from coaching given their age? And, if so, why should a parent pay a coach to work with the young person instead of doing the coaching him or herself? For those of you shaking your heads and throwing up your hands, I encourage you to keep reading. It's okay if you don't get it yet. As I mentioned at the beginning of the chapter, even after all of the years that I have been coaching, I still get quizzical looks followed by the question of "Why do you coach adolescents and young adults?" when I talk about my career. Of course, I am heartened by the fact that just as many people respond to my work with "Wow! That's fabulous. Do you have a business card?" or "How can I do that?"

Skepticism aside, maybe you do get it and can intuitively sense that coaching is something of value for young people. Maybe you see the need in your own children or in other children you know or support. You may think of it from your own perspective, such as, "What if I had been offered coaching when I was in high school or college? What difference would that have made in my life?"

Whether you are looking for some persuasion that coaching for young people is of value or you simply need some concrete talking points to share with those interested in coaching for young people, here are some of the potential benefits of this service to adolescents and young adults. Coaching can help young people do the following:

- identify areas of difficulty and frustration and develop a program for success

- set and attain goals and do so with minimal stress

- increase self-confidence and self-esteem

- learn self-advocacy skills

- create and maintain a healthy lifestyle
- develop techniques for increased focus and concentration
- improve time management and planning skills
- learn strategies for creating a positive, supportive environment
- build skills in all areas of life
- receive ongoing support and encouragement
- maximize productivity at home, at school, or in the workplace
- create a greater sense of balance and fulfillment in life.

Coaching provides young people with the potential for many positive changes in their lives, depending on their particular needs and desires, in the same way that coaching for adults does. As the young person engages in coaching, he or she develops action-oriented plans, greater awareness, structure and support, a new perspective on life, empowerment and self-awareness, strategies for success, exciting opportunities for growth and change, and an upward spiral toward life goals. In short, the young person acquires a whole toolkit of skills, strategies, perspectives, and resources that can be carried wherever he or she goes—at school, at home, at the after-school job, and beyond high school or college graduation.

Judy, the Soccer Player: A Story of Successful Teen Coaching

Judy was a freshman in high school when she first came to coaching. She had a good sense of what she wanted—to get her parents off her back, spend less time on schoolwork, and find more time to play soccer. Up to this point, Judy's parents had managed her schedule and checked her daily assignments because Judy's inattentiveness and distractibility led to late assignments, poor study habits, and missed soccer practices. She would often lose track of time, procrastinate on her homework, or forget her cleats. Now that she was in high school, Judy wanted to be more independent, and her parents were in agreement. They did not want to micromanage Judy but had not been successful in shifting more responsibilities to Judy.

The coaching relationship was valuable for Judy and for her parents. Judy had an opportunity to build skills to enable her to reach her goals without being totally reliant on her parents. Judy's parents found value in the coaching because they were able to step back from the day-to-day nagging and interact in a more positive way with Judy. At first, it was a bit tough to make the transition, and there were some missteps along the way. For example, Judy got better at completing her assignments on her laptop but frequently forgot to grab the work off the printer and take it to school. She and her coach brainstormed ideas to remedy this problem, and once Judy got into the routine, she rarely forgot her work.

A feeling of success built up over time and Judy continued to be more independent, taking the opportunity to partner with her coach to stay on track, learn new skills, and develop good habits. By the start of sophomore year, Judy had found more time to play soccer, thus improving her skills and earning herself a spot on the junior varsity team. Judy had also become more independent, checking in with her parents once or twice a week to go over her schedule and to talk about academic progress and pitfalls without the parental pressure that she had felt in the past.

Teens and young adults are in a unique time in their lives, at the crossroads between childhood and adulthood, which can make coaching not just helpful but also, for some young people, fundamental to their growth. Can most teens and young adults make it on their own without coaching? Certainly. But coaching tends to help them make the transition from childhood to adulthood more smoothly and more effectively. This is because coaching provides young people with a structured, supportive, and safe place to ponder, practice, and acquire the skills and strategies needed to be ready for life's challenges, whether they involve figuring out how to interact with an unfair school teacher, save up money to buy a car, bounce back from getting cut from the school play, or deal with a classroom bully.

As they mature, adolescents increasingly find themselves in situations in which they must make decisions on their own, whether because they are naturally pulling away from their parents or because their life is taking them down a new road. Coaching can serve as a sort of safety net under these adolescents while they test out their "new legs" and figure out how to navigate life with less and less input and direct guidance from their parents. For those in college, the ties to mom and dad have, in large part, already been cut. Thus, coaching becomes a sort of home base to which these young adults can return time and again as they attempt to handle the huge raft of responsibilities they now face—from getting along with roommates, to balancing academics and social life, to staying on top of money matters, to living far from family and childhood friends.

You might think of your own journey in your younger years and how it may have taken several years, perhaps the proverbial hard way, to learn the life strategies and skills you now have. Rather than leaving things to chance or to ad hoc learning, the coaching process provides young people with an intentional means of acquiring the skills that will prepare them for life.

Why Coach the Adolescent Rather Than the Parent?

Decisions, decisions. Parent coaching or youth coaching? Which choice is right for you, your child, or—if you are a coach—your client? When I first started coaching several years ago, I took time to investigate the options. I asked myself, what direction seemed to best serve the parents and young people who crossed my path? For the first couple of years, I engaged in a mixture of parent, youth, and family coaching based on the age of the child and the needs of the family. Parent coaching (in which I worked exclusively with the parent) worked well for those who had young children. Family coaching (in which I worked together with parent/s and their children) was effective in cases in which families were experiencing difficulties with time management and organizational systems and needed strategies for effective daily living. Yet, with time, I discovered that when the child was over the age of 12 years, there was a real value in coaching the young person directly and without parents in attendance.

When narrowing in on the most effective coaching for adolescents and young adults, I steadily discovered that providing a confidential, supportive environment in which young people could explore options, express frustration, and practice new skills was the way to go. For the most part, young people do not like to be told what to do by adults. They want to be independent and make choices; this is a natural part of the growth and maturation process. By bringing in a coach who can support the young person's agenda without any parental pressure and by giving the parent some space to step a bit further back in the picture, coaches can help free up the young person's energy from battling or resisting the parent and direct it instead toward making real progress toward managing and cultivating one's life.

Sure, parents are still involved in the lives of their children. That is to be expected, and coaches are strongly encouraged to tell their young clients that the coaching does not replace parenting and that coaching is not designed to help clients get their way all the time. Parents need to understand that the coach is not stripping them of their parental role but rather enhancing their relationship with their child by shifting the accountability for their adolescent to the coaching process. When parents are able to let the coach and adolescent build a partnership to foster independence and confidence outside of the parental parameters, parents will be able to watch how the young person begins to mature.

A typical scenario for youth coaching follows, which helps illustrate the value of coaching for young people. Dean was a 15-year-old adolescent who had trouble keeping his things organized. As a result, he was always losing his cell phone and leaving his personal belongings around the house. Dean's parents, in contrast, had excellent organizational skills and had a tendency to be short-tempered with Dean whenever he misplaced anything. They would then expect Dean to organize himself precisely as they had instructed. Not surprisingly, Dean would fail repeatedly at the tasks his parents set for him, and, in general, he would not be able to stay organized to his parents' liking.

Dean decided in one of his coaching sessions to discuss his frustration with his parents and explained to the coach that his parents' way of organizing did not work for him. Together, the coach and Dean reviewed his learning style and his skill level and identified where skill building would be valuable. They set up a plan for getting organized in a way that "clicked" for him and agreed on a system for weekly accountability between Dean and the coach. Dean kept his parents in the loop by checking in with them regularly, and they agreed to allow time for his skills to improve.

Coaching directly benefited Dean in a number of ways:

1. Dean was able to express his concerns and his frustration to an impartial party, the coach.

2. Dean had a partner in the process who understood his learning differences and his organizational issues, thus allowing for a more relaxed environment for learning.

3. Dean worked independently with his coach to build skills, becoming more confident and self-reliant in the process.

4. Dean's parents were able to step back and watch his progress in a supportive manner instead of being in a confrontational "just do it" mode.

5. Dean received praise and recognition for his efforts from the coach and from his parents, such that he was able to experience success in an area that had previously been one of failure.

Adolescents and young adults often find themselves increasingly in charge of their own lives while simultaneously being pressured to maneuver through an environment largely ruled by adults. Coaching offers young people a unique bridge from youth to adulthood, where they are invited to create their own rules while in a supportive, trusting, and nonjudgmental relationship with an adult.

The Ongoing Debate: How Does Coaching Differ From Therapy?

How is coaching different from therapy? This is the $20,000 question! Is coach simply a term that can be used to attract more clients into a therapeutic setting without scaring them off or overwhelming them? Is the emerging field of coaching merely a loophole through which people not trained as therapists can hang a shingle and start practicing with clients? Are coaches sufficiently trained to differentiate their role from that of the therapist?

These are just some of the questions that have been swirling around the coaching field since its start nearly 20 years ago. Although the newness and uncertainty that come with every young field can breed early mishaps and even opportunities for a few unscrupulous folks to take advantage of others, coaching has nonetheless emerged as an important field with its own unique focus, characteristics, and purpose. In addition, the majority of trained and certified coaches practicing today do so ethically and recognize the scope of their practice—understanding where coaching ends and therapy begins, or vice versa.

Why have coaching and therapy been linked in the first place? Perhaps it is because both are built on regular conversations between clients and professional and both endeavor to help people enact their best lives. In addition, both coaches and therapists use open-ended questions to help clients work through the issues they bring to the session; both kinds of professionals also put the client at the center of the experience, supporting the client on a journey to find his or her own answers and to draw on personal strengths. In spite of these similarities, coaching is not the same as therapy. An understanding of this difference is essential for coaches to be able to practice ethically and effectively; an understanding of this difference on the part of the individual will also help the individual make choices about whether the desired service at a given time is therapy, coaching, or both.

How is it that coaching differs from therapy? The following table provides a side-by-side comparison of how coaching and therapy compare and contrast with each other. This table is not meant to be exhaustive but is intended to provide a quick overview of some of the important differences between coaching and therapy.

Table 1.1

Overview of the Differences Between Coaching and Therapy

Coaching	Therapy
Provides a trusting, supportive, nonjudgmental partnership and environment in which the client can explore his or her personal agenda	Provides a trusting, supportive, nonjudgmental relationship and environment in which the client can explore his or her personal agenda
Shifts attention toward awareness of a problem or deficit in order to design a plan to change, improve, and grow; the coach will refer the client to a therapist if the client is experiencing significant psychological stress	Guides client toward a better understanding of the clinical diagnosis or pathology in order to gain necessary insight and understanding for healing; helps provide specific tools or coping strategies for that individual
Encourages the setting of attainable goals and the creation of action plans	Invites the client to explore the deeper, unconscious dynamics or the negative thoughts, for example (depending on therapy model), that underlie or occur in relation to the issues brought to the session
Aims to facilitate change through goal-setting, action, accountability, and self-awareness	Aims to facilitate change through self-understanding and insight; goal-setting, action, and accountability may also occur, depending on the therapeutic approach
Supports clients who have mental health conditions only if the client is currently functioning adequately and has the support of a mental health professional; focus is on issues outside of the mental health realm	Supports clients with mental health issues/diagnoses on a path to increase healing, growth, and life satisfaction

How does coaching differ from therapy? Generally speaking, coaches operate out of a belief system in which change is brought about by the client partnering with a coach who supports realistic goal-setting; a clear, achievable plan; action steps; and accountability (i.e., having someone to check in with on a regular basis regarding actions taken or not taken). Although therapists may also value goal-setting and accountability, in theoretical terms, psychotherapists tend to operate out of a belief system in which exploring feelings, developing understanding, and fostering insight create the client's desired change.

As we look at other therapeutic models, it is more difficult to distinguish coaching from therapy. Cognitive behavior therapy (CBT) is a good example. CBT and coaching share many similar approaches; however, CBT differentiates itself as a research-based clinical intervention performed by trained mental health professionals. In CBT, therapists follow theoretical guidelines to address clinical diagnosis. CBT therapists often use strategies such as goal-setting, but they do so as part of a broader protocol to address psychological issues.

Both therapy and coaching play valuable parts in helping people lead more satisfying lives, and both can provide useful support to individuals who seek out assistance. Which service is best for the client will depend on things like the client's current mindset, emotional stability, and mental health status, as well as the nature of the client's goals, personality, learning style, and life circumstances. Note that coaching in conjunction with therapy can also be very useful.

Another key difference to note between coaching and therapy relates to pathology, as reflected in the previous table. When a client is struggling to function adequately due to a mental health issue, this is the realm of therapeutic intervention. As noted by coaching researcher and post-secondary disability specialist Dr. David R. Parker, "people who are dealing with significant and untreated mental health issues often lack the psychological capacity to take the kind of effective action sought by the coaching process even if the motivation to do so is there." Coaches may work with those who have mental health diagnoses, but they will do so only with clients who are receiving treatment for their mental health issues from other appropriate practitioners—therapists, family doctor, psychiatrist, and so on—and/or who have their mental health issues under control or in remission. Mental health conditions do not preclude a person from receiving coaching; such conditions can, however, factor into whether a person is currently "coachable" and/or whether that person needs someone in addition to a coach to reach his or her goals.

Ultimately, clients make a choice about whether coaching or therapy seems right for them at a given time in their lives; coaches and therapists, too, pay attention to what appears to be the best fit for clients, making referrals when appropriate. A clear understanding, on the parts of both client and coach, of the differences between coaching and therapy will make such choices and referrals easier.

When I am considering taking on a coaching client, I am always mindful of what might be going on in that client's life and whether coaching is the appropriate next step for that person. The client needs to be ready, willing, and able to engage in a coaching partnership and to have a clear understanding of the coaching process and what a coach can and cannot provide. If I discover early in the process that the client is seeking the kind of emotional or insight-related support that is better aligned with therapy, I make a referral. Or it may take a few coaching sessions before it becomes clear that the client needs some therapeutic support, whether in addition to or in lieu of coaching. For example, the client may break down and cry every time we talk about his or her family. This type of situation would indicate the client's need to first address an emotional issue that would best be handled in a therapeutic setting rather than in a coaching partnership.

The debate over the differences and similarities between therapy and coaching will continue, and my effort to outline these differences for the benefit of readers is in no way perfect. Yet, I share this analysis in good faith to provide insight into how the two professions align in some ways and differ in others and to encourage additional discussion and exploration of how these two services differ. My hope is that through this process, readers who are potential clients will gain useful information to aid their own decisions about whether coaching, therapy, or both coaching and therapy are right for them. I hope, too, that for readers interested in becoming coaches, some useful knowledge may be attained on the ethical scope of practice for the coaching profession.

Coaches on a Mission

Many of you are reading this book because you want to introduce coaching to adolescents and young adults and can envision the positive change that can occur for them over time with the support of a coach. Although coaching for youth is getting more recognition, the field is still in its infancy. It is up to us as coaches to learn the skills needed to support this budding client base and to establish partnerships that will foster growth and change in a way that most youth have not experienced before, whether at home or at school. Partnership of youth with adults can be a foreign concept, and we as coaches have an opportunity to introduce that concept and to educate others—therapists, teachers, parents, prospective clients, and other coaches—about the value of initiating coaching at an early age. In spite of my enthusiasm for spreading the mission of coaching youth, I nonetheless stand behind the philosophy that coaches need to be well-trained in coaching skills and well-versed in the nuances of working with adolescents and young adults. It is not enough to say that you know how to coach this precious cargo. I encourage coaches, parents, and professionals to learn what it takes to become a qualified professional coach with the skills to effectively and responsibly coach young people. This book can provide a great starting point!

Coaching the Whole Child

When I first decided to coach young people, everyone assumed that I was an academic coach. Although there certainly is an academic component to coaching youth, academic issues are only a slice of the coaching pie. An academic coach focuses on exactly that—academics. The academic coach will observe the client and suggest changes to help the student learn more effectively and improve grades, learning comprehension, and overall academic success. Like life coaches, academic coaches provide encouragement and support. Certainly, academic and life coaches agree that the job of young people is to go to school and do their best to succeed academically. But there is still a difference between academic and life coaches. Not surprisingly, many academic coaches come from an educational background and have experience as teachers or tutors. However, most academic coaches are not trained life coaches and do not offer a full range of coaching services to clients.

There is a place for academic coaching for young people. Yet, in my experience, focusing solely on academics and not on the whole person cuts out a huge portion of what makes a young person healthy, happy, well-balanced, and successful. That is why I created a coaching model that reaches far beyond academics, encompassing all areas of the client's life, including friends, family, self-advocacy, life choices, empowerment, health and well-being, and, yes, academics. Coaches are in a unique position to help bring joy and fulfillment to the lives of children, teens, and young adults. Coaching the whole child, not just the "academic child" or the "athletic child," is the key to a successful and rewarding coaching experience for the coach and client.

If we, as coaches, focus only on academics, we will help foster a young person who becomes skilled in managing his or her academic life—taking clear notes, studying for tests, and remembering deadlines. These, of course, are useful skills, which can be transferred to some degree to one's adult life, for example, while searching for a job or excelling in certain professions. Yet, if coaching focuses on academics to the exclusion of other life skills, like making friends, managing one's money, pursuing relaxation and hobbies, or learning how to self-advocate, coaching may foster a young person who knows how to excel at school (or eventually at a job) but who has a troubled social life or a miserable home experience.

The issue of academic versus whole-life coaching for young people comes up often in the context of youth with ADHD because these young people have a particularly hard time keeping up with schoolwork and mastering subjects because of their challenges with executive functioning, attention, and focus. Parents with adolescents who have ADHD thus often contact a coach in search of academic help for their children. In doing so, parents are understandably responding to the biggest red flags in these young people's lives: their less-than-perfect grades.

Yet, experience has shown me that if these adolescents are struggling at school, they are likely struggling with other life issues as well. As a result, when I offer my support as a coach, I will only do so if the parent is comfortable with the idea that coaching will be provided in a life, rather than solely an academic, context. Whatever goals the young client brings to coaching, the client and I will focus on those—academic or not—that he or she deems feasible and that are suitable for the coaching context. In sum, if coaching focuses only on academics, we may foster intelligent yet ineffectual adults; if we focus on a child's whole life, we will help foster a young person ready to steer through life as he or she blossoms into adulthood.

Whole-life coaching is valuable to youth with ADHD because it can help these individuals develop some of the basic skills and strategies that other young people and adults can take for granted. For example, youth with ADHD may not have the skills to successfully connect and interrelate with other people; as a result, their social life—and self-esteem—may be in shambles. Or consider this: Unless someone stops and asks these children, "What did you do for fun yesterday?" they oftentimes don't even know what having fun really means. And they may lack awareness of their environment, which can cause not only social mishaps but personal discomfort.

For example, one of my clients, an 11-year-old boy, recently came to his session complaining of back pain. When I asked him what was inside the backpack he was carrying, he suggested that it was probably filled with books. And yet when I encouraged him to look inside, he discovered that the problem wasn't books at all. Instead, it was a heavy load of school papers that had been accumulating over several weeks and that simply needed cleaning out. Whole-life coaching helps young people with ADHD address all of the daily challenges they face, not just academics, whether they be keeping one's space organized, sustaining friendships, or choosing a career path.

What Is ADHD Coaching?

ADHD coaching is a specialized type of coaching that is tailored to meet the unique needs of the client with ADHD, delivered by a coach with in-depth knowledge and understanding of ADHD and related issues. For coaches working with those who have ADHD, there is a belief that all clients are naturally creative and resourceful, with, at times, a need for a different approach than would be used in traditional life coaching and an understanding by the coach of how a person with ADHD may struggle in certain life areas. The ADHD coaching process offers clients support, structure, and accountability for their actions, leading to a greater level of success in all areas of life, including those negatively impacted by ADHD, learning disabilities, or other coexisting conditions.

The Institute for the Advancement of ADHD Coaching defines ADHD coaching as

> a designed partnership that combines coaching skills with knowledge of Attention Deficit Disorder, a neurobiological condition. The coaching process enhances quality of life, improves performance and supports growth and change. The purpose of ADHD coaching is to provide support, structure and accountability. Coach and client collaboratively explore strengths, talents, tools and new learning to increase self-awareness

and personal empowerment. Together they design strategies and actions and monitor progress by creating accountability in line with goals and aspirations.

ADHD coaches help individuals to set goals, acknowledge strengths, accept limitations, develop social skills, and create strategies that enable them to be more effective in managing their day-to-day lives. ADHD coaches do this by establishing a pattern of frequent communication with clients to make sure they are focused and working steadily toward their goals.

How Is Coaching Useful to Adolescents and Young Adults With ADHD?

Coaching can be valuable to many kinds of clients, regardless of age or issue. Coaching provides a reliable, trusting environment in which the client can create a vision for his or her life, brainstorm on how to bring that vision into reality, and engage with a supportive partner—the coach—along the way. Now imagine the value of such an environment to a client who not only is young and just gaining access to a world in which he or she has greater responsibilities and more need to direct his or her own life, but who also needs to figure out how to manage all of these things while struggling with challenges in executive functioning, attention, and focus.

For adolescents and young adults with ADHD and learning issues, it can be both difficult and daunting to step out on one's own into the world and try to be successful. This is where a coach can come in and help a young person transform daily life from chaos into clarity. Coaching provides a sounding board, a source for ideas, and a safety net that all help the young person with ADHD try new ways of operating, go after what he or she wants, collect him or herself when things go differently than planned, and then try again, each time growing a little wiser and a little more confident.

From an emotional and life-skills perspective, adolescents with ADHD are typically not prepared for the transition from dependence on parents, teachers, and other important figures in their lives to the increasing independence they face as budding, near adults. These young people are typically behind their peers in terms of their readiness for independent life and lack the skills necessary to make good choices or to understand the consequences of their actions. They often find it hard to understand what's going on around them and don't know how to react appropriately in different situations. Coaching offers young people with ADHD a supportive structure through which they can explore life options, learn new skills, and start to be more independent while in a safe space.

When coaching focuses on social skills, the coach helps young people understand that a future full of friends and positive relationships is out there for them. Clients begin to realize and recognize that they may not get what they want right now, a big area of frustration for the more impulsive and immature clients, but they also learn that with the support of a coach and a solid plan for success, they can move along a path toward their goals in a more independent fashion.

By offering coaching to young people, coaches have an opportunity to help bridge the gap between childhood and adulthood while simultaneously helping parents to step back and allow the maturation process to proceed at a pace that is right for their child. Oftentimes, parents have a difficult time accepting that adolescents and young adults with ADHD and learning disabilities are still in their preteens emotionally. Parents and others often expect these individuals to be mature enough to manage their lives. Yet, there is no "one size fits all" timetable for maturity. Coaches guide and support these young people in getting ready for the future while moving forward at their own pace.

ADHD coaching can help young people with ADHD in a number of ways. For example, it can help individuals

- become organized, learn time management skills, and learn how to prioritize

- develop and maintain focus and concentration

- create and maintain a medication journal (I like to call it "Meds & Moods")

- gain independence and self-advocacy skills

- enjoy a safe space to work on social skills

- manage ADHD issues at home, at school, and at their job.

These positive aspects of coaching are all in addition to the benefits of more general coaching, in which the young person receives support in creating plans and setting goals in an environment of structure, support, and encouragement.

How Does ADHD Coaching Differ From Life Coaching?

ADHD coaching is like life coaching in that it involves helping clients through the process of exploration, goal-setting, identifying and taking action steps, and checking in to maintain accountability, as seen in Figure 2 earlier in the chapter. In addition, as with life coaching, ADHD coaching provides structure, support, and encouragement. Where ADHD coaching tends to be different from life coaching is in terms of the degree of support and structure offered, with ADHD coaching involving an increased amount of support and structure and a higher level of accountability between coach and client to facilitate results. This becomes evident in the kind of questions that a coach poses.

Let's imagine that a young client comes in with the question of "How do I approach my professor with the problems I'm having in class?" If that client doesn't have ADHD, the coach might ask, "How would you like to approach your professor with this problem?" and "What would you like to see as the outcome of your conversation with the professor?" In this case, the coach volleys fairly general questions to the client because the client has the capacity to discover what he or she wants with minimal prompting from the coach and mainly needs a sounding board.

In contrast, if the client has ADHD, the coach will still ask the client some general, open-ended questions, but the coach will also ask more specific or in-depth questions that prompt the client to consider each and every action step needed to accomplish a goal, taking into consideration that the client struggles with initiation and follow-through. So when the client says, "I will talk to my professor sometime this week," the coach might ask, "When will you do this?" "What do you need to do to make this conversation a reality?" and "How will I know when you have talked to your professor?"

Of course, the line between providing ADHD clients the structure they need and not becoming overly directive is an important one. For example, the coach doesn't want to say to the client, "You can't go in to talk to your professor without an appointment!" even if the coach suspects that this is the case. Instead, the coach might ask open-ended questions to help the client think through relevant issues for success, but it is not the job of the ADHD coach to tell the client exactly how to accomplish something. Doing so would do a disservice to the client, who needs opportunities to practice generating solutions and testing out action plans in the real world.

In addition to asking smaller, more specific questions that help a client break action plans into small, achievable steps, ADHD coaches also hold their clients more accountable, which involves a tighter check-in plan between coaching sessions and more frequent contact than in general life coaching. For clients with ADHD, coaching sessions typically occur at least once a week, which is more often than in many life coaching or executive coaching programs.

Check-ins occur between client and coach to provide more structure and serve as a brief connection to confirm action taken or not taken or to update the coach on progress toward stated goals. In ADHD coaching for adolescents and young adults, the check-ins may be set up as often as daily. It is the consistency and frequency of contact that helps make ADHD coaching so effective. Typical means of contact for this regular accountability include e-mails, text messaging, check-in calls, and some form of follow-up if the client doesn't call in at the designated time. The specific details of the check-in plan are best established in the intake and revisited throughout the coaching relationship.

Although ADHD coaching involves greater structure and support than more general life coaching, the structure and support serve as stepping stones for the client, not crutches. Because individuals with ADHD tend to have a track record of falling down a lot, they often have a self-belief of "I can't do anything." By providing these individuals with sufficient structure and support, coaches help them experience success in their lives, often for the first time, so that they start to build a track record of accomplishment rather than failure. Over the course of their work with coaches, individuals with ADHD develop self-confidence that motivates them to pursue goals rather than give up. They build a toolbox of strategies that they can use now and in the future and begin to internalize the voice of the coach into their own thought processes. The coaching work thus often becomes part of the way the client thinks and operates, leading to lasting change.

The Ethics of Coaching Adolescents and Young Adults

Coaches have the opportunity to set an example by modeling professionalism and ethical conduct in their daily interactions with clients. Some young people may not have the cognitive or intellectual ability to understand ethical boundaries from a professional perspective, such as, what are the limitations of coaching, what is considered acceptable behavior on the part of the coach, or what might fall outside the limits of confidentiality between coach and client. Therefore, it is the coach's responsibility as a professional and an adult to hold the boundaries in place and guide younger clients in the proper direction. As the coaching field continues to grow, coaches want to be viewed in the highest regard by clients, colleagues, and other professionals. It is the coaches' responsibility to follow the ethical guidelines and standards set forth by coaching organizations and to conduct themselves accordingly.

For starters, it is important to clearly define the boundaries of coaching. This means knowing what is a part of coaching (questioning, listening, brainstorming, planning, goal-setting) and what is not a part of coaching (telling the client what to do, making a diagnosis, delving into emotional issues, passing judgment) and sharing that knowledge with the client. When the coach is in doubt regarding the appropriateness of an issue raised in coaching, the coach should consult with a mentor coach or a professional advisor. The approach I always recommend to my coaching students is to err on the side of caution: Explain to young clients that you want what is best for them and do not want to overstep the boundaries of coaching. For example, imagine that a client asks her coach what the coach thinks of the local college she is contemplating attending in the fall and, coincidentally, the coach does not like one of the deans at that college. The coach must keep his opinion out of the mix and turn the question back to the client. It would be inappropriate for the coach to unduly influence the client's decision on the basis of his personal opinion.

Next, coaches should take extra care to provide a safe space for coaching. Coaches can explain to young clients the setup of coaching—that it is conducted in person or by phone and computer in a confidential space designed for openness, sharing, and honesty between the coach and client. Coaches can then expand upon the definition of a coaching partnership. Yes, it is a designed alliance between coach and client, but what does that mean? It means that the client is an equal partner in the process and that the coach is not to tell the client what to do or not do. If at any time the client is not seeing the benefit of the coaching or does not like the direction in which the coaching is progressing, the client is encouraged to share this with the coach. This can be done without fear of criticism, retribution, or anger. In return, the coach will be honest with the client and inform the client of any concerns the coach may have about the coaching process and the ongoing partnership. All of this is done in the safe space of the coaching relationship.

Maintaining confidentiality is also a major concern for most adolescents. They fear that the coach is going to run back to the parents and spill the details of the coaching sessions. Coaches need to take ample time to explain the confidentiality clause to the new client and the parents, so that everyone understands the boundaries and the exceptions. On this last point, the coach will take stock of any possible dangers—harm to self or others—and raise concerns with the client directly. When and if problems require contacting the parents, the coach has an ethical obligation to do so. An example of this would be a client who comes to coaching sessions depressed and distraught, unable to control her emotions. The client does not want to worry her parents but admits that she has been feeling like this for weeks. The coach can and will contact the parents if the client refuses to do so, first informing the client of the plan. This is in the best interest of the client.

As noted above, some younger clients may not fully understand the coaching process, and it is imperative that the coach provides clear information to the prospective clients and their parents about coaching before they enter into a coaching partnership. The coach should augment any verbal discussions by providing written materials to client families so that they have ample opportunity to review the coaching guidelines and code of ethics and thus gain a clear understanding of what to expect from the coach and the coaching process. In addition, the coach can refer families to coaching websites and encourage them to ask questions to assist them in their exploration of coaching. Last, the coach should remain open to inquiries about the boundaries of coaching and maintain high ethical standards at all times to facilitate a healthy coaching partnership.

By focusing on these cornerstones of ethical coaching—clearly defining the coaching boundaries; taking extra care to provide a safe space for coaching; and maintaining the confidentiality between coach and client, regardless of age (with the caveat of reporting problems when harm to self or others is feared)—coaches can build trust with the young person and lay the groundwork for a successful coaching relationship and process.

Note to Everyone

Truth be told, young people don't always want to listen to adults, especially their parents. They may listen to their friends, use the Internet as their main information resource, and sometimes make unwise choices out of inexperience or perhaps just to ruffle the feathers of the adults in their lives. Coaches can help young clients find ways to grow, explore, and express themselves in a manner that supports independence after first taking stock of the pros and cons of their choices. Coaches and caring adults have the opportunity to champion these young people and applaud the steps they take in moving forward with greater awareness of the world, their responsibilities, and their abilities.

Parents and coaches need to work together and be a part of the adolescent or young adult's learning process. It may take longer for young people with ADHD to learn new skills, increase self-awareness, and communicate effectively with others than it does for other young people, and it typically requires a greater commitment on everyone's part. It can help to remember that the journey is a steady marathon and not a sprint. Sometimes parents think that the challenges are never going to end, but with coaching, there can be a light at the end of the tunnel. With possible therapy and/or medication, guidance, and support, parents, coaches, and other caregivers can make a difference in the life of a young person with ADHD.

T W O

What Is Your Role?

Do any of the following scenarios sound familiar? You want to help a young person with ADHD, but you just don't know how. Or maybe you thought you helped the young person but realize now that you didn't. Maybe you've read every book on helping children with ADHD only to discover that when you try to implement suggested strategies, they don't work. Or maybe all of the helping techniques you used in the past seem ineffective now that the young person is no longer a child but an adolescent. If you have ever felt confused, overwhelmed, or frustrated when trying to support an adolescent or young adult with ADHD, you are not alone. It can be difficult to know where to start or how to adapt as the child gets older. But I have some good news for you: Help is on the way!

Regardless of your particular confusion or frustration in helping a young person with ADHD, a clear understanding of your role in supporting that young person can go a long way to making your partnership with that young person a success. By role, I am referring to the nature of help that you can offer the young person with ADHD to help meet his or her goals. What does the young person need from you right now? An advisor? A trustworthy confidante? A sounding board? A hands-on helper? How much should you do for the young person? How much should you let the young person do for him or herself?

The nature of help needed by adolescents and young adults with ADHD is distinct from the nature of help needed in earlier and later stages of life. Adolescence and young adulthood represent life phases that are different from those that come before or follow; adolescence and young adulthood are phases in which the young person is entering or moving through a world of budding and ever-increasing challenges. It is the job of coaches, parents, and allied professionals to help foster independence and to meet young people where they are, not where they used to be or where they are one day going. Adolescence is no longer a time for tight hand-holding, but neither is it a time to push the young person out the door without any support.

This chapter provides a clear description of the role that is often most effective to play when working with an adolescent or young adult with ADHD: the role of someone who empowers the young person. This chapter also examines how the different members of the young person's ADHD support team can work well together. If you are a parent, how do you work alongside the coach? Where do you fit into the coaching process? If you are the coach, do you communicate with the other professionals in the client's life or do you leave this work to the client? As a coach, how do you involve the parent in the process? As a client, will the coach be a trusted partner in the process or a mouthpiece for your parents?

As many of the coaches and parents with whom I work discover, working with young people who have ADHD doesn't have to feel confusing, overwhelming, or frustrating. This process can actually feel energizing, rewarding, and fun. When you have a clear understanding of your role in helping these young people, you will be able to engage in that role with confidence. More important, you will be able to offer the kind of deliberate, personalized support that truly helps the young person with ADHD grow. And that's what this process is really about—helping young people stretch to meet their potential and move closer to the lives they desire for themselves.

Your Role? To Empower Rather Than Enable

Take a moment and envision each of the following situations. A mother cleans the room of her 12-year-old son and puts away his laundry while he lies on his bed playing a video game. The aunt of a high school student who is flunking math completes her niece's calculus homework for her without explaining the process. A college professor tells a student who has come in for office hours to discuss a failed test that he will raise his grade simply because the student has asked.

Most people would probably agree with me that something is very wrong with these pictures! A mom cleaning her preteen's room when he is perfectly capable of cleaning it himself? An adult doing a teen's homework for her? A teacher giving a student a better grade without the student doing any actual work to demonstrate additional effort or learning?

In each of these cases, one person—mom, the aunt, or the professor—is trying to help another—the 12-year-old son, the high schooler with the failing math grade, or the college student. Yet, in reality, the mom, the aunt, and the professor are not really helping. Instead, they are enabling—and there is a big difference.

What Is Enabling?

Enabling occurs when someone who means to help does the work for the other person instead of empowering that person to do this work him or herself. It's easy to enable young people because we often forget that they are quite capable of doing most things themselves. It can be even easier to enable young people with ADHD because we might see them as being unskilled or incapable.

Enabling often masquerades as helping because in the short term, acts of enabling make the young person's life easier or better. A quick result is delivered; a goal is met. The preteen's room is now clean and his clothes are ready for the week. The high schooler and the college student have better grades. But what will happen tomorrow? Will the preteen or high schooler or college student be able to meet his or her daily responsibilities and goals? When mom is gone or the aunt is out of the picture or the college professor has been replaced by a boss in the corporate world, will the young person who was once enabled be able to find his or her way?

Even when "help" of the enabling sort has been delivered with care and good intentions, the results of this kind of attention are typically undesirable. Young people who have been enabled are likely to lack the independence, skills, confidence, self-esteem—you name it—needed to thrive on their own as they move into adulthood.

This is because when enabling takes place, a very important agent—the most essential agent—is missing from the operation: the young person him or herself!

When you work with a young person with ADHD, your role, then, is not simply to help the young person. Your role is to help that young person *help him or herself.* The young person does the actual work, and you get to support that young person in the process. Instead of enabling the young person, you empower the young person.

What Is Empowerment?

Empowerment involves helping someone help him or herself. In the context of coaching youth, empowerment is a process of helping the young person identify and apply skills, strengths, and resources to achieving goals. Unlike enabling, which fosters dependence and low self-esteem, empowerment fosters independence and self-confidence.

Empowerment might be likened to the second half of the old proverb, "Give a man a fish; you have fed him for today. Teach a man to fish; and you have fed him for a lifetime." Empowerment is all about teaching young people with ADHD to fish—about helping the young person gain the skills needed to take care of him or herself over the long term rather than to remain dependent or reliant on others.

All young people need to be empowered rather than enabled. All young people need support in acquiring the skills and strategies they will use over a lifetime to achieve their goals and to lead satisfying lives. Yet, for young people with ADHD, empowerment becomes especially important because these individuals often have spent their whole childhood feeling incapable, inadequate, or damaged. Because of their skill deficits, challenges with attention, and other ADHD symptoms, they have continually been treated by others as if they were sick or even "broken."

Thus, when we empower a young person with ADHD, we are helping that young person take a giant leap forward. This is because empowerment not only helps the young person accomplish goals through his or her own effort and action, but it also helps to change the young person's self-image at a fundamental level.

When you empower young people with ADHD, their self-confidence grows, their self-esteem elevates, and their belief in themselves expands. As a result, these young people go from saying things like, "I can't do anything, so why should I try?" to things like, "I believe I can accomplish this goal, so I'll give it a try." Through empowerment, young people with ADHD learn to put forth the effort required to achieve their goals rather than giving up before they even get started.

Regardless of your particular role in the life of the young person with ADHD—parent, coach, school counselor, tutor, therapist, and so on—you will be able to help the young person most when you empower rather than enable.

Parents, this might mean, for example, asking your teen to schedule a medical physical himself once he learns it's a requirement for high school basketball rather than you getting on the phone with the doctor's office.

Coaches, this might mean that when a client sets a goal of improving her SAT scores, rather than directing her on how to meet this goal (sign up for a class, buy a study book, hire a tutor), you would invite your client to generate her own ideas on how she could improve her SAT scores ("Well, I have a friend who took an SAT class...maybe I could do that," the client might say).

Tutors, this might mean that instead of solving the geometry proof for the adolescent, you ask the adolescent questions that encourage him to think for himself about how he might go about solving the math problem.

By inviting the young person with ADHD to do things for him or herself—by empowering the young person—you are giving the young person an opportunity to try out his or her "muscles" and see if they work. In the process, the young person learns that

- he or she has skills, strengths, and resources and identifies exactly what they are

- someone (you!) believes in his or her ability to succeed; over time, the young person may internalize this external vote of confidence and start to believe in him or herself

- if he or she fails at something, life goes on; the young person can get up and try again

- he or she is capable of meeting goals rather than watching someone else do things for him or her.

As noted earlier, empowerment is about much more than helping the young person with ADHD accomplish goals: It's about helping the young person identify strengths and resources; practice thinking about how to solve problems and meet goals; build skills; develop a positive self-image; and, ultimately, lay a foundation for long-term success in the days, months, and years to come.

The Shift of Power—Well Worth the Effort!

Now that I have made all kinds of proclamations about the right role to play when supporting young people with ADHD, some of you may want to close this book or, at the very least, ignore this chapter. Those of you who have experience with adolescents and young adults might be thinking that I don't have a clue about the difficulties adults encounter with young people.

"Ask my 16-year-old to make his own doctor's appointment? He can't even get to school on time!" might be the response of some parents to my earlier suggestion. Or maybe you are thinking, "My son can't survive without me. His food-ridden bedroom would degrade into a nest of killer fruit flies or a minefield of wet towels!"

What can I say? Having worked with hundreds of young people and having raised a teenager myself, I've been there. From an adult's perspective, young people may have a way of seeming uninterested in and incapable of doing what we think is best for them. Conversely, young people often think we adults are asking the impossible of them or making a big deal out of nothing.

Given the frustration that commonly arises in such situations, I want to say up front that I know that it can be tough to work with individuals in adolescence or young adulthood and that it is all the more challenging when ADHD and learning issues are involved. I don't mean to imply that this process is easy or that I have all the answers. I simply offer what wisdom I do have from working with young people with ADHD for the past 15 years, in the hope that this guidance and insight will assist those readers interested in helping these young people have their best shot at a happy life.

With that said, let's go back to the valid concern of parents and other professionals that stepping back and letting young people with ADHD do the work of their lives themselves could lead to absolute failure or unrecoverable heartbreak. Although this might certainly be the case if you were to kick the young person to the curb or throw him, unarmed, into a den of fruit flies, this is not what's actually happening when empowerment is involved.

With empowerment, you aren't completely exiting the young person's life (parents) or sitting mutely in the office while the client speaks (coaches). You are, instead, allowing the young person to engage in the work of life for him or herself while you are nearby, offering support and structure as needed.

Support refers to the trusting, nonjudgmental relationship coaches, parents, and professionals can offer young people with ADHD to help them develop self-confidence and meet their goals. *Structure* refers to the practical tools that coaches, parents, and professionals can offer a young person to help him or her stay on track—or get back on track—on the journey to meet his or her goals.

Support is about believing in the young person with ADHD when the young person is full of self-doubt. Support is about showing this adolescent or young adult that if he or she fails to accomplish a goal, the adult will still be there for him or her, without criticism or judgment. Support is about helping the young person realize that effort alone is a sign of progress and success. Support is about helping the young person celebrate each small and large success.

Structure consists of things like planning; organizing; designing and prioritizing clear, attainable goals with tangible action steps; creating accountability plans; setting up daily routines; and developing a system for managing one's time. Structure is a necessary framework in the coaching process for clients with ADHD. Consider putting a roof on a new home without first constructing the frame. All of the roof planning will be for naught, because there is nothing to which to attach the shingles. In coaching, we work with clients to provide the structure so that the skill-building process will be successful. For example, we guide the client in a structured process of setting clear and attainable goals so that skills like planning and prioritizing can be built. We invite the client to set up the structure of a daily routine so that he or she can build an internal time clock and a sense of how to manage time.

Although the exact support and structure offered to the young person with ADHD will vary somewhat depending on one's role (e.g., coach vs. parent vs. teacher vs. tutor), offering support and structure together will help empower the young person to practice "doing" rather than "being done for" and to accomplish tasks and goals that previously seemed unattainable. The use of support and structure will allow the coach, parent, or professional to step back and give the young person some space to do things for him or herself and work toward goals without attempting this process in a complete vacuum. The end result will be a young person who has strong self-esteem and is able to manage his or her life now and in the future.

Coaches: Teach a Young Person to Fish

Coaches are typically caring, supportive people who strive to see their clients succeed. They are excited to help clients take practical steps forward and to see tangible results. Coaches' caring nature and change-oriented approach to helping is what makes coaches who they are and what puts them in a good position to support young people with ADHD. Yet, the desire to make things better or lessen clients' discomfort can also make it tempting for coaches to enable clients—to do their work for them rather than to empower clients to do the work themselves.

This can be a particularly easy pitfall for coaches with certain professional or personal backgrounds. For example, coaches who were formerly teachers are quite used to rolling up their sleeves and working alongside the young person—reviewing academic lessons, identifying the young person's areas of limited knowledge, providing specific equations or rubrics for the subject matter, and walking through the process with the young person until he or she gets the answer. Although this behavior is perfectly normal and appropriate within the domain of teaching, in coaching, where the goal is to empower the client to apply his or her own skills, strengths, and resources— not someone else's—this approach is too direct and hands-on.

Similarly, for people who have walked in the shoes of the client—as someone who also has ADHD or as the parent or spouse of an individual with ADHD—it is oftentimes difficult to step away from personal feelings and let the client lead the way. When knowledge of one's past personal experiences is put upon a client to influence the coaching plan, the result can be more enabling than empowering.

Resist the Urge: Just Say "No" to Enabling!

It can be tempting to offer one's opinion or assistance. The coach may feel honored that the client has asked for the coach's opinion on an assigned essay on basket weaving in the third century. The coach may jump at the opportunity to dust off technical skills and assist with that quantum physics problem. But coaches should try to remember the principles of coaching and resist the urge to be directive!

Perhaps because of a coach's desire to help the client or the coach's empathy toward the client's struggle, it may come naturally to the coach to get involved in helping the client do the actual work of achieving goals. Yet, doing so will come at a major price.

When the client sees the coach doing the work for the client, that young person will continue to receive a message that he or she is incapable of doing the work him or herself; the myth that the client is broken gets perpetuated. In addition, the client does not have the opportunity to practice doing things for him or herself—even if only to fail and then try again. The client also misses out on the experience and the reward of setting a goal and then accomplishing it. These are just a few of the negative consequences that result when the coach enables rather than empowers young people with ADHD.

One of the things that make it easy to slip into a pattern of enabling young people is that coaches often sincerely believe that they are helping clients when they are actually enabling; coaches' intentions come from a place of true concern and caring. Yet, concern and care can't help the young person if delivered through an enabling approach.

The following examples depict a coach who is enabling a young ADHD client.

- When the client explains that his professor doesn't seem to understand him, the coach offers to call the professor and explain the client's learning disability.

- When the client sets a goal of improving her calculus grade, the coach schedules an appointment with an academic tutor for the client.

- When the client sets a goal of improving his relationship with his dad, the coach offers to contact the client's dad and speak with him.

- When the client misses an appointment with her psychiatrist, the coach offers to reschedule the appointment for the client.

At first glance, in these previous examples, it might seem that the coach is helping the client. In reality, though, the coach is only helping the client in the short term because the coach is doing all of the work for the client rather than supporting the client in doing the work him or herself. In other words, empowerment is missing from the equation. The client does not get any practice resolving his or her own challenges, nor does the client gain the opportunity to build skills and confidence for managing life in the future.

Here's how the previous examples would appear if the coach focused on empowering, rather than enabling, the client.

- When the client explains that his professor doesn't seem to understand him, the coach invites the client to explore how he can handle the situation. The client suggests that he could go talk to the professor to help his professor better understand the client's learning disability.

- When the client sets a goal of improving her calculus grade, the coach gives the client contact information for one or more academic tutors, at the client's request, and leaves it to the client to schedule the appointment herself.

- When the client sets a goal of improving his relationship with his dad, the coach offers to role-play with the client while the client practices what he would like to say to his dad to ask for more understanding regarding his grades.

- When the client tells the coach about a missed psychiatrist appointment, the coach asks the client what she plans to do about it and holds the client accountable for her next steps.

In each of these examples of empowerment, the client presents a goal that is important to him or her, and the coach focuses on providing the support and/or structure needed to help the client work toward that goal him or herself. In the process, the coach is not just staying away from *doing* for the client, the coach is also avoiding *thinking* for the client as well. The client is invited by the coach to do the thinking independently, generating creative solutions that feel authentic.

The empowerment offered by the coach might be described as a sort of dance in which the coach steps back enough to give the client space to think and do for him or herself but at the same time moves toward the client when needed to offer useful structure and support. This dance plays out in the following example dialogue between coach and client.

A Coaching Dialogue: The Dance of Empowerment

Client: I really need to find some colleges—but time is running out. I'm interested in music programs, but I have no idea where to begin.

Coach: What are some of the ways you might find out what colleges are available to you? [The coach inquires rather than provides an answer—empowers rather than enables.]

Client: Gee, I don't know.

Coach: Well, think about it. What resources have other people used? Any ideas you can recall from past conversations? [The coach may know the answer but doesn't give it; she is empowering the client in finding the answer for herself.]

Client: Some people go online.

Coach: Oh, really? Some people go online? [The coach continues to be curious, offering support.]

Client: Yeah, there are different sites. I used one when I signed up for my SATs.

Coach: What was it called?

Client: It's something to do with college searches...but I can't remember the name.

Coach: Oh, are you talking about Collegeboard.com? [Recognizing a short-term memory problem, the coach is willing to prompt the client's memory.]

Client: Yeah.

Coach: I know it can be hard for you to remember things sometimes, so would you be willing to write down the name of the website to help you remember it later? [The coach provides structure, prompting the client to write down the college search site as a strategy for dealing with short-term memory problems; this is not enabling but rather modeling a strategy for the client.]

Client: Okay, that might help.

Coach: Great! What else might you do to find college-level music programs? [The coach is reinforcing the goal and encouraging the client to consider all of the options.]

Client: Well, my music teacher went to a music college. I could ask him about it after class.

Coach: Excellent idea! I am really looking forward to hearing about the schools you find when you do your search and talk with your music teacher. [The coach shows confidence in and excitement about the client's ability to accomplish the college search, a form of support.]

As evidenced by this sample dialogue, the dance of empowerment involves providing enough support and structure to be helpful to the young person while at the same time being careful not to overstep the coaching boundaries and do too much for the young person. To this end, the coach asks the kind of questions that help the client find answers for him or herself; then, the coach offers structure as needed (e.g., "would you be willing to write down the name of the website?")

Thus, as the coach is empowering the client, the coach doesn't simply stay silent and allow the client to flounder on this new journey of doing things for him or herself. Instead, the coach is providing the client with both support and structure as the client becomes empowered to work toward desired goals. In the process, the client's chances of success are increased and the client has a genuine opportunity to increase his or her confidence and skills.

Providing Support

In the context of coaching, *support* is defined as the trusting, nonjudgmental relationship the coach provides to help the client make desired changes. For coaches, offering support will play an important role in helping the client meet goals; in the process, the coach's support also has the potential to help the client develop self-confidence and increase self-esteem.

Providing support for the young person with ADHD involves a variety of tasks on the coach's part, such as active listening, celebrating, championing, clarifying, empathizing, holding the focus, reframing, and requesting. Here are some examples of how a coach might engage in each of these different supportive tasks.

- Active listening: The coach makes eye contact with the client and nods his or her head while the client is talking

- Celebrating: "Congratulations! You set your sights on the lifeguard job and you got it. Way to go!"

- Championing: "Your efforts were fabulous even if you didn't reach your goal."

- Clarifying: "Do I understand your plan for today—you want to go back to your dorm and take a power nap before studying?"

- Empathizing: "I understand how difficult this must be for you."

- Holding the focus: "To keep our session on track, let's return to our review of your goals and action steps."

- Reframing: "I wonder what this situation might look like from your professor's perspective."

- Requesting: "I would like to request that you let me know when you have completed your job application. Is that acceptable to you?"

These are just some of the ways in which a coach can support the young person with ADHD. Whether by expressing an attitude of curiosity to prompt the young person to brainstorm self-generated solutions or by inviting the young person to celebrate each small success, the coach provides the young client with unconditional support that promotes an increase in self-esteem and puts achievement of goals within closer reach.

Providing Structure

In addition to empowering the client by providing support, coaches can also empower clients by providing structure. Within the coaching context, structure refers to the practical tools and strategies the coach offers the client to assist him or her in staying on track—or getting back on track—on the journey to meet the coaching goals. Structure comes in a variety of forms, as noted earlier, such as clear goals and tangible action steps, accountability plans, daily routines, and a system for managing one's time.

The essential structural tool that I use when coaching young people with ADHD is the personal coaching agreement (PCA). The PCA is a written document that the client and I create together at the beginning of coaching to capture the client's goals and the client's desired action steps toward accomplishing those goals.

In addition, when creating the PCA, the client and I develop a plan for helping the client stay accountable for his or her goals and action steps. We also generate a plan for rewarding the client when he or she achieves coaching goals. All of these items—goals, action steps, accountability plan, and rewards—are captured in the PCA.

The PCA provides a tangible touchstone that can be used in the coaching process time and again—first to find out the direction in which the client wants to go and to develop a plan for getting there, then to be the place to return to when the client slips off course or has trouble recognizing the small successes of action steps accomplished.

For example, if a client arrives in your office looking dejected and reports being sidelined from the first baseball game of the season because he was not as skilled in the outfield as other players, you can use the structure of the PCA to help the client see where he did succeed. For example, one of his action steps in the agreement may have been to arrive at practice with all of his gear—cleats, socks, baseball glove, and so on—and he did, in fact, accomplish that step each day he attended practice. By referring the client back to this action step and acknowledging his success in this regard, you are using the structure of the PCA to help the client recognize small successes. In the process, you may also disrupt the client's normal cycle of negative thinking.

In coaching, the process of offering support is integrated with the process of providing structure, with the two processes working together to empower the client. So, looking again at the baseball example, the supportive coach might empathize with the client's rejection from the game's roster, celebrate the client's success in arriving at practice with all of his gear, and also ask how the client wants to address the issue of fielding skills. Might this be a new goal? In sum, as the coach offers support to the client (listening, empathizing, celebrating, championing, etc.), the coach nudges the client back toward the structure of the coaching process, of which the PCA is a foundational part. The coach might suggest, "Let's refocus on your goals and action steps. What next steps are you willing to take to reach this goal? And, if this goal is not resonating for you at this time, what might you do to reframe the goal or replace it with one that works better for you?"

Thus, the coach's role is to combine support and structure to empower the young person with ADHD. Rather than doing the work for the client, the coach provides the client with the kind of support and structure that empowers the client to do the work him or herself—and to grow in the process.

Parents: Let's Do the "Shift"!

Shifting Your Role in the Daily Life Activities of Your Child

Parents' role in supporting their adolescent or young adult with ADHD is, just like that of the coach, to empower rather than enable. This less-hands-on approach may be hard at first, given that parents have probably been directly advocating for the young person for many years: talking to teachers, scheduling appointments, being a homework helper, and much more. In fact, doing things on behalf of the young person may have been a parent's normal mode of operation for as long as the parent can remember—like an automatic response that has been conditioned into the parent's way of being, day in and day out, year after year. Although this approach was likely useful—probably even necessary—when the child was younger, this method of engaging the child becomes outmoded once he or she enters the adolescent years.

In short, the shift from "doing for" the young person to stepping back and allowing the young person to "do for him or herself" will likely involve a huge mental adjustment, especially for parents of a younger adolescent who has just recently reached an age in which this kind of independence is appropriate. Parents of an older adolescent or of a young adult may be more ready to take this step back or may have already taken it, given the more advanced age of the young person and the life experiences that may have already begun fostering independence, such as opening a checking account, having a later curfew, or moving out of the house after high school.

Here are a few examples of what it looks like when a parent enables the adolescent or young adult.

- The parent, upon hearing her daughter complain about her difficulties with one of her high school friends, is reminded of her daughter's social-skills problems in grade school. Although the daughter is older and more mature, the parent decides to call the friend's mother and talk to her about the social issue on her daughter's behalf.

- The parent, upon learning that the adolescent is studying for a chemistry test, sits down and starts quizzing the young person to help him prepare.

- The parent, upon learning that his freshman-in-college daughter has lost her wallet, gets in the car, drives two hours to the college, and takes his daughter to the Department of Motor Vehicles to get a new driver's license.

In each of these previous examples, the parent does something for the young person (enables) instead of allowing the young person to do things for him or herself.

Enabling occurs all the time in today's world of parents and children. The phenomenon is so prevalent, in fact, that a term has been coined for it: *helicopter parents.* Helicopter parents hover close to their children, giving extreme attention to their experiences and challenges and regularly stepping in to stop negative consequences or circumstances from occurring to the child. Helicopter parenting and enabling can occur for a variety of reasons, whether out of sheer caring and love for the child or a basic misunderstanding of the kind of support the child needs as he or she attempts to grow and develop. Although the intentions behind helicopter parenting may be good, this style of parenting ultimately holds back the young person because it eliminates the opportunity for the young person to build skills and gain practical experience managing his or her life.

Here are some examples of what parents can do to empower—rather than enable—the young person.

- The parent, upon hearing her daughter complain about her difficulties with one of her high school friends, asks her daughter what steps she might take to improve the situation. When her daughter suggests that she could speak to the girl at school the next day, the parent offers her support and asks if it would be helpful for her daughter to role-play the scenario with her that evening.

- The parent, upon learning that the adolescent is studying for a chemistry test, says, "Thanks for filling me in. I can see that you're studying and I don't want to distract you so I will give you some quiet time," and leaves the room.

- The parent, upon learning that his freshman-in-college daughter has lost her wallet, which contained her driver's license, empathizes with his daughter's dilemma and asks her to consider all of the options. The parent brainstorms solutions with his daughter, giving her the opportunity to make a decision on how she will get a new license.

When the parent empowers his or her child, the process involves the same kind of dance mentioned in the earlier coaching section of the chapter. First, the parent steps back and gives the young person some space; then, as needed, the parent can step toward the young person, offering support and structure, as in the example of the high schooler with friend problems.

Similarly, after a parent has offered to let the adolescent study on his or her own (giving space), the adolescent may say (asking for support and structure), "Well, actually, you could help me study after dinner. I just need a little more time now to study on my own." In this way, the parent can give the adolescent the space needed to make his or her own decisions and run his or her own life, but the parent is waiting in the wings for the adolescent if called upon or needed.

If a parent is struggling to let go and give the young person the space needed to start advocating for and managing his or her own life, it can be helpful for the parent to remember that his or her role in the young person's life isn't becoming less important, nor is it disappearing. The parent's role is simply changing—from being a hands-on "do-er" to being someone who deliberately gives the young person space and then offers support and structure as needed.

In the context of parenting, *support* refers to the trusting, nonjudgmental relationship that the parent offers the young person to help foster self-confidence and achievement of goals. Structure refers to both the practical tools the parent offers the young person to help the young person stay on track—or get back on track—on the journey to meeting his or her goals and the daily routines and patterns that the parent supports the young person in creating, allowing for freedom, with clear guidelines and reasonable boundaries.

Parents can provide support in a fashion similar to that given in coaching, in a slightly different context. When parents listen to their children, they can empathize with their children's concerns, celebrate successes, and clarify their children's needs and the parent's requests. In doing so, parents will be providing nonjudgmental support. For example, a mom might help her son stay focused on completing his research paper by offering to keep younger siblings downstairs; a dad might help his daughter celebrate a week of on-time arrivals at school by inviting her out to dinner. Parents can provide support by being there and remaining present and attentive to their adolescents and young adults.

As for providing structure, parents can encourage young people to draw on specific tools and strategies from coaching, when needed, such as doable action steps, regular routines, and the use of a daily planner, and to practice self-care, such as exercise, deep breathing, or getting extra sleep. Parents may find that guiding the adolescent or young adult back toward structure can be particularly helpful when the young person appears to be getting distracted, becoming discouraged, or falling off the wagon on the path toward his or her goals.

Parents can also provide structure in the way of accountability. For example, mom might check in at the end of each day and ask, "How is your schoolwork coming?" This lets the young person know that mom cares and is paying attention; it also provides an opportunity for that young person to express concerns and troubleshoot them with mom.

The trick with offering accountability to adolescents and young adults and to communicating effectively, in general, is to switch from closed-ended questioning to open-ended questioning. So, instead of saying, "Did you do your homework?" which can be perceived as nagging or smothering, the parent can ask the adolescent, "How's your homework coming?" Instead of asking the young adult, "Are you studying hard in all of your classes?" the parent might ask, "So, what are you finding most interesting in your classes this semester?" or "What do you like best about your classes?" This open-ended style of questioning sets a nonjudgmental tone that is respectful of the young person's ability to take care of him or herself and thus helps to build self-confidence. It also lets the young person know that the parent is relating from a place of genuine caring rather than trying to meet some personal agenda or to assess some bottom line. In addition, open-ended questioning helps the parent empower the young person because it encourages the young person to think for him or herself.

Here's an example of an empowering, rather than enabling, dialogue between a parent and adolescent.

A Parenting Dialogue:
Empowering the Young Person at School

Adolescent: I really don't understand what's happening in biology class. The teacher doesn't put anything on the board. I want to learn but I'm frustrated. How come it can't be like before when the teacher helped me?

Parent: That sounds frustrating! [The parent empathizes.] How do you think you could improve the situation? [The parent inquires.]

Adolescent: I don't know, I guess I could talk to her after class—but that would be embarrassing.

Parent: Okay, you came in here and made it clear what isn't working for you in class and you did a really good job explaining that to me. I'm confident you can do the same thing with Mrs. Smith. [The parent encourages.] Is there anything else you want to discuss to ease your feelings of embarrassment before you talk to her? [The parent offers support and echoes the adolescent's concern to encourage conversation.]

Adolescent: Well, Mrs. Smith talks fast and I don't always follow the conversation and that is embarrassing.

Parent: Thanks for explaining that. I am wondering if it might help for us to practice right here. I can certainly talk fast and pretend to be Mrs. Smith!

As revealed in this sample dialogue, parents still have a role in being there for the young person with ADHD; it's just a new kind of relationship that involves a shift toward empowerment. Instead of enabling the young person by offering to pick up the phone and call the biology teacher like in the old days, the parent can empower the young person by showing confidence (offering support) in his or her ability to self-advocate and then providing some structure (role-playing) to move the young person one step closer to achieving the goal of communicating more effectively with the biology teacher.

Stepping Back While the Coach Steps Up

Much to the surprise of many moms and dads, the parent's role in the coaching process is actually quite small. After the initial prescreening and intake sessions, the parent will be stepping back again, giving the young person space to engage directly in coaching. At first, this new role may be difficult to understand or accept, but as parents learn more about the coaching process and how it works for young people, it becomes clearer why things work best this way.

If the parent is the one who contacts the coach to engage services for the young person, or if the young person is an adolescent rather than a young adult, the parent will likely participate in a prescreening process with the coach. The prescreening process is used to assess whether the parent truly desires coaching for the young person, because the parent is likely to be the one paying for the services, and whether the parent is willing and able to step back and allow coaching to take place between the young person and the coach without the parent being present.

In the case of adolescents, it is valuable for the parent to be present at the intake session. At the intake, the coach will invite the parent to express any concerns regarding his or her child. The coach will also ask the parent to listen to the young person's perspective and to ultimately allow coaching goals to be created in line with what the young person desires rather than with what the parent desires. The coach will explain, too, that coaching will occur directly between the young person and the coach and that the parent will not be participating in coaching sessions once the intake is complete and regular coaching begins.

If parents find this last piece of news surprising or difficult to hear, they are not alone—many parents struggle with this information. After years of doing so much for one's child, parents are being asked to let go, to do less, and even to become less involved in the details of the young person's life. This may seem scary, strange, or even sad. It can be helpful to reassure parents that it is perfectly normal, reasonable, and understandable to feel uncomfortable as they consider this new role. Parents have been directly engaged in the child's life for years and they care about their child's well-being! This shift may become a little easier if parents focus on the fact that giving the young person additional space as he or she gets older will ultimately help the young person grow and mature into his or her best and most capable self.

Given the potential difficulty of giving one's child some space, parents may find themselves needing some support while shifting from a mode of "doing for" (enabling) to a mode of "supporting in doing" (empowering). Thus, during both the prescreening process and the initial intake session, parents should let the coach know if they are struggling. Parents can express concerns and feel free to ask the coach to help them understand the value and necessity of giving the young person space to take the lead role in accomplishing his or her goals.

The coach is likely to explain, among other things, that this approach allows the young person the important opportunity to practice engaging in the work of life him or herself, to develop skills, and to increase self-confidence. If needed, and if the young person is in agreement, the coach might also be able to schedule occasional check-in meetings with both parents and their child present and/or may refer parents to a therapist or their own coach to help them work through the process of letting go.

Not all parents struggle with shifting to a role of empowerment. For example, some years ago, I began work with a 16-year-old high school student who was given complete freedom by his parents to engage in the coaching process on his own. Other than a quick phone conversation with mom, in which she gave consent for her son to participate in coaching with me, I interacted with the client completely independently of mom and dad. His parents were not even present for the intake session, which the client had driven to by himself. As such, the client and I created a PCA and began our work together without any input from his parents.

It is perfectly appropriate for parents of adolescents to be involved in the intake, but in this case, I followed the lead of the parents, who were fine with staying out of the coaching relationship, much as might be the case for the parents of a college-aged client. This client and I developed a very productive coaching relationship and worked together for five years. In part because of his parents' ability to let him develop independence and work confidentially with a coach, he went from making bad decisions and getting into trouble in high school to graduating college, and he is now studying in seminary.

Coaches: How You Can Help Parents Do the Shift

Coaches can play an important role in helping parents make the shift from *doing for their children* with ADHD to *supporting them in doing for themselves.* Coaches can begin to ease the transition by educating parents on the value of giving adolescents and young adults with ADHD space to practice taking care of themselves. The coach can also invite the parent and client to come up with a mutually acceptable way for the parent to stay connected to what's going on in the coaching process and the young person's life as a whole—ideally, through active communication between parent and client. If needed, and if the client is comfortable with it, brief e-mail correspondence can also be sent to the parent from the coach to confirm that the client is engaged in coaching and completing homework, or occasional check-in meetings can be set up with coach, client, and parent on the phone. Note that the content of coaching remains confidential and secure so that the relationship between the young person and the coach remains protected and intact. Parents are requested to speak directly with the young person to learn answers to questions related to the content of coaching. Last, if necessary, the coach can refer the parent to coaching or therapy to deal, in a supportive environment, with the issue of stepping back and letting go.

Effective communication with adolescents and young adults usually involves asking the kind of open-ended questions mentioned earlier. Open-ended questions help to show young people that the parent does not have a particular agenda and that the parent is interested in hearing whatever it is that the young person wants to share. Here are some examples of the kind of open-ended questions that parents might ask their adolescent or young adult:

- "What are you studying these days?"

- "How are you doing?"

- "What did you think of the movie you saw over the weekend?"

- "I noticed you were reading *A Midsummer Night's Dream.* What part do you like the best?"

- "Wow, you have a lot going on this weekend! How are you planning to fit it all in?"

When asking a young person questions, parents can aim to do so from a context of curiosity rather than judgment. Approaching young people from a place of interest and receptiveness tends to build trust and encourage adolescents and young adults to answer openly and honestly.

How Can Coaches and Parents Work Together to Support the Young Person?

Coaches

1. Partner with the youth directly

2. Support the goals of the client

3. Provide a safe space to try out new ideas without judgment and to discuss the ideas' pros and cons

4. Stay mindful of the parent's concerns

5. Relay concerns about the client to the parent, with the client's knowledge

Parents

1. Respct the boundaries of the coach–client relationship; be open to the information from the coach and client

2. Avoid pressuring the coach or youth to follow parent goals

3. Provide space for the coach–client partnership to develop

4. Ask questions, express concerns; listen to the youth and stay open to possibilities

5. Remain patient and trust in the coaching process

Ultimately, as coaching takes place between the young person and the coach, the parent's role is to observe, support, and applaud the process. For example, the adolescent might ask the parent to be part of her accountability plan—to, for example, ask her each day, "What assignments do you have to turn in tomorrow?" In this way, the parent will be invited to provide support. The parent can also be there to celebrate successes ("Hey, I heard you scored a goal in soccer this afternoon. Congratulations! Your practicing paid off!"). In this way, parents will have an opportunity to applaud the positive results of their adolescent's hard work toward accomplishing goals.

When a parent gives the young person space that is reinforced with support and structure, the young person learns that the parent believes in him or her—just like the coach does—and the chance that the young person will internalize this confidence grows. In addition, when parents learn to empower rather than enable, the young person gains additional opportunities to practice skills for success, identify and utilize strengths, and seek out resources as the parent uses the same supportive approach of the coach—investigating, empathizing, championing, celebrating, and so on.

The Client's Role: Ready, Willing and Able

Just as coaches' and parents' roles are to empower the young person with ADHD by providing support and structure, the young person has a clear and active role to play in the coaching process as well. Overall, the young person's job in the coaching process is to be an interested and willing partner, ready to move forward and work toward positive life changes. In particular, the young person can be asked to participate in coaching by

- communicating openly and honestly

- setting goals and generating action steps

- committing to being accountable and then following through

- calling or arriving on time for phone or in-person appointments, respectively, or canceling appointments 24 hours in advance, if needed.

These expectations are best shared with the client early in the process, ideally prior to or during the intake session. In my practice, I ask clients to read a detailed list of expectations before the intake session, and we discuss them at the actual intake, as needed. My expectations of the client include readiness for exploration, willingness to listen to new ideas, honesty, accountability, timeliness, follow-through, and openness to feedback. These expectations can offer the client insight into the role that he or she is being invited to fill in the coaching relationship. If the client does not express a willingness, an ability, or an interest in meeting these expectations, the client may not be ready for coaching. I also let the client know that he or she may hold me accountable to similar expectations as well. This is an equal partnership, so the coach must be ready, willing, and fully present for the client, too.

A Note for Everyone

The young person with ADHD potentially has many different people in his or her life aiming to assist: parents, teachers, doctors, school counselor, academic tutor, school psychologist, therapist, and maybe a coach. Is it possible for all of these individuals to work together in support of the young person with ADHD?

When my clients have multiple professionals looking after them in addition to parents, I consider working as a team to be the most ideal situation, particularly if we are all on the same page, working to empower rather than enable the young person.

It is interesting to note that the National Institute of Mental Health's Multimodal Treatment Study of Children With ADHD, with its first results published in 1999, reported that children with ADHD who received *multimodal treatment*—who both took medication for the disorder and received behavioral treatment—did better than those children taking medication or receiving behavioral treatment alone. Many professionals in the ADHD community agree with these findings, believing that multiple modes of treatment serve the client better than a single mode of treatment alone. Research continues, and as coaching becomes more prevalent for adolescents and young adults, I am optimistic that there will be more opportunities to understand the positive benefits of multimodal treatment— the coaching intervention included!

Given the multimodal nature of ADHD treatment today, coaches can serve clients with ADHD best when they are knowledgeable on how to (a) reach out to other professionals in the client's life when needed to ensure the best care and (b) encourage the client to reach out to other professionals to address needs that fall outside of coaching. Here are a variety of scenarios in which the coach might reach out or prompt the client to reach out to the other professionals in the client's life.

- The client expresses she has been feeling dizzy from her new medication; the coach asks the client if this might be a good time for the client to get in touch with her neurologist and discuss this symptom.

- When the coach learns that the client has been depressed and stressed out, the coach asks the client, "Would this be a good time for me to contact your therapist?"

- The client, who has used a math tutor in the past, admits to being totally confused about algebra. The coach asks if the client would be willing to reach out to the tutor again.

- The client discusses a problem with his 504 plan accommodations. The coach inquires about the problem and together they determine that this is a matter for the special education contact at school.

- For many weeks, the client has come to coaching sessions thoroughly exhausted. The coach mentions that this seems to be an ongoing problem and asks the client whether she is ready and willing to make an appointment with her doctor.

In most cases, the coach isn't reaching out to the other professionals him or herself but is instead prompting the client to communicate with the professional (empowering rather than enabling). The most common exception to this rule is regarding therapists. Coaches tend to be in actual conversation with a client's therapist more often than with other professionals, with the client's knowledge and permission. Oftentimes, when a client has both a therapist and a coach, there is an overlap in discussions. For example, the client may be working with the coach on improving time management and organizational skills while talking to the therapist about feelings of failure in these areas. The two professionals, coach and therapist, can work together in support of the client's needs.

Coaches, allied professionals, parents, and clients can all be part of the solution for improving the lives of young people with ADHD. Each plays a distinct role—from doctors who help the client manage medicine, to school psychologists who provide expertise on specific educational needs, to therapists who help the client deal with the emotional fallout of having ADHD and coexisting mental health issues, to coaches who help clients generate and accomplish goals for a fulfilling life. Although I don't want to presume to tell other professionals how best to work with coaches or to do their jobs, I do share here a few words for coaches on reaching out to other professionals.

Coaches can work effectively with allied professionals and best serve the client by knowing when to refer the young person to the right specialist, whether for new or continued care. Below is a list of those professionals to whom coaches most frequently refer young clients with ADHD for support or care. I encourage you to take time to talk with various professionals in your community to get a clear picture of each of their roles as they pertain to young people with ADHD:

- academic advisors
- academic tutors
- career counselors
- school psychologists
- occupational therapists
- physicians
  — primary care
  — family practice
  — pediatrician
  — neurologist
  — psychiatrist

- school guidance counselors
- specialized college counselors
- therapists, social workers, and psychologists.

There are many times when a referral is appropriate, even essential. Coaches do best by their clients when they become knowledgeable on the common roles of other professionals in the life of the ADHD client and respond to any cues from the client that it may be time for the client or coach, on the client's behalf, to contact another professional—to meet the client's needs beyond coaching.

As I have attempted to show in this chapter, the common goal of the coach, parents, and allied professionals is to empower rather than enable the young person with ADHD. The coach and parents' roles thus entail helping the young person identify and apply his or her skills, strengths, and resources to achieving life goals. In the process, the young person's sense of independence and self-confidence grow.

When you know your role in helping a young person with ADHD, you will know when to move forward, when to back up, and how to position yourself vis-à-vis the young person. In return, the young person will sense your confidence and clarity and be more likely to develop trust in your abilities to be supportive. In the end, knowing your role allows you to support the young person more effectively, whether as a parent, coach, or other professional. And supporting young people more effectively means that more people with ADHD will be leading more satisfying lives, in part because of the work that you carry on each and every day.

T H R E E
Fundamentals of ADHD

"What will it take for you to complete this project?" When a coach or parent or teacher understands the fundamentals of ADHD, this is the kind of question the adult will know to ask the young person with ADHD who has stopped making progress on a goal or maybe has not even gotten started. When an adult doesn't understand the fundamentals of ADHD, the question asked may be the frustrated or baffled, "Why didn't you do it yet?" The former question recognizes that the young person with ADHD may need extra support and structure to accomplish things; the latter may point to a lack of awareness of the way that young people with ADHD functions and what they may need in their lives to be successful.

Whether in matters of household chores, homework, college applications, personal care, or bill payment, adolescents and young adults with ADHD often need extra support and structure to accomplish their goals, even to complete what may seem like the simplest of tasks to mom or dad or Professor Jones. The more we, the people involved in the lives of young people with ADHD, understand the nature of ADHD—the underlying neurobiology of the disorder, the symptoms that result from this imbalance in brain chemistry, and the way that ADHD manifests itself in different people and responds to different treatments—the more we will be able to meet young people where they are and offer them help that is truly useful to them.

In this chapter, I describe the fundamentals of ADHD to help foster in those unfamiliar with ADHD a basic understanding of what ADHD is, what it isn't, and how this understanding can be used to best support a young person with ADHD. I write this chapter not as a medical professional or a psychologist (I am neither) but as a trained and experienced ADHD and life coach who has worked in the field for more than 14 years and who is constantly testing my knowledge of ADHD in the real world with young clients. This chapter is not intended to be a medical or a psychological reference. Instead, it is meant to provide a practical overview for those new to ADHD who are contemplating coaching young people with the disorder or who would like to gain a better understanding or a brief review of the topic to improve their own ability to support a young person with ADHD.

Over time, as a person gains more insight and understanding into the nature of ADHD, the individual is likely to become better at drawing connections between what's happening behind the scenes for young people with ADHD and what's happening on the surface. An ability to recognize the concrete problems that can manifest themselves in the young person as a result of his or her ADHD may become sharpened, and instead of asking, "Why didn't you do it yet?" the coach, parent, or teacher will have an "aha" moment. The adult's understanding of how the young person "ticks"—in terms of poor organizational skills, low self-esteem, poor short-term memory, and so on—will allow the adult to say, "What will it take for you to complete this project?" The adult becomes able to understand the client well enough to support the client with the empathy, understanding, and flexibility needed to compensate for the issues that may arise. And now, instead of being stuck at an impasse, the young person and coach or other adult can work together to help the young person move forward.

This chapter thus describes the neurobiology of the ADHD brain, common behaviors associated with ADHD, and basic medication issues for youth with ADHD. Also discussed are the executive functioning issues that affect—personally, academically, and socially—young people with ADHD. The chapter also touches on the learning disabilities diagnosed in some youth with ADHD, along with other coexisting conditions (also known as comorbid conditions), such as addiction or depression. The subject of giftedness in youth with ADHD is also addressed.

Why Know the Fundamentals?

Gain Understanding and Recognize Setbacks

For a coach, parent, teacher, or other support person in the life of a young person with ADHD, knowledge of ADHD can be helpful in a variety of ways. First, a basic understanding of the fact that ADHD is neurobiological in nature, caused by brain chemistry rather than by general laziness, poor upbringing, or not caring, will help care providers remain patient and stay focused on the tools that these young people need to overcome or compensate for their challenges. With this kind of understanding, blame can often be avoided and personalized support offered instead.

Second, an understanding of ADHD and how it traditionally presents itself in young people will help the adult be more attuned to setbacks and challenges when they arise. Instead of assuming a missed appointment indicates lack of commitment, a coach will know to look deeper when connecting with the client next time, perhaps by encouraging the client to explore what's making it hard for him or her to show up for appointments. Does the client need a better reminder system? Does the client's medication need some adjusting to help improve focus or memory? Did the client not complete one of his or her action steps and feel embarrassed to report back to the coach? Certainly, a missed appointment can point to lack of commitment, but there are a host of other possible reasons for it, too.

Consider Aimee, a 20-year-old political science major who has indicated that she'd like to write her resume by the end of the month so she can apply for summer internships. In the first two coaching sessions, Aimee seemed excited and committed to the process. She brainstormed with the coach to identify her desired strategy for writing the resume and blocked out five hours each week to focus on creating and editing her resume. Then, Aimee missed the third coaching session. When she finally rescheduled with the coach, she said she didn't really care about getting an internship anymore.

A coach who understands the typical presentation of ADHD—and the mindset that often accompanies it—will know that what is happening with Aimee is common within the context of ADHD. Her reason for stalled progress could be one of many, but the fact that she seems to be faltering and her motivation is dwindling is not necessarily a sign to call her out on lack of commitment or to end coaching. Instead, it is a cue to the coach that Aimee may need some additional support or new strategies to keep making progress. The coach's knowledge of ADHD thus helps the coach put forth a best effort to meet the young person where he or she really is and to help coaching be most effective.

Become More Aware of Coaching Readiness

Knowledge of ADHD and related issues can also help coaches, parents, and other care providers assess whether a young person is currently ready for coaching. When the neurobiological symptoms of ADHD have not been effectively addressed with medication or other targeted treatment, clients may not have a capacity to commit to the work of coaching. If a young person has just started taking a new medication and the dose is still not quite right, might that interfere with the coaching process? When coexisting conditions are present and untreated, how ready is that young person for coaching? Thus, it is valuable for coaches to be knowledgeable enough on both ADHD and possible coexisting conditions to recognize when one or more of these issues could be at play. Is a client showing up with alcohol on her breath? Does the client talk about his anxiety and how it is keeping him from being with others? Does the client disintegrate into tears every time she and the coach discuss her communications with her parents, or does she lash out at the coach in an angry rage when the coach poses appropriate questions? Any one of these situations could be a sign of emotional or mental health issues that need to be addressed before coaching can be helpful.

Knowledge of the fundamentals of ADHD thus provides a foundation for an ethical coaching practice. Coaches need to be sufficiently informed to detect when a client may or may not be ready for coaching, whether because of a mental health condition, a problem with substance abuse, or medication issues that need to be worked out. Along the same lines, an understanding of the various learning disabilities that may accompany ADHD will also provide the coach with valuable information that will help him or her coach effectively. With basic knowledge of learning disabilities and related symptoms, a coach will be in a better position to help a client with learning disabilities to explore strategies relevant to his or her learning style and to seek additional support where needed to help the client reach his or her goals (e.g., hiring a tutor or arranging for special accommodations at school or at work).

Push Past ADHD Myths

Last, knowledge of the ADHD fundamentals can be valuable in dispelling the harmful myths that often surround the young person with ADHD. Too many times, young people with ADHD are misunderstood by those around them— by parents, teachers, sports coaches, friends, and acquaintances. Because the source of these young people's condition is invisible to the naked eye and resides at the level of the brain, loved ones and others may commonly mistake ADHD symptoms in the young person for laziness, lack of caring, indifference, impoliteness, or lack of intelligence. In fact, the reality is often far from the case. I have known many a young person with ADHD who wanted to accomplish his or her goals with the utmost amount of sincerity but yet suffered from a lack of skills and strategies for how to make progress. I have known plenty of others with ADHD who had big hearts but who could come across as uninterested or uncaring because they didn't know how to listen and ask questions of others. And, to debunk the myth that ADHD points to a lack of intelligence, note that scientific genius Albert Einstein has been hypothesized to have had ADHD.

In sum, a clear understanding of the fundamentals of ADHD will provide the coach and other care providers with invaluable information: from how to interpret the behavior of a young person with ADHD, to when to probe for additional information of the young person, to when to refer the young person to other providers outside of coaching for assistance.

What Is ADHD?

ADHD is a neurobiological disorder in which problematic brain chemistry is thought to cause challenges in a person's executive functioning skills. The resulting symptoms relate to hyperactivity, impulsivity, and/or inattention. According to the Diagnostic and Statistical Manual of Mental Health Disorders (4th ed.; DSM–IV), there are three subtypes of ADHD: hyperactive-impulsive, inattentive, and combined hyperactive–impulsive and inattentive, with most young people having the combined type.

ADHD is a congenital, hereditary, neurologic condition. Congenital means it must appear at an early age, generally by the age of 7 years, although many parents can trace back the onset of symptoms in their child to the age of 2 or 3 years. Hereditary means you get it from your family. (This brings up the obvious difficulty that the affected child is often not the only one in the home struggling with the consequences of ADHD.) That ADHD is neurologic means it is clearly a physical condition that changes the neurologic functioning of the brain. It is not a psychiatric disorder.

Researchers are beginning to understand the biologic basis of ADHD. Think of the brain as having two parts, each part being in charge of a different set of functions. One part comprises the workstations of the brain, such as the frontal cortex for thinking, the auditory cortex for language, the occipital cortex for vision, and the motor cortex for movement. Children with ADHD generally have normal workstations of the brain. They have the same abilities—the same strengths and weaknesses—as any other group of children. The second part of the brain is made up of the control sections. It is this part of the brain that

- determines which activities to pursue and which to suppress
- determines how hard to work and how long to work
- suppresses impulses that would interfere with the selected activity.

Researchers now have good physiologic data from studies of adults and children indicating that those sections of the brain that we know to be in charge of control functions operate in the ADHD brain at a very low level of physiologic activity—essentially the same level that most people's brains function at when they're asleep.

With an understanding of this control function, it becomes clear why ADHD is treated the way it is—with stimulant medication—and why that treatment is so successful. Intuition would tell you that giving particularly hyperactive, impulsive children stimulants is about the dumbest thing someone could do. But it works. And it works not because—as medical professionals used to believe—the brain is abnormal and the medication has a paradoxical effect. It works because the brain is normal and the medication works exactly as expected, as a stimulant. Specifically, it stimulates and wakes the brain's control sections, putting the child back in control of his or her own brain.

The human brain is an amazingly complex organ. It has approximately 100 billion cells. Each of these cells has an average of 10,000 to 100,000 connections with other cells. For the brain to work efficiently, a continual complex series of messages is sent between different areas of the brain, with a given message sent along a nerve axon as an electrical impulse. The problem becomes how to pass that electrical message from the end of one nerve cell to the beginning of the next. To accomplish this, the brain uses chemicals known collectively as neurotransmitters. The human brain has 50-100 different neurotransmitters, each serving a particular area and a particular function.

In the case of ADHD, the two critical neurotransmitters are dopamine and norepinephrine. Each of these is produced in a small area of the brain and is widely distributed to the frontal and limbic areas and to the cerebellum. The essential neurochemical difference in the brains of people with ADHD is that they have inadequate levels of dopamine and/or norepinephrine to reliably activate relevant brain areas. Hence, it is difficult to get messages from the control sections of the brain to the appropriate activation area. Stimulant medications act by increasing the amount of dopamine and norepinephrine at those crucial synapses, enabling them to function at a more normal level.

ADHD is clearly a genetic condition. The heritability averages about 0.8. This does not mean that 20% of cases have no genetic association. Rather, unique experiences in the person's life (e.g., prematurity or other significant neonatal illness; disorganized or dysfunctional parents; or in utero exposure to nicotine, alcohol, or illicit drugs) may contribute up to approximately 20% of the likelihood of the expression of ADHD, especially in someone who has some degree of genetic loading for ADHD.

A somewhat unexpected finding is that twin studies have shown a relatively low contribution (0-6%) of shared environmental effects, whereas nonshared environmental events have a greater role (9-20%). Nonshared characteristics relevant to ADHD include head injury, infection, individual exposure to toxins, and prenatal and noxious perinatal events. Among the factors with the highest correlation to ADHD are low birth weight (especially small for gestational age) and maternal smoking during pregnancy. Both of these factors contribute to ADHD independently of maternal ADHD.

Shared environmental effects have much less impact as a cause of ADHD. This category includes such factors as social class, family educational background, general home environment, family nutritional habits, environmental toxins, and family style of child rearing. It is particularly interesting that parenting style has no correlation with ADHD. There is some evidence, however, that having an ADHD child impacts the quality of parental care. In one study, the quality of parenting improved after the child was treated with stimulant medication, reflecting the not surprising conclusion that raising an ADHD child is a challenge. Bad parenting will not give a child ADHD, but an ADHD child can make parenting techniques bad.

General experience would suggest that the number of cases of ADHD with no genetic factors is very small. Most of the time, when environmental effects are present, they are relevant in taking a child with a mild degree of inattention and exacerbating that to the point of impairment.

Young people with ADHD may face a variety of challenges, such as

- memory challenges

- poor organizational skills

- challenges with goal-setting, planning, and task completion

- social challenges

- self-esteem issues

- learning issues

- increased risk taking.

Young people with ADHD are also more likely to follow the crowd and can be easily swayed in their decision making. In addition, they have a tendency to hyperfocus—that is, as noted by Dr. Kenny Handleman, "to completely and utterly focus on one topic or issue, often to the exclusion of others, with precise and productive concentration, until the end result is achieved." As mentioned earlier, those with ADHD may also face substance abuse problems and coexisting conditions, such as learning disabilities and/or mental health issues. As a result of their ADHD, young people may have trouble juggling the multiple demands of life—academic obligations, domestic and family responsibilities, after-school activities, and so on. Even engaging in simple daily living skills, like taking regular showers, remembering to eat breakfast, and finding clean clothes, can be hard for a young person with ADHD.

How Is ADHD Commonly Diagnosed?

Although there are some individuals for whom it takes years to detect or treat ADHD, and some may go a lifetime without discovering the nature of their condition, the journey toward treating ADHD usually begins with a diagnosis. ADHD symptoms are commonly first noticed by parents and teachers. A teacher may say to a parent, "Your child is really bright, but he's having trouble getting work done. You may want to go talk to someone about this challenge." Or it may become evident to the parent that his or her daughter has trouble sitting still at the kitchen table to do homework or that his or her son continually forgets to bring his lunch to school or keep track of things. The young person him or herself may report difficulty following the math lecture or trouble staying on top of schoolwork deadlines.

Once the symptoms of ADHD come to the attention of parents, the journey toward diagnosis can follow a variety or a combination of paths. The most frequent paths to diagnosis and treatment of ADHD include the following:

- Path 1: A teacher raises concerns and the family brings this to their primary physician, who either does the evaluation or refers out to a psychologist or psychiatrist.

- Path 2: The primary physician or specialist attains feedback from teachers and parents—and the young person, when applicable—

- using a behavior rating scale, academic data, and family history.

- Path 3: The parents arrange a meeting with a psychologist, who conducts a psychoeducational report.

- Path 4: The parents or the young adult meets with a psychiatrist if the family is already under one's care or after being referred to one by the psychologist.

The path to ADHD diagnosis can thus involve a variety of professionals, from teachers who give input (without naming ADHD) to analysis by psychologists and doctors. As noted by Dr. Russell A. Barkley in *Taking Charge of ADHD*,

Whether you consult a pediatrician, child psychologist, child psychiatrist, child neurologist, social worker, school psychologist, family practitioner, or other mental health professional seems to matter less than finding someone who is familiar with the substantial scientific and professional literature on ADHD.

No one pathway to diagnosis is necessarily better than any other; what seems to matter most is the care provider's knowledge of and familiarity with ADHD. I would also add to that the importance of the young person and family trusting and feeling comfortable with the care provider.

Behavior Rating Scale From Teachers and Parents

In the first method, feedback on the young person is gathered from teachers and parents using a behavior rating scale. The American Academy of Pediatrics has endorsed the Vanderbilt scales—VADPRS (Vanderbilt ADHD Diagnostic Parent Rating Scale) and VADTRS (Vanderbilt ADHD Diagnostic Teacher Rating Scale)—as their preferred rating scales and has widely distributed them to pediatric offices.

Making the correct diagnosis in pediatric ADHD is especially important today. The Vanderbilt scales follow closely the criteria set forth in the DSM-IV and have been customized to observations made in the home and classroom environments. These rating scales are used to track, review, and quantify the behavioral characteristics of ADHD.

The information gathered in the behavior rating scale is then brought to the pediatrician or family doctor, who will assess the information and recommend next steps for the young person's treatment, if appropriate. The recommended evaluation consists of a semistructured interview in which the doctor looks at current symptoms, developmental history, general health, family functioning, and family history.

If the results of the behavior rating scale, interview, and family history indicate that there is a likelihood of executive functioning issues or ADHD, many doctors will write a prescription for a stimulant medication and suggest that the young person try it for 30 days and report back on the results. For example, if the young person is evidencing a high percentage of problems with focus, distractibility, sitting still, or following through on tasks, the medication can help to alleviate those symptoms.

What Is a Teacher's Role?

By law, public school teachers are restricted from mentioning to a parent the possibility that a child has ADHD. However, teachers may indicate that some issues are going on with a child that could be checked out to help everyone better support the young person. Sometimes this process rolls into the use of the behavior rating scale to capture what is going on with the young person and to provide the parent with valuable information that can then be shared with a doctor.

When there is a family history of ADHD, a doctor may be more likely to write a prescription for a stimulant than would be the case without this history. Some doctors, aware of different treatment options beyond medication, may refer the young person to coaching and/or may suggest adjustments in sleep, exercise, diet, or routine instead of or in addition to medication. A referral to a psychiatrist who specializes in ADHD medication management may also be given.

Psychoeducational Report From a Psychologist

As part of the diagnostic process, the young person will go to see a psychologist (perhaps prompted by challenges at school or at home). The psychologist will take a complete developmental history and an academic history of the young person and will run a battery of tests to determine areas of strengths and weaknesses. Because the psychoeducational report is comprehensive and conducted by a trained psychologist, the results can give very clear insight into what's going on for the young person to inhibit academic success, mood state, motivation, social life, and more.

The results of this process will guide the psychologist toward specific recommendations for treatment, interventions, and accommodations. Recommended interventions may include coaching, therapy (occupational, mental health, etc.), tutoring, and/or medication. If appropriate, the psychologist will refer the young person to a medical professional, such as a psychiatrist.

The psychoeducational report is not only useful for painting a full picture of what's going on for the young person—in terms of psychology and ability to learn—it is also required by most states if accommodations are to be given to the child in the public school system and later on in college. Thus, a big benefit of working with a psychologist to generate a psychoeducational report is that the family will be able to use this report to take advantage of any accommodations that might be necessary for the young person to succeed in school.

Self-Referral to a Psychiatrist

In some cases, when symptoms come to the parent's attention regarding the young person, the parent may immediately set up a meeting with the family psychiatrist to inquire about treatment. This might be the case if one of the siblings is already working with a psychiatrist to treat ADHD or another issue or if mom or dad is under the care of a psychiatrist for ADHD, depression, or another mental health condition. The psychiatrist is likely to take the history of the young person, look over all paperwork and information, and make a decision as to whether a full psychoeducational battery of tests should be run, if one has not already been conducted with the psychologist. Alternatively, the psychiatrist may want to try medication and monitor the young person's response.

A diagnosis of ADHD may be triggered by a teacher's input (although the label ADHD won't be mentioned), identified in the psychologist's office, or detected by the family pediatrician or psychiatrist. Diagnosis, in turn, can lead to treatment. Yet, I also want to point out that a diagnosis of ADHD is not actually required for treatment. Sometimes the family doctor will make recommendations for treating the behavioral symptoms of ADHD without naming the condition for the patient and family. A doctor does not need to make a specific diagnosis to recommend behavioral treatments for specific symptoms. However, most physicians would be loath to prescribe a controlled substance without having at least a tentative diagnosis of ADHD in mind. Other times, an individual will find his or her way into coaching to handle the executive functioning issues associated with ADHD without ever receiving an ADHD diagnosis. Although an ADHD diagnosis can be helpful, it is not required to receive certain kinds of treatment and interventions.

Coaching Without a Diagnosis? Certainly!

Parents sometimes bring their children directly to coaching, skipping the typical paths to diagnosis, when they learn of the issues that seem to be impeding their children's ability to achieve. Oftentimes, poor time management and organizational skills or difficulty staying on track at school are the reasons parents and young adults seek out coaching.

A specific diagnosis of ADHD, executive dysfunction, or learning disabilities is thus not necessary to initiate coaching. For some families, it is preferable to start by focusing on the issues through coaching and consider a full diagnostic workup at a later time. If the initial prescreen and intake indicate that the young person is coachable, the client might try coaching for a while, but if the coaching process becomes inhibited or is made difficult by the young person's symptoms, the coach is likely to recommend that the client go in for psychoeducational testing with a psychologist or make an appointment with a doctor.

For example, I meet young people in coaching all the time whose families have learned of me from friends' parents without ADHD ever being mentioned on either side. "You should try coaching," one mom might say to another. "The coach really helped my son get his grades up." The new young person's parent then reaches out to me to help her daughter with her organizational abilities or some other skill issue without our discussing ADHD. The daughter may or may not have a diagnosis of ADHD—we don't necessarily need to know for coaching to proceed. Coaching is a process focused on goals and outcomes, not on a specific diagnosis. As a result, a diagnosis of ADHD is sometimes deferred and coaching is entered straightaway. If the need for a referral to a psychologist or psychiatrist arises, coaches can then offer the young person the appropriate referral/s.

Regardless of pathway to ADHD diagnosis, the young person should also be evaluated for coexisting psychological and developmental disorders, as stressed by the American Academy of Pediatrics. A complete picture of the young person's diagnosis—from ADHD to potential coexisting conditions such as learning disabilities and mood and anxiety disorders—will provide the young person, parents, teachers, and other care providers with invaluable information for designing an environment suitable for the young person's success.

How Is ADHD Commonly Treated?

Medication: The Basics

As noted earlier in the chapter, ADHD is often treated using stimulants, which have been found to activate the control functions of the brain in individuals with ADHD. For some individuals, nonstimulant medications are the preference. The nonstimulants, such as Strattera, are estimated to have approximately 70–80% of the potency of stimulants. Nonetheless, the nonstimulants have a lower side-effect profile and are valuable treatment options.

According to the National Institute of Mental Health, medications for ADHD can be helpful to some individuals in that they "reduce hyperactivity and impulsivity and improve their ability to focus, work, and learn." Improvements in physical coordination have also been seen. Each individual is unique, and, as with most medications, an individual's response to a given medication will vary. One medication may work for one child but not another; one dose may work in this adolescent but not in that young adult. There is no general formula to predict which will be the best medication and the best dose, and there is a great deal of variability from one person to the next. In general, the correct dose is the dose that works the best, with tolerable side effects.

As indicated by the National Institutes of Health, ADHD medications can be taken in a variety of ways, whether as a pill or capsule, a liquid, or even a skin patch. Individuals have the option of using short-acting, long-acting, or extended-release versions of the medication, depending on what seems to work best for him or her, given the person's reaction to the medication, lifestyle, personality factors, ability to remember medication, and so forth. One of the benefits of long-acting or extended-release medications is the sustained effect of the medication throughout the school day without the drop in focus and productivity that can occur with short-acting medication.

Another consideration involves determining when the medication is most needed—during school, homework time, weekends, or another time. The issue of when to take medication and how to best monitor the level of effectiveness commonly resurfaces in college-aged students who are on a new schedule with erratic study habits, which may create a need to shift the timing and dosage of their medication. Medication management is a fine art and science that may take time, patience, experimentation, observation, communication, and regular check-ins with one's doctor to be worked out.

The coach is in no way responsible for prescribing medication or making direct recommendations regarding dosage and titration. However, a coach may work with a client to

- help the client set up reminders to take medications
- keep a journal to track medication effectiveness and side effects
- follow dosing instructions, such as taking medication after eating or not taking stimulants after a certain time of the day to allow for sleep.

Understanding some basic information regarding the medications prescribed to treat ADHD and related conditions will help coaches to develop a clearer picture of the world within which the client dwells and to have enough knowledge to ask relevant and educated questions. Has the client been remembering to take his medication? Has the client been taking her medication at the right time of day? The coach will likely not come out and ask these kinds of closed-ended questions, but the coach will keep these questions in mind when the client seems out of sorts. A more general "How are things going with your medication?" on the part of the coach may lead to a more specific discussion of where the client may want to take action to improve medication's effectiveness, whether that be learning strategies for remembering when to take medication or realizing that he or she should call the doctor for an appointment.

Coaching

More and more, coaching is being recommended and used as a part of the multimodal treatment plan for those with ADHD. Sometimes coaching is used in addition to medication; other times it is used before medication is considered. The particular treatment plan will depend on the needs and wishes of the young person and his or her parents, as well as on care provider recommendations.

As described in Chapter 1, ADHD coaching is a specialized type of coaching that is tailored to meet the unique needs of the client with ADHD and delivered by a coach with in-depth knowledge and understanding of ADHD and related issues. The ADHD coaching process offers clients support, structure, and accountability for their actions, ideally leading to a greater level of success in all areas of life, including those negatively impacted by ADHD, learning disabilities, or other coexisting conditions.

Coaching can be used to address many of the challenges faced by young people with ADHD and may focus on supporting the young person in areas such as

- improving time management

- establishing routines, rituals, and good habits

- getting to class on time

- studying

- keeping track of things

- doing laundry

- exercising

- eating regularly

- getting to bed

- waking up and staying up

- taking medication.

As noted in Chapter 2, the National Institute of Mental Health's Multimodal Treatment Study of Children With ADHD reported that children with ADHD who received multimodal treatment—who both took medication for the disorder and received behavioral treatment—did better in overall functioning than those children taking medication or receiving behavioral treatment alone. Many professionals in the ADHD community agree with these findings, believing that multiple modes of treatment serve the client better than a single mode of treatment alone. Depending on the needs of the young person and the way he or she responds to certain treatments, medication can be used to activate the control portion of the brain of the young person with ADHD and lay the foundation for academic growth and skill building to come. Tutoring can provide the support the young person needs to achieve academic success in content-related areas, and coaching can be used to support the young person with the processes of daily life.

ADHD Fundamentals:
What's Important for a Coach to Know?

I encourage the students in my ADHD coach training program to read extensively on the topic of ADHD. Although the coach will not be handing out diagnoses, prescribing medication, or identifying needed educational accommodations, the more the coach knows about ADHD, the more prepared the coach will be to help the client recognize issues that may need attention, seek additional treatment where needed, and design an action plan tailored to the client's unique needs. I have noticed several areas of importance when it comes to understanding ADHD:

- executive functioning

- learning disabilities

- coexisting conditions

- behavioral issues

- giftedness.

In the text that follows, I share some of the key issues that may be useful to coaches, parents, and ADHD professionals looking to expand their knowledge of ADHD so they can better support young people with the condition.

Executive Functioning

One of the most important things to understand about ADHD is that it originates in the brain. Although the symptoms of ADHD play out on a behavioral level that we can see with our eyes and notice through day-to-day observation, the source of the disorder can be traced back to an individual's brain chemistry, or what can be referred to as neurobiology. Why is this important to those of us who want to support young people with ADHD?

Understanding that ADHD originates in the brain can help us appreciate the value of ADHD treatments that address the young person's biology and physiology—from medication to exercise to adequate nutrition to sufficient sleep. When coaches understand the neurobiological basis of ADHD and see a client losing focus or acting impulsively, coaches will know to question how the client's medication is working. Is it time to check in with the physician for some medication management? Parents who understand the neurobiological basis of ADHD may find it easier to have patience with the young person and to take the young person's behavior less personally. Instead of saying, "Why didn't you listen when I asked you to stop at the gas station on the way home?" parents can ask questions like, "What will make it easier for you to remember to stop at the gas station next time?" The focus can shift from blame to support, from frustration to helpfulness.

The part of the brain that seems to be most affected in individuals with ADHD is the prefrontal cortex. This brain area is responsible for managing a number of important skills needed to be successful in life, from keeping one's things organized to managing one's time to remembering what someone said a few minutes ago. These skills are commonly referred to collectively, using the overarching term of executive functioning skills. According to Dr. Joyce Cooper-Kahn and Dr. Laurie Dietzel, authors of *Late, Lost, and Unprepared,*

> The executive functions are a set of processes that all have to do with managing oneself and one's resources in order to achieve a goal. [Executive functions] is an umbrella term for the neurologically-based skills involving mental control and self-regulation.

The terms that are used to refer to the different skills affected by executive functioning vary slightly according to researcher. In his book *Attention Deficit Disorder: The Unfocused Mind in Children and Adults,* psychologist and researcher Dr. Thomas Brown labels the affected executive functioning skill areas as

- activation: organizing, prioritizing, and activating to work
- focus: focusing, sustaining, and shifting attention to tasks
- effort: regulating alertness, sustaining effort, and processing speed
- emotion: managing frustration and modulating emotions
- memory: utilizing working memory and accessing recall
- action: monitoring and self-regulating action.

I often use Brown's model to help new coaches understand more about the common symptoms and behaviors of young people with ADHD and how these behaviors link back to executive functioning and the brain.

What does all of this information on executive functioning really mean? ADHD is based in the brain. Further, the brain of a young person with ADHD works differently than the brain of someone without ADHD. Thus, no amount of cajoling, cheerleading, persuading, or yelling will get a young person with ADHD to overcome the symptoms of ADHD unless the neurobiology of the disorder is addressed and/or taken into account. For some young people, this involves medication that addresses and regulates brain chemistry and directly improves executive functioning skills (provides more ability to focus, better impulse control, etc.). Others find that medication lays the groundwork for improving executive functioning skills (or for learning to compensate for weaker executive functioning) in the realm of coaching, therapy, tutoring, and so on. For example, medication might be used to help a young person sit still and pay attention; the young person can then turn to coaching and use this improved ability to focus to learn new strategies for managing his or her homework schedule and arriving on time at school with all of his or her assignments.

Some individuals with ADHD manage to forgo medication altogether, whether because of its lack of effectiveness in their particular case, side effects that preclude use, or a philosophical preference to not use medication. In this case, coaching might be used to help the young person address neurobiologically based symptoms of ADHD with behavioral interventions.

For example, a child who likes to bang his hand on the desk (as a result of his "dancing brain" or his understimulated prefrontal cortex) may learn to move his toes inside his shoes as a safe and nondistracting alternative. The same child might build regular exercise into his lifestyle, which has been found to have a positive benefit for some individuals with ADHD, as detailed by Dr. John Ratey in his popular 2008 book *Spark: The Revolutionary New Science of Exercise and the Brain*. Regardless of the treatment or combination of treatments used to address the symptoms of ADHD, remembering that the disorder has a basis in a person's brain can help coaches, parents, and other adults in a young person's life stay focused on measures that can help the young person address and compensate for challenges to executive functioning due to the ADHD brain.

Learning Disabilities

It's not uncommon for a young person with ADHD to also have one or more learning disabilities. A report by Dr. George J. DuPaul and Dr. Robert J. Volpe indicated that 27-31% of individuals who have ADHD also have learning disabilities, although this range varies according to the specifications used to define learning disabilities.

Thus, when coaches work with young people with ADHD, it's altogether possible that the young person will also be operating with a learning disability. As a result, it's useful for the coach to have a basic understanding of learning disabilities—what is a learning disability and what does it mean to have a learning disability? What are some of the common learning disabilities? And what kind of resources and support are available to those with learning disabilities?

A definition of learning disabilities, according to the Division for Learning Disabilities of the Council for Exceptional Children, is shown below:

> Students with learning disabilities (LD) have difficulty acquiring basic skills or academic content. Learning disabilities are characterized by intra-individual differences [characterized as differences within a student across academic areas], usually in the form of a discrepancy between a student's ability and his or her achievement in areas such as reading, writing, mathematics, or speaking. For example, a student with a[n] LD may be quite successful in math computation and listening comprehension but may read poorly. Other students with LD may read and speak well but have difficulty expressing their thoughts in writing.

Learning disabilities present one way in the early years and may become evident in other ways as a child gets older and schooling progresses. According to LD Online, learning disabilities in the preschool years include "difficulty in understanding certain sounds or words and/or difficulty in expressing oneself in words." In school-aged children, learning disabilities may occur in the form of arithmetic disabilities, reading or spelling disorders, and writing disorders. Learning disabilities are defined differently by different groups, and coaches and parents are encouraged to take time to explore the variety of sources of information on learning disabilities in existence.

Coexisting Conditions

According to Dr. Brown, "A person with ADD is six times more likely to have another psychiatric or learning disorder than most other people." This means that among the other factors that a coach needs to consider when working with a young person with ADHD—unique constellation of ADHD symptoms, personalized treatment responses, and possible learning disabilities—a coach should also stay aware of possible coexisting conditions to the ADHD, which may fall into the realm of mental health issues or other DSM–IV diagnoses.

In particular, young people with ADHD may also struggle with depression, anxiety, or substance abuse or addiction. Other mental health issues that may be present include bipolar disorder, obsessive–compulsive disorder, and oppositional defiant disorder. Addictions may also go beyond drugs and alcohol to include food, the Internet, gambling, or sex. Underlying coexisting conditions may become more evident as a young person gets older or moves into a new environment, such as college.

The goal for coaches is to be able to recognize when something beyond the ADHD is going on with a client. Does the adolescent's panicked physical reaction to school deadlines suggest a referral to a psychologist? Is it possible that after a month of skipping school on and off and sleeping all day, the young person needs to contact the psychiatrist to have his or her antidepressant dosage evaluated? General knowledge of the possibility of coexisting conditions, as well as additional insight into the nature of various mental health diagnoses, can provide coaches with the information needed to recognize when something more than ADHD may be interfering with a client's progress.

In some cases, the status of a coexisting condition may interfere with coaching to the point that the young person is simply not coachable at the present time. Coaching may need to be put on hold or terminated altogether. A young person in the throes of an addiction will not have the mindset, resources, or capability to commit to coaching, compared with someone who has gone through rehab and therapy for an addiction. A college student who is so depressed that he or she can't make it to class is unlikely to be able to function at a level that makes coaching effective. Once a coexisting condition has been treated and/or stabilized, the young person may find him or herself ready to engage or re-engage in coaching. Coaches should not think of termination due to a coexisting condition as a failure. Instead, success can be measured in terms of making appropriate referrals: extending the young person the kind of support he or she truly needs at a given time and not enabling the young person with the pretense that coaching will be useful when he or she is not yet ready for it.

Behavioral Issues

Behavioral issues often accompany ADHD. Dr. Russell A. Barkley, in *Taking Charge of ADHD*, made the interesting observation that "from early infancy, children with ADHD are often reported to be more demanding and difficult to care for in their general temperament than are non-ADHD children." Behavioral issues that a young person with ADHD may exhibit include defiance (exhibited through lying, arguments, and general pushing back against others' statements and ideas) and risk-taking behaviors, such as reckless driving, unprotected sex, drug use, and activities that produce an adrenaline rush, such as bungee jumping.

Adolescents and young adults with ADHD and behavioral problems may benefit most from added structure and clear consequences for their actions. Use of the time out or behavioral reward systems such as sticker charts are no longer appropriate. In the majority of cases, when behavioral issues present themselves during coaching, a coach will discuss the issues with the client and parents, suggest that a referral is needed, and note that the client is not currently ready for coaching.

Gifted Young People With ADHD

The part of the brain thought to be related to ADHD affects executive functioning—one's ability to be organized, arrive on time, stay focused, remain in control of one's impulses, and so on—and is not related to a person's intelligence. As a result, a young person with ADHD may not only be smart but may also fall into the category of gifted (defined as someone with exceptional talents, high achievement potential, and oftentimes intrinsic motivation). One of the challenges for gifted children with ADHD is that their intelligence, talents, and abilities may hide their ADHD, leaving the disorder undiagnosed and unrecognized. These young people may then be left without much-needed treatment and support that could help them be even more successful in their lives.

Dr. Felice Kaufman, Dr. M. Layne Kalbfleish, and Dr. F. Xavier Castellanos found that gifted children with ADHD were seemingly experiencing more impairments than were their nongifted ADHD peers. This may mean not so much that gifted children with ADHD have more difficulties than their nongifted peers with ADHD but that gifted children with milder forms of ADHD are simply being missed.

Gifted children with ADHD face a variety of challenges. As mentioned, their ADHD diagnosis may be missed or may not come until later in their lives. This can be problematic because, as noted by LD Online, young people belatedly diagnosed with ADHD run the risk of "developing learned helplessness," they may become chronic underachievers, and they will not have access to useful educational accommodations. Another important issue to note: It is also possible, as noted earlier, that a child with ADHD will have his or her giftedness go undetected. It can therefore be very valuable to have young people with ADHD reevaluated for giftedness after they have begun treatment.

Although gifted children with ADHD will have an intelligence level that is higher than that of their nongifted peers, they nonetheless are likely to fall behind their peers in cognitive, social, and emotional development. As a group, ADHD children tend to lag two to four years behind their age peers in social and emotional maturity. Gifted children with ADHD are no exception. This finding has important implications for educational placement. As a group, gifted children without ADHD tend to be more similar to children two to four years older than children their own age in terms of their cognitive, social, and emotional development. As noted by LD Online,

> When placed with other high ability children without the disorder, ADHD children may find the advanced maturity of their classmates a challenge they are ill prepared for. Also, gifted children without

the disorder may have little patience for the social and emotional immaturity of the gifted ADHD student in their midst. This is not to say that gifted ADHD students should not be placed with other gifted students. The research is clear that lack of intellectual challenge and little access to others with similar interests, ability, and drive are often risk factors for gifted children, contributing to social or emotional problems.

The balance between feeding the intellectual curiosity of a gifted young person with ADHD and supporting that young person's ADHD-related issues can be challenging for teachers, parents, and coaches and very frustrating for clients.

In addition to giftedness, many young people with ADHD are highly creative. When comparing scientific data, Dr. Bonnie Cramond found similarities in brain structure, temperament, and mood between those who were considered creative and those with diagnosed ADHD.

Doreen Lorenzo, mother of a son with ADHD and author of the article "The Unique Brain: The Link Between ADHD and Creativity Is Turning a Problem Into a Gift," gives insight into the value of identifying the interests of a child with ADHD, whether in the creative realm or otherwise:

> Discovering my son's "sweet spot" didn't happen right away. We tried sports and various camps but they didn't work. Then in the summer before he entered third grade he went to a writing camp. The requirements were two composition notebooks and a pen. The camp counselor encouraged the children to write through various activities. My son wrote an entire novel. We were amazed, as was his third grade teacher. He couldn't even sit in a chair, but given something he loved to do and the right environment in which to do it, he was able to focus. His teacher encouraged me to test him for the gifted and talented program at his school. That program allowed him to explore creative areas he had never experienced.

Identifying whether a young person with ADHD is gifted (and whether a gifted child has ADHD) provides valuable information for the coach, parent, and young person. Awareness of giftedness can be used to connect young people who have ADHD to the appropriate academic track and to challenging intellectual experiences; awareness of ADHD in the gifted child is essential for getting the young person access to the special accommodations he or she may need to be most successful in life. In addition, an awareness that having ADHD does not mean one is without talents or gifts can be very powerful. Those who support the young person can look to connect the young person with the activities and resources that will stimulate and support the young person, while the young person may receive a significant boost of self-confidence from insight into his or her strengths.

Coaching the Whole Person, Not the Disorder

Although I have spent the bulk of this chapter defining and describing the symptoms of ADHD and coexisting conditions, all of which can lead to significant challenges in a young person's life, I want to be sure to underscore that I believe wholeheartedly in seeing each and every client as a person and not a disorder. The moment we view a young person with ADHD as broken or deficient, we risk robbing the young person of his or her power lest we inadvertently convey this perspective to the young person. The coach should not be looking at a client from the viewpoint of having ADHD, coexisting conditions, or learning problems. Operating from this perspective skews the coaching process and places the focus on all the things that are "wrong" or all the things that have to be "fixed."

Instead, coaches, parents, and care providers can help young people with ADHD reclaim their strengths and build their self-confidence. The first step in doing so is to opt out of the myth that the young person is broken. For us coaches, the second step is to stand by ready to offer support to the young person with ADHD in all areas of life: goals for at home, in one's love life, at school, on the sports field, and so on. Just as coaches support the whole person when working with adults in a life coaching situation, in ADHD coaching, coaches are supporting the whole child—not just the student or the college applicant.

Sadly, negative messages are a part of the lives of many young people with ADHD. The coach may be the first person in the life of a young client who models behavior of acceptance and respect for the client, regardless of any diagnosed or undiagnosed disorder. The goal of coaching is to shift the young person's perspective to the positive and the appreciative, reducing or eliminating negativity that the client has typically associated with this disorder. Clients and parents alike appreciate the fact that someone values and accepts the young person for who he or she is.

One caveat: Although the focus of coaching needs to be on the whole client and the specific goals stated in the coaching plan, the ADHD and related issues do require that the coach set limits and create structures to best support the client. It is important to address the issues of hyperactivity, lack of focus, and social faux pas, for example. These are often the reasons why the client's family has sought a coach out—because the coach has ADHD expertise, skills, and experience. Thus, the coach will be helping the young person address his or her goals within a context of ADHD while acknowledging that the young person is not the disorder but a whole person with needs that span all areas of life: personal, emotional, social, academic, familial, and more.

A Note for Everyone

If you are going to coach or support young people with ADHD, it likely comes as no surprise that there is tremendous value to becoming informed on the nature of ADHD, common symptoms, and coexisting mental health or learning issues. In addition, understanding that ADHD is a brain-based condition puts the young person's challenges into useful perspective and helps us all remember the very real hurdles that the individual with ADHD faces. It reminds us of the young person's need not for mere prompting to get something done but for personalized support, structure, and strategies to achieve goals. This is not a case of laziness or obstinacy or not caring. It is the case of a person facing very real challenges at the level of the brain, which make fundamental life tasks incredibly challenging: from remembering to take one's medication, to engaging in a normal conversation with peers, to sitting still through a history class and remembering what was taught.

A qualified coach will maintain a sound knowledge base not only on ADHD and the latest research but also of possible coexisting conditions with ADHD. This information will help the coach know when to refer the client for additional support. Such knowledge is useful, too, in helping the coach be able to recognize when the timing may not be right for coaching. Perhaps a client needs to work through emotional issues first in therapy, or maybe the client needs to work with a psychiatrist to get his or her anxiety under control. Alternately, there may be indications that the client is abusing alcohol, which make it clear to the coach that the client simply isn't ready to participate in coaching. Knowing when to refer and when to terminate are essential components of proper ethical conduct in coaching.

A cursory understanding of learning disabilities can also go a long way in helping the coach best support the young client with ADHD and possible learning disabilities. What are the signs that the client may have a learning disability? What resources are available to help the client identify, treat, or accommodate learning disabilities? Awareness that a learning disability may be complicating a client's ability to succeed provides the coach and client with useful data for understanding what's going on in the client's life and for designing an action plan that truly meets the client's needs.

Perhaps the most important knowledge a coach, parent, or care provider can gather on ADHD is an understanding that young people with ADHD are not broken or faulty. Even with the potential obstacles and impediments these young people face, they are nonetheless creative, resourceful, and whole. They have everything they need inside of them: With the support of their particular treatment—from medication to coaching to good nutrition —

young people with ADHD can apply their efforts in focused and strategic ways to achieve the goals they set for themselves. By asking questions and really listening, the coach can empower the client to come up with everything he or she needs to be successful: from clear goals to rewards that motivate, from action steps to strategies for success. And by supporting the client in going into the world and testing his or her wings, the coach sends a message of faith and confidence, saying, "I believe in you." Very often, this confidence is contagious, and with even a few successes experienced, the young person with ADHD can start to believe in him or herself, too.

I extend many thanks to Dr. Richard Steinberg for his important contributions to, and review of, this chapter. Dr. Steinberg is the father of three adopted sons with ADHD, from whom he learned much of his basic understanding about ADHD. He also devotes most of his clinical practice time to the diagnosis and treatment of ADHD.

F O U R

Getting Ready for Coaching: Prescreening the Parent and Client

Ready, set, go! The coach receives a call from a mother who absolutely wants her child to receive coaching and an appointment is scheduled for the intake session. The coach is excited to add a new client to his base and thrilled that the parent seems so ready to sign up for coaching services. But the day of the appointment arrives and 20 minutes into the intake session, mom explodes with anger because the coach explained that she will not be sitting in on most of the coaching sessions. She wanted coaching for her child— but not that kind of coaching! How will she know whether the coaching is working? How will she know whether her child is making any progress or telling the truth when she says that coaching is going "fine"?

What went wrong in this situation? On the phone, mom seemed so eager to get coaching started. Now, she is looking at the coach with angry eyes and it's unclear whether coaching can actually take place. If things fall apart and mom decides to pull the plug on the arrangement, the coach will have wasted valuable time e-mailing intake paperwork to the parent and client, reviewing the paperwork before the intake session, and blocking out two hours or more on the schedule for the actual intake session.

This chapter covers a process that can help coaches avoid the time, hassle, and frustration of meeting with a young person and parent for an intake only to discover that one (or both) of them isn't ready to engage in the coaching process. This process is known as *prescreening*. The chapter that follows is dedicated to highlighting the benefits of the prescreening process as well as to providing guidance on how to formally conduct this invaluable early stage of coaching.

Identifying Coaching Readiness

1,001 Reasons to Conduct the Prescreening

A common complaint I hear from coaches all over the world is, "I thought the teenager wanted coaching, but it turns out the mom did." When I hear these words, I know that the coach forgot—or simply didn't know how—to prescreen. The purpose of prescreening is to, as best possible, confirm that the adolescent or young adult is ready, willing, and able to enroll in a coaching partnership and that the parent is willing to let that process take place. The prescreening process is useful with prospective clients of all ages and is offered free of charge. In addition, prescreening often takes place in a phone call of 30 minutes or less. Some parents and young people (as well as coaches) prefer to meet in person, in which case the prescreening can be conducted in the coach's office or in a neutral spot like a coffee shop.

Prescreening can eliminate uncomfortable surprises from occurring during the intake session. This is because when prescreening is properly conducted, an unnecessary intake never gets scheduled, because it's clear from the prescreening that the parent or young person isn't ready for or desirous of coaching. If an intake session does get scheduled after the prescreening, it typically goes more smoothly than it would have without the prescreening because the young person and parent have already been partially educated on the coaching process and have shown a willingness and/or motivation to play by the coaching rules. The young person and parent are also less likely to feel confused or deceived over the course of the intake session, when the coach continues the process of discussing what coaching is and how it works.

There is never a guarantee that a successful prescreening will lead to successful coaching—like with any new relationship, it takes time to build trust and create a partnership—but in many cases prescreening can help determine early on that a young person or parent is not ready for or interested in coaching.

Prescreening, Decoded

Prescreening involves a brief process of gathering information from the parent and young person and sharing information with the parent and young person to make sure that

- the parent and young person really want the services the coach has to offer

- the parent is truly ready to support the coaching process

- the young person is truly ready to engage in the coaching process.

You may have noticed that I've put the word *parent* before *young person* in the previous text, and perhaps this ordering surprised you. By now, you are probably familiar with my insistence that *coaching takes place with the adolescent or young adult, not the parent!* Although this is still true, in this early stage of the coaching process, coaches are likely to come in contact with the parent first—in the case of adolescents, anyway. When kids are in their teenage years, parents are typically going to be the ones to reach out to a coach on behalf of the teen. As a result, prescreening begins first with the parent; if prescreening goes well, the coach will then ask for an opportunity to speak with the adolescent. In the case of young adults (those beyond the high school years), it is possible that the young adult him or herself will contact the coach. In these cases, it is common to not talk directly to parents, except sometimes when the parents are helping to finance the coaching. The young adult is the point of contact, so the coach can immediately begin prescreening the prospective client. The complimentary prescreening session provides a no-pressure opportunity for both the coach and the prospective client. If the coach senses that the parent or the young person is not ready for coaching, it is much easier to decline the prospect before money changes hands. Conversely, the family has an opportunity to learn about the coach and the coaching process without obligation. No fees are paid until the intake session, at which point all parties have agreed to move forward.

Is the Parent Ready?

Prescreening can begin as soon as the parent makes contact with the coach. When the parent initiates contact, the coach should listen, ask, observe, and feel, with the goal of assessing whether the parent is really ready for the kind of coaching offered. With each word that the parent shares with the coach—whether by e-mail, on the phone, or in person—a message is being communicated.

Maybe that message is "My son's therapist told me he needs coaching so I'm calling you but I really don't want to pay for coaching!" That might be a message of resistance. Or the message might be one of desperation: "My daughter keeps coming home late every night and I've lost total control and I don't know what I'll do if you don't help me!" Or maybe the coach explains to the parent that coaching is based on the young person's goals—not the parent's—and the coach notices dead silence on the other end of the phone line. That might be a message of uncertainty about coaching.

Parents give off all kinds of messages when they first call for coaching, but if coaches are not tuned in to what parents are communicating or do not make a concerted effort to gather all of the information needed to determine whether this parent and young person are a good match for coaching services, coaches can end up going down a road to nowhere.

Prescreening is an essential first step to the coaching process, which enables the coach to assess whether the parent is truly interested in coaching (as opposed to, e.g., tutoring or therapy) and to assess whether the parent is willing and able to allow coaching to take place directly between the coach and the young person, without the parent being present.

X-Ray Vision: Learning to Read the Parent

Each parent brings his or her own unique traits and experiences to the prescreening process, which will affect his or her comfort level with a coaching plan that does not include the parent every step of the way. Nonetheless, four common factors can be assessed to gain valuable insight and understanding into how a parent might react to the knowledge that the coaching process does not involve the parent:

- the age of the prospective client

- how involved the parent has been in the child's day-to-day life up until now

- how independent the prospective client is

- the level of disability or difficulty experienced by the prospective client.

For example, parents of younger adolescents may express significant concern about not being present at every coaching session, when their norm up until now has been day after day of hands-on involvement in the life of the child. In contrast, parents of older adolescents and college-aged kids may be far more ready to turn their respective children over to the coaching process, having already watched them grow independent by getting a driver's license, landing a job, or moving away from home. Similarly, parents of children who struggle with learning disabilities in addition to ADHD may not believe it is possible or beneficial to let go.

By gathering information on the context in which the parent is currently operating, the coach can get a better sense of the parent's readiness to support the coaching process and the degree of hand-holding the parent might need to be able to let go. This information will also help the coach identify how strong of a boundary needs to be created between the parent and the coaching process. For example, a parent of a college-aged student best supports his or her child by getting out of helicopter mode, allowing the young adult an opportunity to grow, explore, and learn without mom or dad hovering and requesting daily updates on progress. Conversely, the parent of a young teen can be an integral part of the daily progress of the child, supporting the coaching with, for example, a daily backpack check to ensure that everything is ready for school the next day, as outlined in the personal coaching agreement.

The prescreening process begins with a call or an e-mail inquiry from a parent or a young adult. Phone tag aside, prescreening usually takes place over a week's time, including contact with the prospective client and the parent, when applicable. With that said, it is important not to rush the decision-making process. Prospective clients are encouraged to think the opportunity over without pressure from the coach or the parent.

To effectively assess a parent's readiness to support the young person in the coaching process, a coach's work will involve two aspects:

- gathering information from the parent

- sharing information with the parent.

Let's make these two steps even more specific.

- First, during prescreening, the coach aims to gather information from the parent that will help determine *whether the parent really wants the services being offered and is willing to let the young person be coached.*

- Second, in prescreening, the coach works to share information with the parent on the *services the coach is capable of providing* so that the parent can assess whether the services being offered match those the parent desires for his or her son or daughter.

Once the coach has thoroughly conducted each of these steps of the prescreening, he or she will have significant information to help assess whether the prospective parent is ready to participate in the intake session and to hire coaching services for the young person. The text that follows provides details on these two aspects of assessing parental readiness: information gathering and information sharing. Note that although the prescreening of parents comprises two distinct stages—gathering information and sharing information—these two processes are often happening in a continuous, integrated fashion that appears seamless to the parents.

Gathering Information on the Parent's Openness to Coaching

Imagine for a moment a wild scenario. You have a 13-year-old daughter with an unusual disorder that causes her hair to grow in purple. Because of the nature of this disorder, your daughter's hair is very brittle and, if it is not cut in a very special way, her hair will break off at the root, leaving her with patches of unsightly bald spots. This condition can be very embarrassing. As a result of her hair condition, since the time your daughter was a preschooler, you have been working closely with hairdressers, doctors, psychotherapists, and even her teachers to make sure that your daughter not only gets the kind of haircut that caters to her special needs but also has the support she requires to deal with the physical, social, and emotional repercussions of her disorder. Before your daughter knew how to speak up for herself, you would. When no one would advocate for your daughter's needs, you were willing to speak on her behalf and get her the support she needed. Taking care of your daughter is how you keep her safe. Speaking up for your daughter is a natural part of who you are as a parent, almost like living and breathing.

But now you've walked into the office of a prominent researcher who is telling you that he has a very helpful treatment for your adolescent daughter but that it will only work if you are willing to step out of the picture. To make things worse, all that the researcher can tell you as the treatment is taking place is things like "Your daughter is regularly participating in sessions and following the treatment" and "If you'd like an update on how things are going, speak to your daughter."

By now, you have probably figured out that this hypothetical—if a bit ridiculous—scenario represents my not-so-veiled attempt at providing insight into the experience of a typical parent of an adolescent with ADHD as he or she makes contact with a coach. After years of doing everything for his or her daughter or son, the parent of an adolescent with ADHD, upon speaking to a coach for the first time, learns that the parent is no longer allowed to be part of the process! In essence, the coach tells the parent, "Thank you for all of your great service these years, but you are no longer needed."

Admittedly, that language is a bit more extreme than the language that is actually used by coaches, and we coaches know that the parent's role in supporting his or her child with ADHD will continue throughout the coaching process and beyond. Yet, by the time the child has reached adolescence, the kind of support that the child needs from parents has changed greatly from the days of primary school, when it was the parent who was doing all of the talking for the child. By adolescence, it is the young person's turn to practice speaking on behalf of him or herself and it is the parent's turn to step back and let the adolescent manage daily life, even if that means the adolescent struggles or even suffers a series of disappointing setbacks. It can be incredibly difficult for parents to watch their children fail at making friends, passing a course, being selected for the school play, or getting a date to the homecoming dance, but the only way for their children to grow and develop is to get practice negotiating the world around them without mom and dad always stepping in.

One of the coach's jobs during the prescreening process is to assess the parent's readiness and willingness to change roles. Will the parent be able to step back from being the advocate for the young person to being an observer and supporter while the young person learns to advocate for and take care of him or herself?

Of course, this all presupposes that the parent really wants coaching in the first place. The prescreening process is also about making sure that the parent really wants coaching for the young person—not something else, like homework help or psychological counseling.

To address this latter point—does the parent really want coaching for the young person—the coach will ask some questions to investigate what kind of services the parent desires for his or her adolescent or young adult. This can occur through a variety of questions posed by the coach to the parent, such as

- What kind of services are you looking for from a coach?

- Do you understand how coaching differs from tutoring or therapy?

- What is your understanding of the coaching process?

- How do you hope coaching can be helpful to your child?

As the parent responds to these questions, the coach listens to see whether the parent's desires are aligned with what coaching is and the kind of services the coach can offer. If the answer to this question is "yes"—they are aligned—the coach can affirm that the parent has come to the right place and then go on to assess parental readiness to let go and allow coaching to happen. If the answer is "no," the coach can take the misaligned expectations and use them as an opportunity to educate the parent on what the coaching process looks like to see if this is indeed something the parent would like for the young person.

During the information-gathering stage, the coach is also doing some early investigating into the prospective client's interest or motivation for coaching. To this end, the coach might ask questions like "Is your son/daughter aware of the fact that you have contacted me on their behalf about coaching?" "Has your son/daughter expressed an interest in working with a coach?" and "When might I expect a call from your teen to briefly connect and discuss the possibility of coaching together?" The parent's answer will give the coach some insight into the prospective client's motivation level for coaching.

Sharing Information With Parents:
What Happens During Coaching?

The information-sharing aspect of the prescreening process involves educating the parent on what coaching is, what coaching is not, and what the coaching rules (i.e., expectations and boundaries) are. This is an excellent opportunity for the parent to get a clear idea of what the coaching process entails before the coach speaks directly to the young person or the intake session is scheduled.

When I educate the parent on what coaching is, I explain that coaching involves my creating a direct partnership with the adolescent or young adult, supported through regular meetings and check-ins in which the parent is not present or involved. During these regular meetings and check-ins, my role in working with the young person is to empower him or her to achieve goals and enhance the quality of life through actionable steps the young person has laid out. In the process, I aim to foster independence in the young person by empowering that young person to discover and apply his or her own resources, skills, and strengths. I also make sure that the parent understands that when I work with clients, I do more than focus on academics with the young person. I will offer *whole-life coaching* and *ADHD coaching* rather than merely academic coaching.

After explaining what coaching is, I also explain to the parent what coaching is not. Coaching is not therapy. Coaching is not homework help. Coaching is not monitoring the young person and then reporting back to the parent. Equally important, I let parents know that coaching is not doing the work for the client or enabling him or her to be dependent.

For example, if an adolescent has set a goal of saving money to buy a car but is having trouble managing his allowance, I do not take out a piece of paper and create a budget for him. Instead, I invite the client to explore how he might go about managing his money better. As his desired process for managing his money unfolds, I support him in that unique process, asking questions that guide him on a journey toward discovering his own personal strategies for better money management. If he suggests creating a budget for himself, his coaching homework for the week might be to draw up a draft budget. So, instead of creating the budget for or even with the client, I allow him to engage in this work himself.

Some of the phrases I might use to explain to parents what coaching is and what coaching is not include the following:

- "Coaching occurs in partnership with the coach and the adolescent (client). After the initial intake session, the parent is not present during sessions."

- "Coaching revolves around the client's goals, not the parent's goals."

- "The parent's input from the prescreening and intake session will be taken into consideration and reviewed with the client as we design goals and action steps for success."

- "I employ life coaching and ADHD coaching methods, which go beyond academic coaching. This means I support your child in meeting goals that support all areas of his life—academic, as well as other areas, such as social, emotional, and vocational."

- "Because I'm not an academic tutor but a coach, I can help motivate your child to do her own homework if this is one of the goals we have set for coaching, but I won't do her homework for her."

As I go about explaining to the parent what coaching is and what coaching is not, I am also informing the parent about the coaching expectations and boundaries. Some of these expectations and boundaries are evident in the list of example statements just presented. The following section discusses coaching expectations and boundaries in more detail.

Coaching expectations and boundaries. When I am prescreening parents, I also take time to educate them on the parameters of coaching—the expectations and boundaries I ask parents to meet to help the coaching process be most effective.

The expectations I typically present to parents include the following:

- The parent will be willing to participate during the intake session by answering questions and sharing information.

- The parent will listen to the adolescent's perspective during the intake session and will keep an open-minded attitude toward that perspective.

- Using the personal coaching agreement as a guide, the parent will hold the adolescent accountable for missing sessions with the coach.

- The parent will be willing to step back and let the coaching process take place between the adolescent and the coach.

As you may have noticed, I used the word *adolescent* in many of these expectations. This is because these particular expectations tend not to apply when the coach is working with a college student or other young adult. In such situations, the parent is typically not involved. If the parent is involved in such cases, these expectations can, of course, be discussed.

Coaches: Don't Fall Into the Parent Trap!

There is sometimes an expectation on the part of parents that the coach will base services around whatever it is that the parent wants instead of asking the young person to set goals and then building the coaching around those goals.

It's the coach's job to be on the lookout for parent directives and to be careful to not fall into the trap of serving the parent rather than the client. Setting clear expectations and boundaries during the prescreening process will help the parent know how coaching is supposed to unfold and what guidelines should be followed during the coaching process.

This does not mean that the parent's concerns are ignored. Instead, the coach invites the parent to discuss those concerns openly with the coach and client, and the coach then creates an opportunity to compare and contrast the parent's concerns with those of the client. If there is agreement on the part of the client that the parent's concern rings true, the coach helps the parent and client work together to ascertain the level of priority for that particular concern amid other coaching concerns and goals.

Sometimes clients decide they want to address the same goals that their parents have suggested, such as getting to sleep earlier in order to arrive at school on time in the morning. Other times, clients decide a concern is not important enough to focus on in coaching, such as making their bed every day, because it will divert energy from other important goals, like remembering to take morning medication or being focused and ready to ace the calculus test.

The boundaries I typically discuss with parents include the following:

- The parent will not be present at coaching sessions other than the initial intake session.

- If the parent would like progress updates on the coaching, the parent is encouraged to speak directly with the adolescent or young adult.

- If the parent desires to speak to the coach, the coach will only do so if the client agrees. Preferably, such discussions will take place with the client present.

- The final coaching agenda is the client's agenda, not the parents' agenda.

- All information between coach and client is confidential unless otherwise specified in the contract.

Although there are a variety of ways to word these coaching boundaries, they represent the fundamental areas I have discovered in my own practice to be particularly essential to effective coaching with adolescents and young adults.

As you can see, a theme of confidentiality runs through the majority of these boundaries, and they are all "client-centric" rather than "parent-centric." Confidentiality with the client is incredibly important, not only for ethical practice but to help build a trusting relationship between client and coach and to help foster independence in the client. By providing the client with a safe space in which to grow, outside of his or her family setting but within the supportive coaching office (virtual or otherwise), the coaching space becomes a place of transition where the client has more structure and support than if the client was thrown out into the world on his or her own but less support than if he or she was coddled by the parent. This special environment can go a long way to foster independence and increase self-esteem in the young person with ADHD.

Over time, most coaches develop their own preferred style of communicating expectations and boundaries to the prospective client. They also become skilled at identifying how in-depth they need to go in sharing this information with parents: Some parents need only a little information; others need quite a bit more to feel comfortable with coaching or to get their mind around how the process works. Depending on preference and needs, the coach may word the previous expectations and boundaries differently than shown here or the coach may add additional expectations and boundaries to the list to suit the style and seeming preferences of both coach and client.

The little details of coaching. Somewhere during the prescreening process, it is also important to inform the parent of the practicalities of coaching: fees (typically charged beginning with the intake session), delivery method, frequency of sessions, duration of each session, and typical length of the coaching relationship. Coaches will want to define coaching services in advance and then be clear on informing the parent of the practicalities of their particular coaching business. If the coach has flexibility in certain areas, he or she can explain this to the parent as well. As with expectations and boundaries, over time, the coach can customize services to best suit his or her style and preferences while at the same time working with the unique needs of each parent and young person.

Parent to parent, the prescreening process will vary greatly. Sometimes it will consist of only a 10-minute conversation in which the coach is able to quickly get a read on the parent's readiness; other times, the prescreening process might consist of a 45-minute question-and-answer session that gives the coach and the parent the information needed to decide whether to schedule an intake. In some cases, prescreening might also involve the coach requesting that the parent and prospective client review written coaching expectations and acknowledge a basic understanding of the coaching process before scheduling an intake session.

If the prescreening process of the parent reveals that the parent truly desires coaching for the young person and that the parent seems willing to give the space needed for coaching to take place directly between the coach and the young person, the coach will be ready to assess the young person directly for his or her readiness for coaching. If, instead, the parent seems to desire services other than those offered or is struggling to accept that he or she will not be part of the regular coaching sessions, the coach can consider making a referral (in the first case) or spending more time in conversation with the parent (in the second case) to help the parent feel more comfortable.

Supporting Parents: Is Coaching the Best Choice?

In some cases, it will become clear early in the prescreening conversation that coaching services aren't a match for the parent's needs. Dad might be calling to get help for his son in algebra. Or mom may really be looking for a therapist to help her daughter deal with depression. When it becomes clear that the parent desires services other than coaching, the coach can then make a referral to a qualified professional that could meet the parent and young person's needs: tutor, psychotherapist, psychiatrist, or whomever provides the services required.

If the parent does desire coaching for a young person but is having trouble with the idea that the parent will not be sitting in on the coaching sessions, different options are available. The coach can educate the parent on the value of one-on-one coaching without the parent present, refer the parent to a therapist or other coach to support him or her in letting go, or discuss the possibility of adjusting the process to include occasional check-ins among coach, client, and parent.

Educate the parent. When a parent is struggling with the fact that he or she will not be part of the regular coaching process, I take extra time to explain why this act of stepping back is necessary. In particular, I let the parent know that this boundary in the coaching process has been created to provide the client with an opportunity to gain skills, develop problem-solving abilities, explore new perspectives, and ultimately become more confident and self-sufficient.

Instead of the parent sitting in on sessions as an intermediary between the young person and the coach, the young person gets to engage independently in the coaching process. This provides an environment in which the client can practice advocating for him or herself within the coaching session. The coach then encourages the client to self-advocate outside of the coaching space, too—at home, school, and work; in sports or band practice; and so on.

Ideally, the initial coaching the parent has received about giving the young person space to be coached will also make it less tempting for the parent to jump in and advocate for the young person in daily life beyond the coaching process. Thus, as the young person gets practice in self-advocacy, the parent simultaneously gets practice at giving the young person space to do so. This is an important and useful by-product of the coaching boundary that keeps parents outside of the coaching relationship.

I also highlight for the parent the need for the coach to build a trusting partnership with the client and note that this can more effectively take place when the parent is taken out of the equation. The coach provides a safe space in which the client can share his or her goals without fear of judgment or repercussion and without triggering any of the psychological dynamics that can take place within the family context. This safe space can best be created without the parent present.

When I am able to place the client–coach relationship within the context of what's best for the adolescent or young adult, parents sometimes have an increased understanding that helps them accept this boundary of the coaching process and move forward with the engagement.

Refer the parent to coaching or therapy. Other times, parents respond with concern to my explanation of the value of stepping back, saying, "You don't understand. My child will suffer so much if I don't stay involved" or "I've been taking care of my child's day-to-day life for years. I don't know how to let go—even if I wanted to." When this occurs, I ask the parent if he or she would like some coaching or therapy to help work through any concerns. "Would you like some extra support in managing your trepidations about letting go?" I might ask. Depending on the nature of the parent's issue, I might offer to coach the parent before starting a relationship with the young person (I make a practice of not coaching the parent and the young person at the same time), or I might refer the parent to another coach or therapist, as needed. I also offer the parent a referral to a therapist when I notice the parent struggling with family or emotional issues that would not be addressed in coaching, such as fighting among parents or a mom's struggle to deal with empty-nest syndrome now that her child is in college.

Investigate the possibility of check-ins. Sometimes a different solution can put the parent at ease. Instead of getting coaching or therapy for the parent, investigating the possibility of setting up occasional check-in meetings between the client, coach, and parent can also be sufficient to allay some parents' concerns. In this case, I explain to the parent that we can ask the adolescent or young adult if he or she would be willing to have monthly check-in meetings in which the young person, the parent, and I are present. If the client agrees, we can then proceed in this manner, although I am sure to let the parent know that the client always has the right to change this agreement.

I also let the parent know that the client can give me permission to talk with the parents without the client being on the phone. I let parents know that when such conversations take place, they are likely to be generalized and occur along lines like these:

- "Your son/daughter is participating in coaching."

- "Your son/daughter is following the coaching plan."

- "Your son/daughter is having a good week."

- "If you have specific questions, I encourage you to discuss those directly with your son/daughter."

If parents feel uncomfortable with the idea of going directly to the young person for information, I highlight that this, too, is part of the growth process of coaching. By referring parents to their children for coaching updates, I aim to give clients opportunities to communicate with their parents rather than having me do the communication on their behalf. Similarly, this situation provides parents with opportunities to sharpen communication with their maturing children. This kind of improved communication will be beneficial to the parent–child relationship for years to come.

Sometimes parents are willing to proceed with coaching after we have a deeper discussion or we agree to investigate setting up check-ins. Other times they are not. To determine parental readiness at this point, I might pose any of the following questions:

- "When you called me, you made it clear that there were certain areas in your child's life where you felt coaching was needed. Are you willing to let go and give coaching a try?"

- "Would you agree, mom and dad, to take two steps back and let me take three steps forward and be there to support your child?"

- "What is your primary concern or hesitation about coaching or the coaching process?"

If the parent's answer indicates that he or she is not ready, this is when I might let the parent know about the other options available to him or her—to get coaching or therapy for him or herself or to seek a different kind of professional (e.g., a family therapist or a tutor for the young person).

If the parent's answer indicates a willingness to step back and allow the coaching process to take place and I have a sense that the parent is sincere in that answer, I am ready to prescreen the adolescent or young adult.

Is the Young Person Ready?

Prescreening the young person actually begins during the prescreening call with the parent, except in cases of young adults that have contacted the coach to begin the process. In particular, at the end of the parent's prescreening, I request that the parent have the adolescent or young adult call me in the coming week. If the parent has a handle on the young person's schedule, I might even suggest some tentative times for the call to increase the likelihood that the young person will reach me rather than my voice mail. For example, if the parent mentions that her daughter comes home from yearbook club every night at 6:00 p.m., I might share that I'm available to speak from 6 to 7 p.m. on Tuesday and Wednesday evenings.

Setting up the process so that the prospective client calls me directly allows me to gauge motivation for coaching. If a prospective client is not willing to call me, then I take this as a sign that the young person is not currently ready for coaching and I do not schedule an intake, even if a parent is insistent. Of course, I don't take this approach to be mean or unfair; experience has simply shown me that coaching cannot be successful until the young person is motivated to engage in it.

Several years ago, I learned the hard way the importance of speaking directly with the young person to assess readiness for coaching before scheduling the intake session. In this particular case, after two long phone calls with the young person's mom, the sending of intake paperwork back and forth, time prepping for the intake session, and a long drive to the young person's home (nowadays, I meet with clients in my office, but in the early days of coaching, things were different), I followed the mother into the living room to meet her 13-year-old son and begin the intake. What happened next? I took one look at the young man and had the sense immediately that he had absolutely no interest in being coached!

I had asked the mother during our previous contact no less than four times, "Does your son want coaching?" and she had emphatically assured me each time yes, he wanted to be coached. Yet, when I arrived for the intake session, her son refused to speak to me about coaching. His mom admitted that, in fact, she had never asked her son if he wanted to be coached and hoped that when I arrived I could talk him into it!

If I had spoken to this young man during my initial contact with his mom, I would have been able to determine early on—before I had spent so much time, travel, and effort—that he was not currently "coachable." Or perhaps I could have spoken to him in a way that engaged him and started to build trust, opening the door to coaching. Instead, when I arrived at his home, the young man felt tricked, not a good environment in which to begin the coaching process.

Prescreening the young person—not just the parent—allows you to avoid wasting your valuable time and effort preparing for work with a young person only to find out that he or she does not want to be coached. It also begins the process of building a trusting relationship with the young person early on, such that the intake session to follow can go a little more smoothly than it otherwise might.

Investigating the Young Person's "Coachability"

During the client phase of the prescreening process, the goal is to assess whether the adolescent or young adult is ready, willing, and able to be coached. In other words, is the young person coachable? Much as with the prescreening of the parent, you will be both gathering and sharing information during the prescreening of the young person.

One of the typical questions I use to begin the prescreening process with the potential client is "Did your parent explain who I am and what I do?" If the young person says "no," I go on to tell him or her more about what coaching is and how I can be of service. If the young person says "yes," I ask the young person to tell me a little bit about what he or she knows about coaching. I then build on the information the young person shares to educate him or her further on the coaching process. During this process, I touch on coaching expectations and boundaries.

For example, I highlight that other than the intake session, our sessions will be private and that they will be focused on whatever goals are important to the young person. This helps the young person see that coaching is about him or her, not the parent, and sometimes helps to excite or engage the young person in the process. I also let the young person know that I won't be doing things for him or her but instead helping the young person do things for him or herself. On the one hand, this sets boundaries—for example, I will not call the young person each morning so he or she is on time for class. On the other hand, it lets the young person know that I believe in him or her—it sets the stage for building the young person's confidence and self-esteem.

During a phone prescreening, I also like to ask if the parent is in the room at that moment. Parents have a way of hovering at times like these, and I want to give the young person an opportunity to speak freely without any pressure. I might ask, "Is one of your parents in the room by any chance?" If the young person says "yes," I'll ask, "Where could you go in the house so you have some privacy and can say what you want to say?"

The young person could choose the bathroom or a closet for all I care (although some parents have been known to try to follow their kids even in there!)—I just want him or her to find a space to speak openly and honestly. And if the young person can't find a private space, I can still ask a closed-ended question to get a sense of whether the young person is sincerely interested in coaching, such as "Were you pressured into calling me?" or "Are you calling of your own free will?" If the youth indicates he or she was forced to call, I let the youth know that's okay—this lets me know that the young person is not currently interested in coaching and I can let the young person get back to his or her activities.

As the prescreening process unfolds, I mentally try to answer questions such as

- Does the young person sound ready for coaching?

- What is the young person's motivation for coming to coaching?

- Are there any red flags related to maturity, ADHD, or other conditions that would make coaching difficult or impossible?

- What might be happening in the young person's life that could get in the way of coaching?

While I keep the previous questions in my mind, the following questions represent those that I might actually ask the young person.

- "What do you hope to get out of coaching?"

- "Are you ready and willing to make changes in your life?"

- "Are you ready and willing to learn?"

- "Are you comfortable having a partnership with an adult?"

The goal of asking questions in the prescreening is to gather basic information to assess whether the young person has an interest in the coaching process and whether the timing is right for coaching. Later, at the intake, I will have the opportunity to assess the goals and desires of the young person.

In actuality, there are a host of questions beyond the previous four that I would like the prospective client to consider, but I also don't want to bombard the prospective client or make him or her feel grilled. So I often share a written list of questions with the prospective client, by e-mail or fax, before we have the initial, brief prescreening session. Once we are on the phone together, I ask the prospective client to look the questions over again and then let me know if any of the questions give him or her pause. Are there any that the prospective client would like to know more about?

For example, prospective clients are sometimes put off by my expectation regarding coaching homework. When they bring this topic up, this provides an opportunity for me to further educate the young person on what I mean by *homework* so there aren't any surprises later and for him or her to express any concerns or questions. (*Coaching homework* refers to the step the client agrees to take toward his or her goals before the next coaching session and is unrelated to academic homework.)

If the Shoe Fits: Are the Young Person and Coach Compatible?

The prescreening process is not just a time to assess a young person's readiness for coaching; it's also a valuable chance to consider whether the coach and the young person are compatible with each other and whether the two want to work together. Yes, I said it: *Coaches have the freedom and right to decide whether to work with a particular young person!* Not every prospective client will be right for every coach, and that's okay. The reverse is also true. The coach might not be the right match for every prospective client. It's nothing personal, really—adolescents sometimes just don't connect with some adults.

The prescreening process provides coaches with a valuable opportunity to assess compatibility between the coach and the young person before the coach spends time and energy exchanging paperwork, making appointments, and maybe even trying to twist the arm of a young person who just doesn't feel comfortable talking or whom the coach has no real desire to get talking. If the coach determines that the young person is not a good match (on either side) but still is coachable, the coach is encouraged to refer the young person to another coach for prescreening.

What Makes Adolescents Tick?

In addition to assessing the young person's readiness and the compatibility between the young person and the coach, the prescreening process is about laying down a foundation for the coaching relationship to come. From the start, the coach's goal should be to build trust with the young person and to help the prospective client feel comfortable communicating openly and honestly with the coach.

Some coaches have the tendency to treat adolescent and young adult clients like very young children—by talking down to them or directing them rather than asking questions and listening. Doing so not only runs the risk of perpetuating dependence rather than independence, but it also can make prospective clients feel put off, uncomfortable, or even angry with the coach.

From time to time, after I refer a young person to another coach because of scheduling conflicts or some other reason, I might get a call back from the young person saying, "Do you have a different coach I can call? She was too much like my mother," or "He treated me like a baby." When this happens, I can guess that the coach forgot to adjust his or her interactions with the young person to be well suited to the young person's age and maturity. It's important to remember that adolescents and young adults are quite different from children of younger ages and that they require an approach that is far more open-ended, collegial, and collaborative in nature. Speaking from a place of respect for the young person's autonomy will go a long way toward build a trusting coaching relationship.

Declining a Prospective Client

Oftentimes, the prescreening process leads to taking on a new client. Parents are commonly interested in coaching services once they understand what they are, and they often express a willingness to step back and allow the coaching process to take place, even if this is a new phenomenon for them that takes some getting used to. The young person too may show motivation and interest in receiving the support of a coach and engaging in the process.

Yet, from time to time, the prescreening process may provide the coach with information that indicates it would be best to decline a prospective client. Even when coaches have a sense that a young person or parent isn't ready for coaching, they sometimes have trouble saying "no" to taking the young person on as a client. This can occur for a variety of reasons: because the coach needs the new business, because the coach wants to prove that he or she can handle any kind of client, or because the coach feels so much empathy for the parent or young person that the coach doesn't want to let the person down by declining to work with him or her.

Taking on a Client for Financial Reasons

One reason that coaches accept clients even though the prescreening has revealed they probably shouldn't is because the coach is excited to have some new business or worries about the financial repercussions of declining a client. The coach might think, "I can't be choosy." But consider the importance of coachability and the client–coach match. If a coach takes on a client and then runs into constant obstacles with the client because he or she isn't ready for coaching or because of personality conflicts with the coach, will that be fair to the client? Will it be ethical? In addition, what kind of frustration will the coach feel in trying to work with a client who isn't able to successfully engage in the coaching process? What services might the client actually need that the coach won't be recommending as a viable alternative to coaching at that point in time?

When I work with coaches who are afraid to turn business away for financial reasons, I remind them of the need to treat clients and prospective clients with fairness and respect by referring them to the right professional, even if that other professional is simply another coach better suited to work with the young person. I also encourage coaches to have trust that when one door closes, another one opens. In fact, time and again I have seen coaches turn business away in spite of some financial worry only to gain new business that was more suitable to them in a matter of days.

Taking on a Client to Prove Oneself as a Coach

Another reason that coaches find it difficult to decline a client is because they believe that doing so shows a weakness on their part. They want to prove to themselves that they are capable—that they can work with any client who comes their way. And so they accept a client even though their instinct is telling them that another coach or even a therapist would be better suited to work with the client.

When I speak to coaches who feel compelled to take on clients to prove themselves—rather than because they are excited to work with the client—I ask them to consider viewing what it means to be a capable coach in a different way. Perhaps being capable is more about coaches knowing their limits and having a keen sense of when they are a good match for a prospective client and when another coach or professional would be a better match.

Ultimately, it's okay for coaches to trust their gut and say, "This client is not for me." None of us should be expected to work with every young person, no matter how good of a coach we happen to be. The truth is that I've been working in this field for a very long time, and I still regularly refer clients to other coaches, not only because of time constraints on my schedule but because I recognize when a client is not a good match for me or when I am not a good match for the client.

Taking on a Client Because One's Heart Strings Are Pulled

A third reason that coaches sometimes have difficulty declining a prospective client is because they feel empathy for the parent and client and don't want to let them down. For example, the coach might have the sense that the young person isn't ready for coaching, but the parent sounds desperate. "Please, you don't know what we've been through," the parent might say. "If he doesn't get coaching, I don't know what we'll do!" Then, the coach feels terrible turning the parent away. Or the young person breaks down crying on the phone and says, "Thank you for listening! You're the only adult who's ever cared about me." The coach has the nagging feeling that the client really needs therapy but worries about making the young person feel rejected and so decides to take the client on.

When I work with coaches who face this particular challenge to declining a client, I again remind them to think about what is most fair and helpful to the client. No matter how much the coach wants to help the young person, if the coach has assessed that the prospective client isn't ready for coaching or needs something besides coaching right now, taking the person on as a client won't truly be helpful. I encourage these coaches to channel their helping energy into referring the parent and young person to more appropriate resources for the current time and to communicating this in a way that is caring and respectful. The coach can also remain helpful to the parent and young person by inviting them to follow up with the coach and share how the referral process is going. In this way, the coach doesn't leave the parent or young person without support.

Regardless of the reason, there may be occasional circumstances in which the coach might have a sense that a prospective client needs to be referred elsewhere, but instead of listening to that thought or feeling, the coach says, "Oh, well. Why not?" and agrees to coach that young person. I try to encourage the coaches with whom I work to trust that sense that a young person isn't ready or should be referred and follow it rather than override it. Once these coaches give themselves permission to say "no," they often share their relief with me. They are able to admit, "It just wasn't going to be the right situation for me or the young person." They give themselves the freedom to refer the young person elsewhere and this enables the young person to pursue other options.

Coaches: How to Say "No"

- Coaches, if you decide to decline a prospective client, here are some basic guidelines that can help the process go smoothly.

- Maintain a professional, helpful, and upbeat demeanor at all times.

- Provide support and encouragement and remain positive throughout the referral process.

- Provide names of other coaches if coaching is appropriate but just not going to be right with you.

- Recommend that the young person interview other coaches before making a final decision. This leads to clarity and a greater commitment to coaching if the young person comes back to you for coaching.

- Offer resources and referrals that may be beneficial to the young person and the family.

  — This may include therapists, doctors, treatment programs, coaches who work in specialty niches, and professional organizers.

  — Invite the young person to contact you for additional information or to let you know that the right match has been found.

  — If the young person seems uncoachable, the parent might choose coaching for him or herself.

There are a number of things a coach can do to decline a prospective client in a respectful manner, as well as in a way that allows that young person to get the exact help that he or she needs.

A Note for Everyone

There are times when the parent is unable to let go of the adolescent and allow coaching to take place. There are times when an adolescent does not want to be coached or simply isn't ready. There are times when the coach feels overwhelmed at the thought of working with a particular prospective client, and there are times when the prospective client expresses discomfort in working with a particular coach.

Prescreening is an invaluable first step in the coaching process that enables the coach to identify early on whether the young person, parent, and coach are ready to engage in the coaching process. It involves gathering and sharing information with the parent and young person to make sure they are both clear on what the coaching process is, what the coaching process is not, and what boundaries and expectations guide the coaching process.

When coaches prescreen prospective clients, they are going through a careful process of deciding which individuals to engage and which individuals to refer elsewhere. They are unwilling to take on any and every client, and they will make every effort to avoid taking themselves and the client down a path to nowhere.

The prescreening process can offer reassurance to allied ADHD professionals that coaches are selective about which clients they engage and that they make every attempt to avoid accepting clients who are not the right match or who are unable to benefit from their services. The prescreening process is also a sign that a coach has no interest in taking business from other professionals better suited to help the client.

Thus, professionals interested in referring young people to ethical and effective coaches are encouraged to assess whether a coach prescreens in some form or another. Doing so will help these professionals get a better sense of a coach's ethics, approach, and outlook.

In sum, a coach who prescreens is a coach who shows deliberateness, care, and skill. A coach who prescreens wants the best for the young person—even if that means referring the young person elsewhere or offering coaching to the parent first to lay a foundation for effective coaching of the young person in the future.

F I V E

Building a Foundation: The Coaching Intake Session

The intake session is a time of information gathering unlike any other part of the coaching process, and I often liken it to detective work. Coaches, do you have your Sherlock Holmes deerstalker hat on and a magnifying glass in hand? (No pipe required.) Young people and parents, are you ready for an open-ended dialogue? Are you willing to share honestly and be fully present? At the start of the intake, the coach will possess only a small amount of information about the client—whatever data were gathered during the prescreening to assess the client's coachability. By the end of the intake, the coach will likely have a much more complete picture of the client—who the young person is, what's working for the young person right now, and what the young person's desires are for coaching.

The coach's work during the intake session is not unlike that of a detective: It will involve the coach not only listening to what the young person and parent are saying directly but also using traditional coaching skills of observation and intuition to read between the lines and get an even clearer picture of what's going on in the life of the young person. Each cue from the client and parent—whether verbal, tonal, visual, or something else—provides the coach with a valuable opportunity to get the real picture of what's important to the client and what he or she hopes to gain from coaching. These cues can also prompt the coach in facilitating the discussion during the intake session.

For example, if the coach hears the young person parroting mom's goal as his or her own ("I want to get better grades"), but the young person's tone seems to indicate some resistance on his or her part, the coach might use this opportunity to ask the young person to put mom or dad's wishes aside for a moment and consider what he or she as the client really wants to do in coaching and in life. It is helpful for coaches to explain that coaching is a collaborative process in which the young person's opinion and choices count. By listening to the client and parent during the intake session as well as observing what's going on for each individual beyond the realm of words, coaches will gain the insight they need as the session progresses to conduct a supportive coaching experience for the young person and ultimately to gather a sound body of information on the client and his or her desires for coaching.

How do coach and client get from Point A to Point B in the intake session? The coach leads the process, skillfully eliciting information from the young person—and, for younger clients, from the parent—while simultaneously building a rapport with the young person so that he or she will stay engaged in the process. Clients participate in the discussion, while parents offer their perspective to provide additional insight into the situation. Ideally, clients avoid being defensive and parents contribute in a respectful way while doing plenty of listening.

This chapter outlines a process that coaches can use to facilitate an effective intake session, from sharing coaching ground rules with the young person and parent to reviewing the coaching process, from gathering information from the client and parent to identifying the client's preferred learning style. In this chapter, I also discuss the primary goals of the intake session to highlight how and why the intake session is so important. Clients and parents can use this chapter to learn more about what to expect during the intake session and to gain insight into how to get the most out of this valuable start to the coaching process.

The intake session—an intense information-gathering session with both client and parent present (except in some cases of young adults, in which only the client is present)—is like no other part of the coaching process. At its hardest, the intake may be a time when old grievances are aired by parents and when clients feel put on the spot or grilled. At its best, however, the intake session is a time for clients to learn that they do have a voice in their own lives and that coaches and parents are there to support what it is that they desire for themselves.

Goals of the Intake Session

Deepening the Learning:
Educating the Client and Parent About Coaching

The intake session is an opportunity for the coach, client, and parent to continue the educational discussion about what coaching is that began during the prescreening session. Confusion often exists for parents and clients regarding the details of the coaching process. The intake is a time for explaining the coaching process in detail, so that any confusion that might exist is reduced and, one hopes, eliminated. Also important to consider is that parents of a new client may have their own attention problems, making repetition and review of the coaching process a good idea for them as well as the young person. It is essential for coaches to be open to answering questions and responding to requests for clarification of the coaching process. By doing so, the coach shows respect and consideration for both client and parent and lays the foundation for an effective coaching process to come.

Getting to Know the Client

In addition to serving as an informational opportunity for clients and parents, the intake session also provides information for coaches that is foundational and enables the coach to discover relevant knowledge about the client. Every young person is different, and the intake session will provide the coach with valuable information on how to structure the coaching process and how to be an effective coaching partner for that particular young person. What is the client's predominant learning style—visual, auditory, or kinesthetic? What's important to the client? What's working right now and, conversely, what obstacles should coach, client, and parent plan to be on the lookout for as coaching unfolds? Coaches will gather the information needed to answer these and other essential questions with an eye to serving the client best, on the basis of his or her sincere desires and unique needs. Coaches will do well by opening the intake conversation with the new client rather than the parent. Let the young person speak first, if he or she is ready and willing, as this is one more way to build rapport and continue to solidify the coach–client partnership.

In this getting-to-know-you phase, the coach will also be learning about parents' concerns and background data on the young person's strengths and areas of difficulty. Because both the parent and the client fill out coaching information forms before the intake and, when available, provide psychoeducational reports, the coach can use these data to spark conversation and learn more about the young person. Some parents have a tendency to overdo the background information.

For example, one client family with whom I worked provided two large three-ring binders filled with years of data. Although I did not need all of that information for coaching, it was evident that blood, sweat, and tears had been spent in search of the best support for the adolescent, and the parent wanted to share that with me. It is helpful for coaches to be open to what comes their way, while also being able to explain that they will use the basic background facts but begin anew from that day forward in coaching the young person. Comments about moving forward can be reassuring for the young client, who can become embarrassed or anxiety ridden when his or her life history is presented to the coach.

Note that during an intake session with a young adult, the parent may not be involved in the process at all or may provide information in writing or by phone, at the client's request, to fill in the blanks on pertinent information. The intake session then proceeds in a similar fashion as an intake with an adult client might, with the coach addressing the parents' notes with the young adult as a part of the discussion.

Building a Positive and Trusting Relationship

In addition to educating the client, the intake session also serves as an important time for relationship building. In all likelihood, this will be only the second time that coach and young person have communicated with each other, so the relationship between the two will still be in the early stages. The intake provides a valuable opportunity for the coach to begin fostering a connection, building trust, creating a positive rapport, and engaging the young person in the coaching process. How the coach conducts him or herself during the intake session can have a major impact on whether the client will choose to continue working with this particular coach and whether the coaching process will ultimately be successful.

Relationship building helps both the coach and the coaching prospect evaluate readiness and rapport, and it initiates trust and confidence within the relationship. According to the co-active coaching model, the coaching relationship is a designed alliance. The coach and client work together to design the plan that will meet the needs of the client. The client plays a fundamental role in designing how he or she wants to be coached and learns that he or she is in control of the relationship and ultimately the changes that he or she makes in life.

Getting Ready for the Intake Session

In the lead-up to the intake session, the coach will typically follow the procedure below.

1. **An intake appointment will be scheduled with the young person and his or her parent/s** (parents of college-aged clients typically do not attend the intake session). Coaches, clients, and parents should plan for the intake session to take two hours. It is advisable for the coach to ask whether the client would prefer two 1-hour meetings to break up the time to accommodate for hyperactivity or information overload. In addition, the coach should be sure that everyone agrees to the date and time of the session.

2. **The coach will communicate the fee for the intake session** and explain that it will be due at the time of the meeting.

3. **The coach will send paperwork to the client and parent for completion** and request that it be returned in advance of the intake session. This will allow the client and parent to review all of the information and be prepared for the meeting. Coaches should consider providing a handout on coaching expectations as well.

4. **The coach will review client and parent paperwork.** If the coach receives the paperwork in advance, he or she can spend time looking over the data on the forms to formulate the questions that are most important for that family and the young person.

The Intake: Time to Jump In!

An appointment has been set (for an in-person or over-the-phone meeting), and the coach has learned a little more about the client by reviewing the completed paperwork. The day of the intake finally arrives. If you are a coach, how should you plan to direct the process? If you are a client or a parent, how should you expect the intake session to unfold? The intake session typically involves the following components: a discussion of the intake plan and any ground rules for the session, an explanation of the coaching process, an interview of the client and parent by the coach with a focus on what can change, a request by the coach to parents to step out of the room (or hang up the phone), drafting of the personal coaching agreement (PCA) by the client and coach, and a closing discussion with the client and parent to take care of any final intake details.

Although there is sure to be some variation in how any given intake session goes, this list more or less presents a chronological timeline for how a coach might conduct the intake session. Specific information on the key steps of the intake process follows.

"What Is Coaching, Again?"

In the intake, the coach will want to continue the education process that began during prescreening. This will involve answering any client or parent questions on coaching and on how to actively and appropriately engage in the coaching process. Some of this information giving may be a review from the prescreening conversation/s; some of it may involve additional color and details that expand on what the coach has already shared with the client and parent. Additional time spent educating the young person and parent on coaching can be invaluable. The more clients and parents understand the nature of what's to come in coaching, the smoother the process to come can be.

Intake plan and ground rules. The education process can begin with the coach reviewing the plan and ground rules for the intake session itself, with the coach explaining that this is an opportunity for all parties to share their thoughts and concerns in a nonjudgmental manner in support of the new client. Logistically, the session will begin with a conversation between coach, client, and parents to gather information about the client. What's working? What's not working? What are the goals of client? What are the concerns of parents? The parents will then be asked to step out of the room or hang up the phone, and the client and coach will have time to speak independently. The intake process commonly occurs over a two-hour period, with the first 45 minutes dedicated to parent–client–coach conversation and the second 45 minutes set aside for conversation between coach and client alone. The last 30 minutes of the intake can be used to bring the parents back into the session and to wrap up logistical aspects of the appointment, such as payment and paperwork completion. Regardless of the length of the intake session (one 2-hour session vs. two 1-hour sessions), the coach may offer short breaks, stretches, and a bit of deep breathing to help everyone stay focused and energized throughout the process.

The intake session is a fee-based service. The intake is a foundational part of the coaching process and represents the beginning of the coaching relationship. The fee for the intake covers the coach's time during the actual intake as well as any time spent reviewing forms and psychoeducational reports and, at times, placing a brief call to a doctor, therapist, or school counselor to gather information pertinent to coaching.

During prescreening, the coach will have communicated that a fee will be charged for the intake session; the coach also will have noted the exact fee for this service and for subsequent coaching sessions, as well as acceptable methods of payment. Some coaches prefer to take care of payment and contractual issues at the start of the intake session and then move on to the intake without further discussion of monies. This is at the coach's discretion, as long as all parties understand that the fee is to be paid by the end of the intake process. Young adults who will be arriving for an intake alone when parents are paying for coaching may also appreciate a reminder before the intake to make payment arrangements in advance of the meeting.

Discussing the coaching process. Once the plan and ground rules for the intake session have been communicated—equal opportunity for the young person to speak, a nonjudgmental attitude displayed on all sides, parent present for only part of the time, payment collected by the end of the session—the coach can move into reviewing the coaching process as a whole with the young person and parent. Once the coach has gauged the knowledge level on coaching for client and parent, the coach may review the coaching process to the degree necessary for this particular client and parent.

In brief, coaching consists of a partnership between client and coach to help the client move forward with his or her agenda. ADHD coaches combine knowledge of ADHD and its neurobiology with life coaching skills to help affected individuals set goals, acknowledge strengths, accept limitations, develop social skills, and create strategies that enable them to be more effective in managing their day-to-day lives. Coaches do this by partnering with the client to design an action plan for success. The coach establishes a pattern of frequent communication with clients to help them stay focused and working steadily toward their goals. Also important, ADHD coaching focuses on the whole person and the whole life, such that it may include but also goes beyond academics to touch on other life areas relevant to the client, from making friends to getting on the sports team or into a sorority, from managing money and staying fit to dating and finding the right apartment.

When explaining the nature of the coaching process, coaches will ideally highlight the importance of boundaries. A parent may need to be reminded that coaching takes place without him or her present (save for the intake session) and that the issues discussed during regular coaching sessions between the young person and coach will be kept confidential. Although the coach can share with the parent (during check-ins to which the young person has agreed) that the young person is following the coaching plan, content and details of coaching will need to be discussed directly between young person and parent.

A parent's ability to trust and recognize that a child is now a young adult is vital to the self-confidence and self-esteem of the young person. Coaches may invite parents to consider coaching to be an opportunity for growth and change on everyone's part. The confidentiality boundary is also important from the young person's perspective, as it helps to lay the groundwork for the trusting, positive relationship that needs to be developed between the coach and the young person for coaching to be effective. When clients learn that their parents will not be privy to the content of coaching, they often show visible signs of relief—a sigh, a shift in posture, or a smile.

There is an expectation on the part of some parents that the coach will to do what the parent wants instead of focusing on the needs and wishes of the young person. In such situations, the coach will attempt to set boundaries and determine what is appropriate for coaching and what might be considered a directive from the parents. The coach has an opportunity during the intake to help the family set reasonable expectations for coaching and discourage parents from overstepping their bounds. The coach will build the confidence level with the family and will consider providing resources for the parents to help them manage change. When the parents are comfortable about the coach's knowledge and professionalism, they will trust the coach to coordinate the coaching process and work with the young person.

In addition to having a discussion on boundaries in coaching, the coach may also spend some time talking about the fundamental coaching piece known as accountability. *Accountability* refers to the expectation in the coaching process that the young person will follow through on the plans and action steps he or she agrees upon with the coach and be responsible for communicating the status and progress of coaching-related action items in between sessions. Accountability is often put into practice through regular check-ins in between coaching sessions, whether through telephone calls, e-mails, text messages, or faxes. The coaching sessions themselves also provide opportunities for progress updates and regular accountability. Whatever the coach and client agree upon is to be carried out.

Coaches often ask parents if they are willing to hold the young person accountable at a different level than they have in the past. This new level of accountability may include checking in with them less often and giving the young person a chance to be more independent. If there are times when the young person stumbles, will the parents consider that a learning experience? Some parents are ready to do so, whereas others have a harder time letting go. When there is a solid relationship between the parent and young person, both parties may have difficulty transitioning and shifting the accountability to the coach–client relationship.

Educating Clients With Recent ADHD Diagnoses on the Condition

For some clients, particularly those who have recently been given the ADHD diagnosis, it can be very helpful for the coach to take some time during the intake session to educate the client and parent on the nature of ADHD and related issues. If the coach is unclear on a client's ADHD knowledge, the coach can gauge his or her present level of understanding by asking questions about ADHD. When the young person responds, the coach may listen for the level of understanding as well as for acceptance from the client. This will guide the coach toward the best resources for the individual.

For example, when a client tells the coach that all he knows is that there is something wrong with him and he can't do things without taking medication, this is an opportunity for the coach to share a few books and websites on ADHD geared to the client's age group. The coach can also ask if the client would like the coach to explain in more detail what is going on in an ADHD brain and how and why medication can be helpful.

It is helpful for the coach to offer information from a variety of sources (e.g., Internet, campus counseling services, books, support groups) so that the client can choose the format and location he or she prefers. The coach can also let the client know that a trained ADHD coach is a resource. Next, the coach can discuss the benefits of structure and systems for clients with ADHD and explain how creating a plan with a coach can make a positive difference. All of this is ideally done with a supportive attitude that emphasizes the client's strengths and ambitions!

Parents: Get the Most Out of the Intake Session

The intake session is meant to serve as a time of discovery for you, your child, and even the coach. During this session, the coach will invite you to share your concerns regarding your child, as well as to provide background information that you believe will help the coach best support your child. Because your son or daughter is the actual client in the coaching process, the coach will give him or her the first opportunity to speak. You will then be invited to add additional information. The coach will also want to give your child some time to share thoughts, feelings, concerns, wishes, and goals in a private and confidential setting, so you will be asked to step out of the room for the second hour of the intake session. This can be a good time to fill out any paperwork; review handouts from the coach; take a break; discuss things with the other parent, if present; and generally regroup after the sometimes intense discussion that can occur during the intake.

Some parents find it to be a challenge to step back and allow coaching to take place between the child and the coach. It can be helpful to remember that the coach is inviting you to step back and allow your child to take more ownership over his or her life because this is what's most effective for adolescents and young adults. Not only do young people often crave increased independence, but they actually require practice doing their own thinking and making their own decisions if they are to become prepared for the adult world that awaits them only a few years down the road.

Take a moment to pat yourself on the back for having the courage and the wisdom to connect your child with a coach—someone who has special knowledge in working with youth with ADHD and who is 100% dedicated to helping your child succeed. Success for your child won't always be defined in the way you envisioned, but it will be defined in terms of what your child dreams of doing in his or her life to feel healthy, hopeful, and happy.

Finally, you as a parent can still play an essential role in your child's life at this stage. Young people with ADHD do best when they have regular accountability, and if your child feels it will be helpful, you can reinforce the accountability already being offered by the coach by holding your child responsible for missed coaching sessions or missed check-in e-mails or phone calls. Last, you can be your child's cheerleader by maintaining a positive outlook about potential progress and praising your child's positive actions taken, large or small.

Building the Relationship

As the intake session unfolds, the coach and client will be engaging in an incredibly important process: building a positive and trusting relationship. It will take weeks for the coach–client relationship to grow, develop, and crystallize; the intake session (following in the wake of what, one hopes, was a positive prescreening experience) is the coach's opportunity to begin laying the foundation for this relationship.

It's not hard to imagine how difficult the coaching experience might initially feel to the young person. The young person has likely spent most of his or her life receiving criticism or at least correction from the adult world; the praise and successes the young person has seen peers and/or siblings receive have been elusive to him or her. Now the young person is being put in front of another adult, and it is all too likely that the young person fears that the coach will judge or find fault with him or her. This has often been the young person's experience with adults to date. By treating the young person with respect and speaking to the young person like the blossoming young adult he or she is becoming rather than the child he or she used to be, coaches can lay a solid foundation for a positive, trusting, and honest relationship.

Some new coaches fall into the trap of treating their new clients like babies, speaking about them in the third person to the parent, or not talking to them in a way that is appropriate for their age. This is often experienced by adolescents as a sign of disrespect, even if done by the coach with good intentions. Every so often after referring a young person to a coach, I will receive a call back in which the young person says something like, "She was a nice enough person but she reminds me of my mother and I don't want to work with my mother." I am reminded in such moments of the importance of treating young people like responsible, capable, independent beings.

Adolescents and young adults don't want to be spoken down to, told what to do, or humored. Instead, they crave a relationship with someone who has a sincere interest in what's most important to them and who will support them rather than push or persuade them in any given direction. One of the ways I start to build rapport with my young clients is to say, "I appreciate that you are taking time out of your day to talk to me." I might also say, "It is important that you feel comfortable and want to partner with me in coaching. By the end of this meeting, or maybe when you get home, would you agree to let me know if you are comfortable and still want to coach with me?" Or I might simply show respect by inviting the young person to tell me more about him or herself. "In reviewing your coaching information form, I noticed that you are a musician. That's fantastic! What type of music do you like?" or "What instrument do you play?"

When I talk about building a positive relationship with the client, the goal isn't to become buddies with the client; it is simply to create the necessary conditions for our work together. Without trust and connection between client and coach, the rest of the process cannot occur with any success. With trust, the client will feel safe enough to share feelings openly and goals honestly. This will allow for authentic progress to take place as client and coach formulate goals, action plans, and incentive systems reflective of the client's real needs.

The intake session is often a particularly delicate, uncomfortable, or heated time for the young person. The parent might be in the office venting years of frustration regarding the child's struggles with ADHD. The client may feel ashamed or enraged by the parent's complaints. Complicating matters, the coach might presently be reviewing a psychoeducational report from the young person's school or doctor that the young person is embarrassed to have the coach see or that the young person has never even seen before. All of these possibilities make for a touchy situation in which a coach's relationship-building efforts will be particularly needed and valuable.

The high emotional temperature that may develop between family members and permeate the coaching space requires the coach to become expert at managing his or her own emotions, reactions, and opinions during the intake. As Laura Whitworth, Karen Kimsey-House, Henry Kimsey-House, and Phillip Sandahl noted in *Co-Active Coaching,* "coaches are human, too, and sometimes, the conversation, a subject or just a word, sparks a reaction on the coach's part." If the parent or young person starts to yell, the coach's stress level may rise. If the tissue box comes out—and it often does—the coach's heartstrings may get pulled and cause the coach to lose focus. Each coach will experience the intensity of the intake session in his or her own way, depending on personality and experiences. Regardless, all coaches will do well to master their emotions and sentiments during the intake when those of the young person and parent start to run high.

In the coaching world, this is called *self-management*. Effective self-management will help the coach stay in control of the intake session so that he or she can help keep the young person and parent on a course toward positive change for the young person. In the process, the coach will continue to build rapport with the young person, who is likely to be reassured by the coach's calm and nonjudgmental presence in the face of upsetting tensions with mom or dad.

Getting to Know the Client

Here's where Sherlock Holmes appears on the coaching scene. Once the coach has finished with the preliminaries of reviewing the nature of the coaching process with the young person and parent, the coach is ready to bring out the figurative magnifying glass. This is the part of the coaching process where the coach begins to take an up-close look at the life of the young person—what's working for the young person and what's not, the challenges the young person and mom and/or dad predict may occur during the coaching process, and the young person's hopes and dreams for coaching and for life.

The reason I use this metaphor of Sherlock Holmes is not because I encourage coaches to aggressively dig into and invade the young person's life but instead because I hope to highlight the value of employing a *mindset of curiosity* during the intake (as well as during all of coaching, really). I encourage coaches to make no predictions and to assume that they don't know any of the answers, regardless of how many hours of coaching experience or work with youth that the coach already has under his or her belt. This curiosity-based approach is not only respectful to the client as a unique person but also prepares the coach to hear what the young person and parent are really attempting to communicate.

Engaging the client. During this portion of the intake session, the coach will focus on finding out more about what brings the client to coaching, offering the client (rather than the parent) the first chance to speak. What is it that the young person would like to change or improve upon in his or her life? What's working now? What might get in the way of progress? What are the goals of the young person? Answers can bring up goals that range across many areas of the young person's life, including home, school, social, and extracurricular activities. ADHD is whole-life coaching—not academic coaching—so the client has room to explore all of the parts of him or herself during the intake, not just those related to grades, academics, or college acceptance.

The intake is also a chance to gather background information that can have an impact on the coaching process: What is the young person's favorite subject at school? What accomplishments is the young person proud of? Has anyone ever explained ADHD to the young person so that he or she really understands it? Has the young person ever worked with a coach or professional organizer to assist with ADHD or learning disability problems? If yes, when? What did the young person work on and did he or she like it?

The information gathered from the parents is usually filled with details, while the form for the client can be more open-ended and fun. Get curious about your clients. For example, what is their favorite food, band, or sports team? What do they enjoy doing in their free time? Do they have any free time? What's their favorite movie or book?

Last, how does the young person see the future and possibilities for change? Does the young person have an outlook that is conducive to self-growth? Is he or she ready and willing to give coaching a chance and work in partnership with the coach? Not all young clients are highly motivated at the onset of coaching. An inkling of interest, a glimmer of a connection, or a smile may be the indication that the prospective client is ready to move forward.

As the coach engages with the young person to elicit information, parents may want to jump in with their reasons for wanting a coach. Instead of deferring to the parent, coaches can use their expert diplomatic skills to invite parents to first listen to their child and try to appreciate his or her perspective on the situation.

Posing a wide variety of questions to the young person during the intake session can be helpful. Of course, this can get exhausting or overwhelming. As a result, I recommend designing a comprehensive intake form for the young person and requiring that the young person complete and return it in advance of the intake meeting.

By having the young person (and parent) answer questions in the form of intake paperwork, the coach will increase his or her ability to gather a maximum amount of information in a reasonable time frame. Although the coach most likely won't have time to discuss each and every question answered on the intake forms, the coach can plan to raise any issues that seem particularly relevant for the young person and to ask any clarifying questions that have arisen. The coach can also direct the young person to the intake paperwork and ask the young person if there are any issues in particular that he or she would like to discuss during the session. Further, in situations where the client is reluctant to share information verbally during the intake session, the coach can leverage the intake forms by viewing them during the session and then leading with the information the client provided there to initiate a discussion.

Engaging the parent. Once the coach senses that the client has had a sufficient amount of time to answer the coach's questions and discuss any concerns, the coach may turn to the parent and gather the information that the parent has to offer to provide better insight into the young person's current situation. In all likelihood, the shift from client to parent may not be clear-cut if the parent interjected information while the client was speaking or the client looked to the parent for answers.

What's important is that the coach gives the client an opportunity to speak first and share as much information as he or she chooses. Next, the coach will listen to parent concerns and hopes for coaching as the coach gathers more information about the client from the parent's perspective. The parent should also have completed an intake form, which can be used by the coach, if needed, to lead the discussion.

Questions on this form—some of which might also be discussed during the actual intake session—include the following:

- When was the young person's ADHD first diagnosed?

- Are there other family members with an ADHD diagnosis?

- Does the young person have any coexisting (comorbid) conditions or issues that need to be taken into consideration during coaching or that may impede the coaching process: depression; anxiety; substance abuse; or other mental, behavioral, or environmental conditions?

- Does the young person have special accommodations per an Individualized Education Program/504 plan?

- Has the young person worked with a tutor? If yes, in what subject(s)?

- Does the young person's family use a calendar? Who maintains that calendar?

The coach's questions to parents during the intake session are intended to help the coach gather relevant history on the young person, assess what resources are currently available to the young person, and gain insight into the parents' concerns and the obstacles parents anticipate on the young person's path. Parents have most likely invested time, energy, and resources—financial and emotional—to support their child with ADHD and related issues. They understandably want to be heard and to voice their concerns. The intake session is an opportunity for the coach to listen with the understanding that although parental input is valuable, the final coaching plan will be developed between the coach and the young person.

As the information-gathering portion of the intake session unfolds, the client and parent may find it easy to slide into a complaint mode. Parents are typically feeling very frustrated by the time they connect their child to coaching; young people are often feeling totally overwhelmed by their academic and life responsibilities and maybe even feeling hopeless about their future. The kinds of obstacles faced by young people with ADHD can understandably lead to the young people developing a mindset of pessimism or negativity.

It is the coach's role to help the young person and parent focus on what can change for the better in the future rather than getting mired in the past. Coaches can do this by sharing the value of gaining new perspectives, maintaining a positive outlook, and focusing on the potential for a successful future rather than getting stuck in the problems themselves or going over the past in great detail. Coaches may ask the client, "What is it that you would like to change or do differently?" and "What do you hope to improve upon?" By helping the client and parent focus on the potential for positive change, the coach can shift negative energy toward positive energy, lending an air of hope to both the client and the parent.

An exploration of learning style and learning disabilities. While the coach is gathering information from the young person and parent, the coach may also take some time to investigate what kind of learning style is most effective for the young person. Does the young person learn best by seeing things (visual learner) or by hearing them (auditory learner)? Or does the young person instead retain information best when he or she is in motion (kinesthetic learner) or is involved in a hands-on way (tactile learner)? Everyone learns differently, and most people utilize a combination of learning styles to understand new concepts or develop new skills. In all people, one style will nonetheless always be dominant. A variety of resources are available to better educate oneself on the different learning styles in existence. A quick search on the Internet will reveal many resources to explore. These guides will help both coach and client understand how to capitalize on the client's preferred learning style(s) and allow them to adapt the coaching modality and coaching strategies accordingly.

Knowledge of a client's learning style will provide the coach with valuable information on how to tailor coaching to meet a client's unique needs, from how best to deliver the coaching (e.g., over the phone vs. in person) to which methods will be most useful when a client is trying to absorb and retain plans for coaching homework. What might work for the client: Writing the coaching homework down? Speaking the homework into a tape recorder? Walking over to the computer and typing in the coaching homework for that week? Although the coach is careful not to tell the client what to do, the coach will regularly encourage the client to consider his or her predominant learning style when making plans. For example, when talking with a client, the coach might ask, "Do you remember those things that were recommended for visual learners? How might those tips help you with your work today?" For a kinesthetic learner, the coach might inquire, "What are some of the things that you can do kinesthetically to help with your hyperactivity and to stay focused when your body still wants to move?"

I find that about half of my young clients have at least a loose sense of their predominant learning style, while the other half are unaware that learning styles even exist or what theirs happens to be. In either case, I typically find it helpful to offer clients an assessment for identifying their particular learning style. Once the client has identified his or her predominant learning style, the coach can then discuss the practical applications of the learning style and provide the client with a handout on the topic. Even clients who come into coaching knowing their predominant learning style are typically not well informed on how to actually use this information to improve their learning and retention. The coach can help the client discover the practical applications of knowing his or her learning style as well as encourage the client to design his or her action plans in accordance with the learning style. In the process, the coach may help the young person see him or herself in a more positive way, for example, by helping him or her understand the challenges related to the less dominant learning style and by embracing learning strengths.

Beyond mere learning style differences, some clients may also have a learning disability, such as an auditory processing deficit, which makes it particularly important to capitalize on the predominant learning style during coaching and beyond. In fact, there appears to be a connection between ADHD and learning disabilities, with research indicating that there is a 40-60% overlap between ADHD, learning disabilities, and giftedness, as noted by Dr. Susan D. Mayes, Dr. Susan L. Calhoun, and Dr. Errin W. Crowell. Further, according to Dr. Joanne Rand Whitmore and Dr. C. June Maker, "It is not unexpected, then, to find a significant discrepancy between the measured academic potential of these (gifted) students and their actual performance in the classroom." This can be confusing and frustrating for parents and teachers, who expect high achievement from the gifted child and don't see results because of the impact of ADHD and learning disability on the child's ability to achieve.

In many cases, there may be a larger percentage of overlap of learning disabilities in individuals with ADHD because of the difficulties that ADHD causes with focus and processing. These difficulties may not result in diagnoses of specific learning disabilities, yet the processing deficits and inattentiveness manifest as learning difficulties or learning differences. Because of the overlap between ADHD and learning disabilities, coaches are advised to combine the discussion of learning styles and learning disabilities/learning differences during the intake session, keeping in mind the question "How does the ADHD impact the learning and the ability of my client to learn effectively?"

Parents may come to the intake and say, "My child doesn't have any learning disabilities. It's just the ADHD. I want you to work on organization and time management." Yet, parents may be missing important pieces of the puzzle in such situations. When a client comes to coaching and is consistently having problems in a specific subject in school or complains of being unable to understand what others are saying (missing bits and pieces of oral information), there may not be a diagnosed learning disability, but the ADHD is still having an impact on learning and on connection to others. As educated coaches have specific knowledge about ADHD and learning issues, coaches are advised to put on their "teacher" cap and explain to clients and parents that although there may not be a diagnosed learning disability, ADHD itself does create difficulty when it comes to staying on track, focusing, and taking in large amounts of information. The question becomes "How does ADHD impact the ability of the client to learn effectively?"

Discuss Goals and Action Steps

Once the education and getting-to-know-you phase of the intake is complete (about 45 minutes into the session), the coach will ask the parent/s to step out of the room so the second part of the intake can be conducted with only the young person present. Doing so will give the coach an important opportunity to discuss the young person's coaching goals openly and honestly, as well as to gather any additional information that the client may feel most comfortable sharing after the parent has stepped away.

Although the young person may have already shared his or her goals earlier in the session, revisiting the discussion during the one-on-one session will provide the young person with a safe space to explore his or her goals even further. Maybe the young person doesn't want the parent to hear certain goals because the parent is focused on academic achievement. Or maybe the young person is in agreement with his or her parents' goals but wants to come up with a plan to reach those goals without the parents' getting too involved. Whatever the reasons, young people will benefit from having a parent-free space in which to explore goals during the intake session.

During the intake, a discussion of the client's goals will take place to pave the way for creating the full PCA in the next regularly scheduled coaching session. The PCA is the written agreement between client and coach that captures the client's goals, action plan, and incentives for change, and the intake session is the ideal time to begin laying its foundation. This discussion is a chance to begin clarifying goals mentioned in the earlier conversation. For example, the coach might say, "I was wondering which of the goals you mentioned earlier is the most important to you right now?" or "I recall that you said that you wanted to take guitar lessons but your parents won't allow that until your grades improve. Would you be willing to design your PCA to reflect action steps toward better grades and an incentive of guitar lessons?"

As this discussion of client goals proceeds, it is quite possible that you and the client will remain in a formative process and not actually come to a clear decision on the client's specific goals for coaching. That's fine; formulation of exact goals can be picked up again in the first full coaching session. In many cases, so much has been said during the intake—with parent concerns swirling around the room and an overload of questions posed to the client by the coach—that it's neither realistic nor fair to expect the young person to come to any set decision on his or her goals for coaching. This time can simply be an opportunity to start the process of goal formulation in a structured fashion. When the client heads home with goals in mind and an understanding of how the PCA will be crafted, he or she can consider the choices he or she wants to make, as opposed to feeling pressured by others. The result is commonly a more client-centered, engaging PCA in which the client is invested.

The coming week can then serve as a period of private reflection for the client, who may be more ready to select goals in the next session after having gotten some distance from the intake experience. (Note that goal-setting sometimes proceeds more quickly with young adults than with adolescents because parents have not been present during the intake session, opening up more time for the discussion of goals and eliminating excess static from parent input.)

Evan, the Musician: Overview of an Intake Session

Evan Miller and his parents arrived at the coach's office for the two-hour intake session with the coaching information forms in hand. The coach had given the family the option of two 1-hour sessions, but they chose to have the one longer meeting. Evan was 16 years old and had ADHD inattentive type. He also had a visual motor impairment that made handwriting difficult. Mrs. Miller initiated the coaching process by calling the coach with a complaint that her son just would not do what he was told to do by parents or teachers. She was frantic that Evan would never have the grade point average needed to get into a good college.

In the prescreening call between the coach and Evan, Evan expressed interest in coaching to find out how he could do better in school and to get his parents to leave him alone. It was not clear how much time he was actually spending on his academics, how his ADHD was affecting him, or what he did for fun. He and the coach agreed that Evan would do his best to fill out the coaching forms and the two of them would discuss some of the questions during the intake. Evan appreciated the coach's concern for his handwriting difficulties.

The coach focused her attention on Evan during most of the session, and when Mrs. Miller interrupted Evan to answer questions for him, the coach calmly redirected the questions back to Evan. Mr. Miller did not interrupt and appeared comfortable as the "fly on the wall," so the coach asked him what he viewed as Evan's strengths and areas of difficulty.

At the end of the first hour, by which time Mr. and Mrs. Miller had been given an opportunity to share their concerns about Evan, the coach asked for one-on-one time with her new client. Evan's parents knew about this in advance, so they calmly took the coaching contract and handouts on ADHD and coaching and waited in the next room. For the next 30–45 minutes, Evan and his coach talked about Evan's interests (academic, social, musical), his goals, and his concerns. Evan was frustrated that his parents thought he made no effort in his life when, in fact, he had tried to do things many times and had simply failed. The coach brainstormed some short-term goals and action steps with Evan, based on his comments and the data on his coaching forms. Evan agreed that he wanted help to improve his academic performance and to get his parents to reduce their current daily homework and activity monitoring. The coach asked Evan about higher education, stating that she was curious about his interest in college, given that having Evan to go college was one of his mother's goals.

Evan said that he was not sure and requested that they talk about college later on in the semester because he wanted to focus on other goals first.

Evan now had a short list of goals and action steps to ponder until the next session, at which time he and his coach would create a PCA. Evan asked his parents to come back into the office, and they discussed the details of the coaching contract and schedule. Mr. Miller wondered about guarantees for progress. The coach explained that there are no guarantees in coaching. However, she made it clear that with clear communication, effort, and a willingness to learn and make changes, Evan could make progress with coaching. She reminded them that she would be monitoring progress with Evan along the way and making adjustments to the coaching plan as needed.

Wrap-Up

The intake session is nearly complete. The coach and client have reviewed the nature of the coaching process, time has been given to building a positive relationship between the coach and the young person, and the coach has gathered all kinds of information from the young person and parents to help design a coaching process that supports the client and his or her needs. Now just a few logistical issues need to be wrapped up. The parents are called back into the coaching session for the last 20 or 30 minutes. Once parents are back in the room, the coach can review the coaching contract, coaching plan (frequency, duration, and method), and parent involvement and boundaries, as well as collect payment and review future fees and appointment times. During the wrap-up of the intake session, the coach can also answer any remaining questions on the part of the young person or parents.

A successful intake helps parents respect the boundaries of coaching and know how to support the young person. It helps the young person begin to think about the goals that are important to him or her for the coaching journey, as well as to relax into the idea that the coach is the young person's advocate, not the parents'. And the coach him or herself now has additional knowledge to inform the coaching process: things like client learning style, possible coexisting conditions, and desired areas for growth.

A Note for Everyone

The intake session is an information-gathering time unlike any other during the coaching process. Whereas the client will be in control of the agenda at regular coaching sessions to come, during the intake, the coach follows a clear and standard plan. As noted earlier, the intake session typically involves the following components: a discussion of the intake plan and any ground rules for the session, an explanation of the coaching process, an interview of client and parent by the coach, a request by the coach to parents to step out of the coaching session, drafting of the PCA by client and coach, and a closing discussion with client and parent to take care of any final intake details.

During the intake session, the coach uses powerful questioning and active listening to get a full picture of the situation, as well as the wants, needs, and desires of the client, in a nonthreatening, curious manner. A thorough coaching intake session provides an opportunity for the new client and the parents to share their concerns and expectations. With all of the cards on the table, the coaching plan can be developed with more clarity.

In the intake process, the coach considers all perspectives—those of the client; parent/s; and other professionals, such as teachers, therapists, and doctors—and shares those perspectives with the new client as he or she begins the coaching journey. This information can be valuable throughout the coaching relationship, especially to a young person with ADHD who is unsure or unaware of how he or she is viewed by others.

During the intake, coaches also have an opportunity to share knowledge about ADHD and related issues with the client's family. This may be the first time that ADHD and the impact on the client have been discussed openly. In addition, coaches often speak (with permission) to the client's doctors, therapists, teachers, and case workers to get a full, accurate picture of the client and the areas of difficulty. This information, in addition to data from the client and the parents, helps to provide the big picture, which helps the coach and client set the coaching agenda.

Finally, during the intake session, the coach and the client begin to establish trust and develop rapport. If there is hesitation on the part of the client, this is an excellent opportunity for coaches to slow down and discuss the value of moving forward. Coaching is a process, and it is important for the coach to move at a pace that is best for the new client. When conducted effectively, the intake sets the foundation for a solid, well-designed coaching partnership.

S I X
Moving Forward:
A Motivational Approach
Toward Success

I hear parents of young people with ADHD say things like the following all the time: "If he cared about getting A's, he would study for his tests," or "He says he wants to clean his room, but then he never follows through. He just doesn't care." Where there's a will, there's a way, right? When someone is motivated to do something—when a person *wants* to do something—the person will go ahead and successfully accomplish his or her goal. This is a premise that many of us operate on, regardless of context.

I have learned over the years, however, that for young people with ADHD, having the will to do something is not always enough. These young people may have all of the will and desire in the world to accomplish something— what's called *motivation*—but lack the skills needed to get from Point A to Point B. So they may appear unmotivated to the rest of us when really they just don't know how to proceed. And for those who do lack motivation, it's not simply a matter of these young people not caring. Something is actually happening in these young people's brains (their neurobiology) and likely their life experiences, too, that makes motivation difficult, if not impossible.

This chapter explores the complex nature of motivation in young people with ADHD so readers can better understand the challenges that these young people face and, in turn, provide them with the kind of support they need to start being successful in their lives. The remainder of the chapter will explore how the components of the personal coaching agreement (PCA) are indeed an integral part of the plan for accomplishing the client's goals and the development of a client's confidence.

Through a three-pronged motivational approach, young people with ADHD can begin moving forward in their lives, implement changes, make progress toward their goals, and experience success, often against a backdrop of months or years of past frustration. A rewarding cycle of motivation, progress, and success often ensues, in which motivation leads to progress and success, that success then fosters more motivation, which then leads to more progress and success! When this cycle gets put into motion, it's very exciting for coaches, parents, and other professionals to observe.

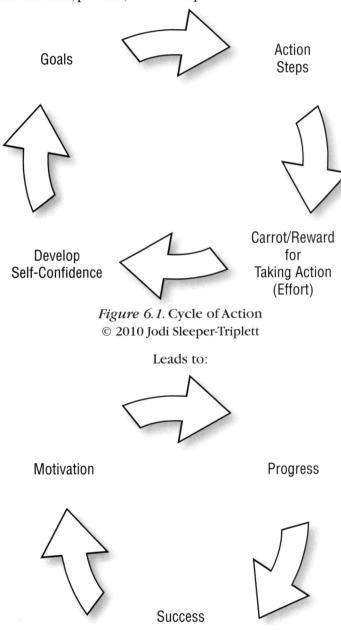

Figure 6.1. Cycle of Action
© 2010 Jodi Sleeper-Triplett

Leads to:

Figure 6.2. Cycle of Success
© 2010 Jodi Sleeper-Triplett

What Do We Know About Motivation and How Does It Relate to Young People With ADHD?

One of the major challenges that parents and teachers identify in young people with ADHD is that these individuals lack motivation. Although there is certainly some truth to this statement, motivation in young people with ADHD is far more complicated than the notion that these individuals simply don't care or lack a desire to be successful. In fact, the contrary is often the case. After years of failing to meet the grade, falling short of their own or their parents' hopes and expectations, or struggling to master even basic tasks like showing up for activities on time or completing homework and household chores, these young people are often walking through their daily life with broken hearts and defeated attitudes because they want more than anything to succeed at life, but they lack the skills, know-how, and experience to do so.

Chris A. Zeigler Dendy notes frequently in her book *Teenagers with ADD and ADHD* that teens with ADHD often appear to be unmotivated and lazy to those around them. The low energy, daydreaming, or "spaciness" of an ADHD inattentive-type teen can appear to adults, peers, and others as disinterest, laziness, and lack of motivation. Sadly, these young people have often been told by others that they are ill-behaved, uncooperative, ungrateful, uncaring, or even stupid. Although it's true that motivation to work is often a problem for young people with ADHD (as noted by Dr. Thomas E. Brown in his book *Attention Deficit Disorder*), a lack of apparent motivation in young people with ADHD does not equal laziness. Both Dendy and Dr. Brown stress the need to develop and strengthen executive functioning skills, which are necessary for goal-directed behavior, in young people with ADHD.

Motivation has been studied for years by psychologists, educators, workforce specialists, and others; thus, countless variations of what motivation is and how it can be fostered have been described in literature emerging from an array of fields. Within the context of coaching young people with ADHD, I define motivation as the desire to take action toward achieving one's goals. Thus, a perceived lack of motivation in young people with ADHD pertains to the absence of momentum and drive to achieve their goals. This lack of momentum is often fostered by a lack of skill or other inability to achieve one's goals and doesn't mean that young people with ADHD are being obstinate, willfully disobedient, or inflexible.

Oftentimes, these young people simply have trouble getting started because their executive functioning capacity is underdeveloped or they have yet to acquire the skills needed to get started on accomplishing their goals. Other times, these young people have trouble getting started because they are used to their efforts toward achieving goals being met with failure rather than success. Somewhere along the way, these young people have become tired or even fearful of trying, believing that one more disappointment awaits them around the corner. Many of my young clients have trouble initiating tasks, especially difficult ones. Although these problems may seem insurmountable, especially to the clients, I have found that by chunking down a task into small steps and offering a "carrot" for taking just one step at a time, I am able to help clients move forward with greater momentum and less resistance. Despite their past experiences, these clients discover that they can gain the momentum to complete the task.

Thus, lack of motivation in young people with ADHD is not simply about making a choice not to act or about choosing to do less than is expected of them. Lack of motivation in these young people stems instead from the neurobiology of ADHD and the resulting challenges to their executive functioning, which often result in an insufficient skill set and demoralizing life experiences. Fortunately, the neurobiological, skill-related, and life-experience components affecting motivation in young people with ADHD can be addressed, whether through proper medication management, therapy, coaching, or some combination of these. Before examining possible means of doing so, for greater insight and understanding, let's look a little more closely at the components of motivation in young people with ADHD.

Lack of Motivation Due to Neurobiological Issues

A key culprit related to lack of motivation in young people with ADHD can be found in one realm of the brain. A youth with a prefrontal cortex that is asleep in some way because of a neurochemical imbalance related to the biology of ADHD can easily be mistaken for a young person who simply does not care or is unmotivated. For the young person to feel motivated, this part of his or her brain first needs to be sufficiently stimulated. Until then, we as coaches, parents, and adults can try to jumpstart these young people into action until we're blue in the face, but we're likely to see no tangible results if their brains are not sufficiently activated. Only when the young person's brain is sufficiently activated (i.e., regulated to have the proper flow of neurotransmitters, such as dopamine and epinephrine) can we even begin to hope to see motivation in the young person. Without this brain regulation, motivation is simply an unrealistic expectation.

As you may recall, I began this chapter with the mantra of "where there's a will, there's a way." This is a sentiment expressed by many of the adults I meet who are feeling frustrated when trying to support young people with ADHD. Here's what we all need to remember, though: Because of the brain-based biology of ADHD, motivation is not about will or choice for many young people with ADHD; it is about a neurobiological condition that runs counter to natural feelings of motivation. If these young people could, they would choose to engage in actions to meet their goals. The problem is that these young people really and truly have trouble getting started—not because they don't care, per se, but because they lack the physical sensation of "get up and go" that would exist if their brains were regulated properly. When a young person with ADHD seems unmotivated, the young person is not usually being willfully disobedient or purposefully choosing to do less than what's expected. The case is simply that the young person's brain-based executive functioning capacity is underdeveloped and needs activation.

Piper, the Writer: How the Brain Affects Motivation

My client, Piper, was a talented 16-year-old writer. Teachers raved about her skills and gave Piper high marks—when she completed her assignments. That was the problem! Piper was perpetually stuck and unable to initiate the tasks needed to get her work done.

It was easy for Piper's parents and teachers to assume she didn't complete her assignments because she didn't care—because she was unmotivated —but our work together revealed that the source of the problem was actually related to her brain-based executive functioning challenges. As it turns out, Piper's mind was actually racing when she would try to make progress on her assignments, with her brain busy creating all of the variations of the first paragraph of the weekly English essay. By the end of an evening, Piper usually had notes on a few topics or a sentence or two written and rewritten, but she couldn't get further than that because she would get stuck on the next step, unable to sustain the momentum she needed to complete the steps.

One day, Piper stayed late at school to talk with the teacher about her unfinished essay. While waiting for her teacher to finish with another student, Piper started to write her weekly English essay and was finished with a first draft in about 20 minutes! When Piper told me of her experience—her burst of creativity and energy—I explained the concept of a body double in coaching: the mere presence of another person sitting and working nearby that keeps the person with ADHD more focused and on task.

Piper decided to test the theory of the body double the next week and, when she did, she once again completed a first draft of her essay. From that point on, the action plan was set up to include a weekly after-school session with the English teacher, not for direct help, but for Piper to sit in the classroom and work independently in the presence of her teacher. Piper was motivated to repeat this activity because it lowered her stress level and feeling of failure and provided her with external praise and good grades for her accomplishments.

So, if motivation appears to be an issue with a young person with ADHD, you may need to support the young person in investigating what's going on at the level of the brain. Before any real work in coaching can take place, it may be necessary to support the young person in working with the multimodal support team to make sure that the young person's brain is sufficiently activated and thus ready to engage in activities that require motivation and work. This kind of attention, directed at addressing the biology of ADHD, can involve a range of solutions, whether through medication management, exercise, nutrition, sleep, waiting out the ups and downs of puberty, or some combination therein.

Once we are successful at getting the frontal lobes to wake up—once we have the correct brain activation in the young person with ADHD—we have the right setup to begin working on the other factors that may contribute to lack of motivation or to begin working toward the goals at hand. Although a higher level of activity in the prefrontal cortex of the brain does not guarantee an external display of motivation in the young person, it does lead to a higher probability of seeing motivation in the client than if the brain were not adequately stimulated.

Lack of Motivation Due to Insufficient Skills and Negative Life Experiences

Problems with motivation for young people with ADHD begin in the brain— where an imbalance of neurotransmitters may rob the individual of any natural feelings of motivation or "get up and go"—but, unfortunately, these motivational challenges don't end in the brain. Instead, they may carry over into other areas of the young person's life, further complicating the young person's ability to feel motivated.

Insufficient skills. Over the course of the young person's life, his or her imbalanced brain chemistry has led to weakened executive functioning skills, such that the young person may have trouble concentrating, focusing, organizing thoughts, sustaining effort, or utilizing working memory. As you can imagine, this kind of compromised brain functioning makes for a very challenging learning environment. While the young person's peers are observing social behavior—learning how to make friends, communicating effectively with adults, and effectively modulating their emotions—the young person with ADHD is missing the chance to acquire the same skills because his or her mind has created an environment not conducive to learning. While classmates are learning from their own parents' modeling of how to manage one's time, keep one's living space organized, or make conversation at a family gathering, the young person with ADHD may be unable to observe, absorb, or acquire those skills because of challenges with executive functioning.

How is this all relevant to motivation? Reliable executive functioning isn't just needed to accomplish goals; it's needed to *acquire the skills* used to accomplish goals. As a result, a lack of skills can lead to an adolescent who is frozen with uncertainty on how to proceed on a given task. The outward picture of a young person without skills may be an individual who doesn't turn assignments in, who doesn't study for tests, or who avoids writing college application essays. However, if we were privy to the young person's internal world, we could see that he or she may actually feel trapped or paralyzed because of a lack of skills. The young person may be filled with the desire to be successful but be deficient in the skills needed to identify or engage in the action steps that will lead to success. The young person's lack of skills inhibits him or her from taking action. Until the young person has developed those skills, achieving many of his or her desired goals will be as hard as walking a tightrope or taming a lion without any circus training.

Here's another scenario that may provide greater understanding into the world of the young person with ADHD. Imagine that a vacationer who doesn't know how to swim is out on a snorkeling boat with a tour guide and some fellow passengers. When the tour guide asks everyone to jump into the water as the boat approaches a coral reef, the vacationer who doesn't know how to swim will likely lack the motivation or desire to jump off the boat, because doing so will be not only uncomfortable and fear provoking but also outright dangerous. How does this relate to ADHD? Many times, without realizing it, parents and teachers are asking young people with ADHD to jump off the proverbial boat when these young people don't know how to swim yet and aren't even wearing a life jacket.

Parents sometimes say, "If he cared, he would just do it," without considering the possibility that a young person can care with all of his or her heart but, without the proper knowledge or skill set, be completely unable to take even a first step toward action. As indicated by renowned developmental psychologist Erik Erikson, if we want young people to be able to meet their goals, we have to first help them develop the skills and attitudes needed to work productively.

Negative life experiences. A lack of skills can lead to a lack of motivation in young people with ADHD, but there's even more contributing to challenges in motivation for these young people. Another source of nonmotivation can be the demoralizing nature of many of the life experiences encountered by the young person so far in life. For example, a young person with ADHD might have experienced many failures in his or her lifetime, such as receiving poor academic grades, encountering difficulty making lasting friendships, or repeatedly struggling to initiate a task, due to the challenges of ADHD. The life experiences that begin to accumulate for the young person, then, are typically marked by disappointment, letdown, or even defeat.

Imagine that every time you tried to scale a climbing wall, you fell to the ground. Imagine that no matter how much time you spent building a model airplane, the darn plane would never actually fly. What would be learned in the process? Might you eventually stop trying to scale the climbing wall in the first place? Would you leave the next model airplane in the box?

When we look at examples as simple as these, it's not hard to understand how this cycle of effort followed by failure followed by effort and then more failure could slowly wear away at a young person's motivation to put forth future effort to achieve goals. Who wants to keep trying to climb a wall if the result will be bruises or broken bones? Why spend hours building a model that seems sure not to do its job when you are done?

The thinking in young people with ADHD often goes something like this: "Why bother trying? I know I'll just mess up." A vicious cycle thus gets created, in which effort followed by failure diminishes a person's desire to apply future effort. The trick with young people with ADHD is helping them to move into a cycle of action followed by success (see Figures 6.1 and 6.2), which, in turn, can help to motivate the young person to put forth more effort as he or she becomes more able to anticipate possible success. Coaches also want to help the young person develop and discover tools for handling failure, so that when goals aren't accomplished, the young person is not totally demoralized and demotivated.

In sum, not knowing what steps to take (i.e., having insufficient skills), along with having had so many failures in the past, can make it truly difficult for young people with ADHD not only to complete their goals but also to even to get started working toward these goals in the first place.

Problems With Motivation: What's the Source?

If you are working with a young person with ADHD who seems to lack motivation, consider each of the following areas: degree of *brain activation*, sufficiency of *skill* set, and quality of *thoughts and beliefs* in regard to the young person's ability to generate success from his or her efforts. These three areas work together to help a young person with ADHD experience the motivation needed to put forth effort and work toward goals. Questions to ask include the following:

1. **Is there underactivity in the brain that needs addressing?** If lack of motivation seems apparent in the young person, take some time to make sure the brain is properly activated. Work with the young person's multimodal support team to examine and address any relevant neurobiological issues. If you don't help the young person become more attentive in thought and initiation, it will be next to impossible for him or her to be motivated to do something.

2. **Are sufficient skills in place?** Next, look at the current skill level of the young person. What skills does the young person need to build to initiate tasks and sustain motivation? Request a self-report of areas of difficulty and frustration in addition to areas of strength and skill. Then partner with the young person and his or her support team to create a plan for effective skill building in all life areas.

3. **Do negative thoughts or beliefs from a history of failure need to be addressed?** As a result of a past record of letdowns and failures, the young person may be caught in a trap of viewing the glass as half empty rather than half full. Negative or pessimistic thinking can undermine attempts to build skills; self-defeating thoughts can interfere with motivation and effort. What will it take for the young person to look at the future with a new perspective and a more positive outlook? Help the client become aware of common negative thought patterns and work together to create an affirmation, such as "I will be successful" or "I can do it."

A Framework for Increasing Motivation

Motivating adolescents and young people to do something is often not an easy task. Add ADHD to the picture and the challenge becomes all the more difficult. Yet, by building on some basic principles of motivation and enabling the young person to stay at the center of the coaching process, you may be surprised at how much you are able to help a young person get moving. These principles, which do double duty as the steps one follows to increase motivation, include setting goals, creating a step-by-step action plan to accomplish goals, and identifying desirable rewards and incentives. There is a fourth principle I would add to the motivational process, too: fostering confidence in the young person.

These four principles work together to help the young person get motivated to start moving. Of course, these tools go way beyond helping the young person get started: They also help the young person actually accomplish goals. The text that follows offers an overview of these four principles/steps and how they work together to help motivate the young person to put forth effort and find success in the process.

Set Goals

The first step in generating motivation in the young person is to help the young person figure out what he or she wants to do in the first place. What is it that the young person hopes the coaching process can help him or her accomplish? Does the young person want to spend a semester abroad? Would the young person like to go to music camp? Does the young person want to save up for a new computer? Identifying a young person's goals is the first step in the motivational process. After all, it's hard to get motivated if you don't know what exactly you're trying to accomplish.

A key piece of motivating young people (and the rest of us!) is to keep the coaching process tied to what it is that the young person wants and to avoid falling into the trap of advocating for mom and dad's goals. A basic principle of motivation is that individuals are more likely to attempt to achieve something if the end result is desired by the individuals. For example, when a young person is reading an exciting mystery and wants to know how it ends, he or she will be motivated to spend the time and energy needed to read the book until the mystery is solved. Staying aligned with the young person's goals—directing him or her to find out what these really are—will play a very important role in the motivational process.

Client-Centered Goal-Setting and Parents: Do the Two Mix?

A big dilemma coaches often face during the goal-setting process is how to keep the coaching centered on the client but not ignore mom and dad. It's a delicate balancing act to make sure that parents feel heard at the intake without alienating the young person by pushing the parents' agenda. Although coaching is based on client goals, the coach can still provide an opportunity for parents to express their wishes for the young person and the coaching process. Not only are parents often paying for coaching and expecting some acknowledgement of their goals at the first intake session, but parents often have valuable insight into the life of the young person that can be useful in informing the coaching process. Being respectful of parents' goals by acknowledging them in the presence of the client while also explaining that the process is client directed will go a long way toward keeping the process on track. Coaches are encouraged to share with the parents that time will be spent during the goal-setting session with the young person discussing whether the young person would be interested in considering any of the goals suggested by the parents.

Although the coach won't be forcing the young person to adopt the parents' goals, the coach will give the young person a chance to assess whether any of those goals are of interest. Oftentimes, the parents' big-picture goals, such as graduation from high school, are aligned with the client's goals of improving grades and getting his or her parents to provide more breathing room. Thus, the coach can plan to discuss the parents' requests during the goal-setting session with the client and aim to help the client see different perspectives on a situation without pressuring the client to choose a parent-centered goal. The client may decide that a parental goal is too rigid, whereas a variation on that goal fits just right. The coach can be a valuable facilitator of the goal-setting process with adolescents and young adults.

An essential element to being motivated is having a target to aim for—a defined goal that the young person wants to attain. In young people with ADHD, having a goal alone is not likely sufficient to get the young person motivated (remember, there's often fear of failure and a belief that he or she is incapable of achievement), but it is necessary. If one wants to find the motivation to move forward from Point A, it's important to identify where Point B is exactly. Once the young person has a defined target to aim for, the other motivational elements can fall into place.

Create a Clear Action Plan

Another essential step for helping motivate young people with ADHD is the creation of a step-by-step action plan that will help them make actual progress toward their goals and learn the skills needed to accomplish other goals in the future. The creation of an action plan in and of itself may be a new experience for the client, one that the client can add to his or her skill set for use again and again in the future.

For example, a client may have a goal of being first chair violinist in the high school orchestra. The coach inquires, "What action steps are required to meet this goal?" And the client begins to break down the process: (a) practice daily, (b) meet with my violin teacher each Monday afternoon, and (c) remember to take my violin to school.

The action stage of the process is a time when very sincere intentions on the part of the young person with ADHD can easily break down. Maybe the adolescent knows she wants to get into college (goal), and yet she has no idea what steps she needs to take to apply for and be accepted into college. Maybe she doesn't know what she needs to do and, even if she did, she may not have the strongest skill set for engaging in the necessary work. Without the support of a coach or her parents, she may never take even the first step toward working to achieve her goals. Those observing from the outside may identify this apparent inertia as laziness or obstinance—as a lack of motivation—when, in fact, it may simply be the case of a young person who lacks the skills to get her personal project off the ground.

Our society has a false assumption that we can just kick young people out the door on their 18th birthday and expect them to be ready, willing, and able to make it on their own. This becomes more problematic for young people with ADHD. Because, as Dr. Russell A. Barkley points out, youth with ADHD are often less mature than their peers without ADHD, and because they may have had trouble over the years picking up and retaining the skills needed to be successful at daily life, much less accomplishing loftier goals like college acceptance or moving into one's own apartment (for the college-aged set), these young people need some supportive hand-holding to help them cross the bridge from the idea stage to the action stage: from goals to motion. A clear and realistic step-by-step action plan can serve as an invaluable tool for young people with ADHD who might otherwise grow overwhelmed by the prospect of working toward their goals and remain stuck.

Ben's History Grade: Turning Goals Into Action Steps

Ben, a coaching client with ADHD, had a goal to improve his history grade but was inconsistent with reading the assigned text and related articles. He found the information presented in the readings to be boring and had a difficult time sitting still for extended periods of time. The coach explained that this was not an uncommon experience for young people with ADHD and asked if she could share a strategy used by other students.

"Sitting still is a challenge for many of my clients. Some of them have found that reading for 15 minutes while sitting in a chair and then taking a break for a minute or two is quite helpful. I understand that that sitting is really uncomfortable for you. Would you consider using a timer so you'll know when you're time is up and can take a break? If you want to try this out, I encourage you to get up and celebrate when you've met your goal of 15 minutes of reading—do the Snoopy dance or whatever. And if you don't accomplish your goal, don't punish yourself. Just try again."

The coach helped Ben move from goal stage (improve history grade) to action stage (read for 15 minutes a day) by suggesting a strategy that she knew had worked for other young people. She also reminded Ben that he had the option of coming up with his own strategy for accomplishing the reading if the coach's strategy was not to his liking and invited him to brainstorm alternatives.

By helping clients think through the practical nuts and bolts of how they are going to accomplish a goal—by mapping out the individual steps needed for success—coaches can provide clients with an important motivational boost. A great and overwhelming burden of stress may get lifted from the young person with ADHD once the action plan is in hand, because instead of facing chaos and uncertainty, the young person now has a tangible, line-by-line, realistic set of instructions for how to proceed in order to meet goals.

It's not that the coach designs the action plan for the young person with ADHD; instead, the coach will guide the client through the process of developing a step-by-step plan and will support the client in creating his or her own plan, one that feels right and is based on personality, learning style, comfort level, and so forth. The coach can then jump in as needed along the way to offer specific strategies, support, and structure for constructing the plan. Coaches use their coaching skills to help the client stay focused, consider all perspectives, step back, look at the big-picture goal, and then zoom in on the specific action steps needed to accomplish the goal.

Identify Desirable Rewards and Incentives

Goals and a step-by-step action plan work together to clear the way for a client to act. Yet, for motivation to be sustained beyond a discussion in a coaching session or over a period of weeks or months, youth with ADHD often need more than goals and a plan—they also need a reward system for achieving those goals. This is a basic fact of human nature: To have the motivation to do something differently, a person needs to find something positive in achieving it. Another way of stating this is to say that individuals engage in new behavior when they anticipate a reward for that behavior. That reward can be external, such as money, a vacation, a trip to one's favorite coffee shop, or a new "toy," or it can be internal, such as feelings of pride, integrity, and/or acceptance garnered from praise from others or from self-satisfaction with a job well done.

Identifying goals is another one of the essential steps in motivating young people with ADHD, but because these individuals have a lot to overcome to get from here to there, external rewards are a particularly important part of the motivational process. Setting a goal will turn the young person in the right direction. Creating an action plan will put a roadmap in the young person's hand. And helping the young person create a reward system for meeting those goals will provide an important impetus for the young person to exert the effort needed to actually move forward.

I find it valuable to include a question about rewards on the parent intake form: "Do you currently use a reward system with your child? If not, are you willing to work with the coach to develop a system?" The answers give me a sense of the parents' level of acceptance of the use of rewards and incentives to shape new behaviors, thus helping to guide the conversation on this topic during the intake session. The reward system is discussed briefly during the intake, and both parents and young clients are provided with an opportunity to share their opinions and ideas.

The most effective method for landing on acceptable rewards is to give the family an opportunity to discuss rewards in the comfort of their own home. In my experience, new clients are reticent to ask for a reward, and they often report that they don't deserve anything. It may take a discussion of human nature and basic principles of behavioral change to help both clients and parents understand that this is not a bribe but rather a part of the process that leads to greater success.

Incentives or rewards can be designed to help the young person find the energy, wherewithal, and determination to work toward their goals. What will the young person receive in return for achieving a goal? The range of rewards my clients explore is incredibly wide, from cash to sports equipment, books, and electronics to activities like a trip to the movies with friends, going out to dinner with mom or dad, or a trip to the paintball course. Sometimes the reward is the accomplishment itself, but that approach takes time, a certain level of maturity, and better overall self-esteem on the part of the client.

As with goal-setting, the process of identifying rewards and incentives needs to be client centered if it's going to be effective. Given that adolescents still live at home and young adults are sometimes still financially dependent on parents, the rewards the client brainstorms as being appealing will often need to be approved by the parents, but the ideas need to originate with the young person him or herself. There's one sure way to make a reward system ineffective, and that is to pick something as a reward that the young person doesn't care about. Instead, working with the young person to identify a desirable reward will help create an environment conducive to change.

Rewards Versus Incentives?

Before I go further in explaining how a reward system can play out as an important motivational tool in coaching, I want to acknowledge that some parents find the idea of giving the young person a reward for doing something he or she is supposed to do distasteful, or they may even consider this approach to be bad parenting. These parents are coming from a school of thought in which it would be a violation of parental values to give external rewards for fulfilling one's responsibilities, for example, money for good grades or a new video game for cleaning one's room. Or they may want to teach the value that hard work yields internal rewards (e.g., satisfaction, pride, a sense of accomplishment). This reality highlights the fact that rewards will not only vary by a young person's interests but will also have to be moderated using a framework within which parents are comfortable and able to be supportive.

After clients brainstorm possible rewards for achieving their identified goals, I always direct them back to their parents so they can have a conversation to gauge parents' willingness to sign off on providing (or agreeing to) these rewards. If you find that parents are opposed to the suggested reward system, it can be helpful to guide the client to work with the parent to identify rewards that would be palatable to the parent. For example, maybe the parent is unwilling to give the young person money for academic improvement but is comfortable with taking the young person out to a restaurant of his or her choice to celebrate this success, and this sounds appealing to the young person. You may also find that parents respond better to the term *incentive* than *reward*, because an incentive is more closely related, by definition, to motivation and encouragement, as compared with the misconception for some that a reward is a bribe. Choose the term you wish to use on the basis of your own preferences and those of the client and his or her family.

Everyone needs some promise of a reward—whether external or internal—to feel motivated to work toward a goal. But for young people with ADHD, the promise of a reward is particularly important, because these individuals are often stuck in a quagmire of past failure and need something truly compelling to help spring them out of this trap of inactivity. As mentioned earlier, many young people with ADHD have continually experienced the negative consequences of their failings in life—and, when interviewed in the coaching intake session, they often point out that they never get anything for their efforts or for their attempts to improve or change, so they simply choose to stop trying. Because they don't get rewarded for effort, young people with ADHD often lose motivation to work toward goals.

It is interesting to note that there is also another group of young people with ADHD who have simply been unable to internalize or remember, because of their ADHD and related issues, the rewards and the praise they received for their efforts in childhood. These young people report that they never received rewards or positive feedback from their parents or that it was very infrequent. Even though this may not have actually been the case, these young people's sense of not ever receiving rewards for their efforts may have created in them a chronic lack of motivation.

To be effective, the incentive system should reward clients for taking a step forward—making an attempt—rather than holding the reward until the larger goal has been reached. Motivation in incremental steps is key! Many years ago, when I was starting out as a coach, I had a teenage client who was promised a brand new car if he got his grades up throughout the school year. This was to be accomplished through coaching, after-school help from teachers, medication for increased focus, and support from the school's special education department.

Halfway through the school year, the client was not making much progress and the progress that had been made was inconsistent. The parents called a meeting with the school personnel and I was in attendance. I remember clearly the assistant principal looking at my client and stating, "Your parents are offering you a new car. What is keeping you from doing your work and earning that car?" My client replied, "The car is so big and so far off that it does not mean anything to me. What about now? What do I get for trying?" This was a turning point for my client and a valuable learning experience for his parents as well as me.

By supporting the client in creating a reward system and reviewing that reward system from time to time, coaches and parents add something new to the life of the young person that has the potential to get the young person excited about trying again. The promise of something special or desired can go a long way to draw young people with ADHD out of their seeming state of disinterest. They still may not know how they are going to accomplish the goals they've identified, but identifying rewards helps them generate some valuable energy and excitement around rolling up their sleeves and putting in the effort needed to achieve their goals one step at a time. Until these clients can begin to develop and experience internal rewards like satisfaction and pride, the use of external rewards, or the "dangling carrot," is invaluable.

Developing Confidence

The fourth piece of motivating young people with ADHD has to do with building their confidence level. Remember that young people with ADHD have often experienced a lifetime of feeling like they are letting others down. On the flip side, many of them have never experienced the kind of rewards, successes, or reinforcements for their efforts that would help them develop a positive belief in their ability to accomplish what they set out to do. As a result, you may find that the young person is skeptical when he or she first sets out to follow the action plan created in collaboration with the coach. This is because the young person is basing expectations on past experiences rather than on the fact that the young person is now doing something different: namely, following a step-by-step guide to action with a coach's continual support.

In the beginning, when the young client is tentative or fearful, a coach's ability to show belief in the client's capacity to accomplish goals will stand in for the client's own lacking self-confidence, thus giving a little motivational boost. Over time, as the client achieves small successes, he or she will start to build confidence. The coach can support this process as it unfolds through continual confidence-building gestures. When a client reports a success, the coach will be one of the first to congratulate the client ("Way to go!" "Fantastic!"). When the client expresses uncertainty, the coach will remain steady, encouraging the client to give something new a try. And when the client does not complete an action plan or meet goals, the coach will also accept the client. The coaching partnership is nonjudgmental.

In truth, confidence, at its core, involves believing that a person is a worthwhile human being, however and wherever that person is on life's journey. By lightening up on young people with ADHD—by showing support regardless of outcomes—coaches and other adults can help these young people gain insight into a new perspective on themselves. The young person may start to think along the lines of the following: "Hey, my coach thinks I'm a good person even if I make mistakes or I forget to call in for coaching sometimes. Maybe that means I really am okay as I am, no matter what." As a result of this nonjudgmental, supportive approach, the consequence for not doing something does not become a withdrawal of support, encouragement, or positive regard. The result is simply whatever natural consequence follows from the young person not executing a particular action. So if the young person didn't talk to a teacher about retaking a test, his or her overall grade might suffer. If the young person didn't get home in time for curfew, he or she forgoes the reward that was built into the PCA for five on-time arrivals.

When the young person experiences natural consequences for his or her actions (or lack of actions), motivation tends to be increased. In contrast, the application of random negative consequences, such as being grounded, losing unrelated privileges, or being required to perform a chore, does not connect to the client's goals and actions and does not motivate the client to work harder or smarter toward achieving goals.

Ultimately, developing confidence increases motivation. Imagine a new inspirational speaker is getting up in front of a group for the very first time. He is stressed, he keeps telling himself that he doesn't want to do this, and he is not sure if sound will come out of his mouth when he begins speaking. Then, a miracle occurs! His vocal cords work well, his points are right on track, and the audience nods in affirmation. The presentation is a success. The new speaker feels more confident than before, ready to take on the next presentation that comes his way. He is motivated to try again as a result of his success and the increased confidence created by that success. The process works in a similar way for young people with ADHD, even if it takes some time and practice to experience success and ultimately feel confident.

So many times I have begun work with a client who appeared to parents and teachers as unmotivated, only for everyone to discover that when the young person and I spell out specific goals; create a doable, step-by-step action plan for success; build rewards and incentives into that plan; and work together to increase confidence, the young person moves out of a state of seeming inertia into a state of activity and progress. What once seemed insurmountable—for the young person and everyone else—suddenly becomes more attainable.

The PCA: An All-Encompassing Tool for Motivation

I use the PCA as a formal tool for motivation. The PCA is initiated during the intake session and completed during the first coaching session that follows. It includes a client's goals, a step-by-step action plan for accomplishing goals, and the chosen reward system for meeting those goals. In other words, it captures the motivational framework suggested for use in this chapter.

The action plan is designed to include daily and weekly steps that the client has agreed to take, leading to incremental rewards for effort and achievement. Knowing that there is value in trying, the client is more likely to feel comfortable and ultimately confident about forging ahead to meet the goal. The amount of reinforcement provided by the coach will vary depending on the client. The coach is not reinforcing just for the sake of hearing him or herself shout praise but to reach clients in a way that sparks and sustains motivation.

The PCA is not the only tool that the coach can use to motivate someone. For example, for older clients such as young adults, a verbal discussion of concrete goals and action steps for reaching those goals can be enough—these clients may not need or want the piece of paper that is the PCA, or they may decide to go home after a session and create their own write-up of goals and action steps. In addition, these clients don't always need to select an external reward to get themselves motivated. Instead, the promise of an intrinsic reward like pride, satisfaction, or security may be enough. Or the accomplishment of the goal itself—getting a job, acing a final, or making new friends—may be the reward for the client.

Yet, the PCA is the tool that I find most useful with young people who have ADHD because it provides a concrete structure and point of reference from which the client can progress. (Note that motivation is only one of the by-products of the PCA. It also provides a structure for the coaching process and strategies for the client to follow toward his or her goals.) The PCA is discussed in detail in the following chapter.

A Note for Everyone

It is common for adults to view low motivation and procrastination as "not caring." Parents, teachers, and other professionals are encouraged to acknowledge that skill building and support are required to assist adolescents and young adults with ADHD in moving forward to meet their agendas. By doing so, we open the door to possibilities for young people who want to move forward but find themselves stuck, whether because of a neurochemical imbalance, a lack of skill, the fear of failure, or a combination therein. Goal-setting with built-in rewards and action steps for progress and accountability have shown great promise with young clients with ADHD. According to Dr. Nancy Mather and Dr. Sam Goldstein, "the appropriate application of positive reinforcement has repeatedly been demonstrated to increase both on-task behavior and work completion." Dr. Mather and Dr. Goldstein's work and other studies have shown that positive reinforcement is the best way to promote motivation in all children and adolescents. In addition, when a structural framework is incorporated into the coaching plan, adolescents with ADHD learn and thrive.

Each person has a unique motivational key. When supporting young people with ADHD, take time to explore the young person's likes and dislikes, passions and trepidations. Through that exploratory process, you will be able to better identify the motivators that will open the door to possibilities and changes.

S E V E N

The Personal Coaching Agreement: Cornerstone of Support and Structure

If I could offer a secret ingredient to success when it comes to coaching youth with ADHD, would you want to learn about it? If there were a magic formula to motivate youth to change their behavior and try new strategies that might help them to reach their goals, would you want to know what it was? The personal coaching agreement (PCA) is possibly the most valuable ingredient I can offer when it comes to maximizing the success of ADHD coaching. No, the PCA won't work actual magic, and its use can by no means guarantee results, yet I have seen the power of the PCA demonstrated time and again as I have worked with young clients to create and use this powerful tool. I never tire of watching the amazing growth that can occur in a young person who is ready and mature enough to engage in coaching and who is willing to work hard to put all of the elements of the PCA into practice.

On the surface, the PCA is a rather simple document with clearly defined parts: client goals, action steps with an accountability plan, and rewards. At a deeper level, the PCA is more complex because it needs to be created and followed within the context of the young person's unique goals, changing life situation, and increasing self-awareness. In the real world, each client will bring distinct goals to the coaching experience and will be working to achieve these goals using his or her own set of personal strengths and weaknesses. Add to this unique client "fingerprint" the changing environment in which the young person lives (e.g., a new school, a change in extracurricular activities, a new job, a move to a new town, a boyfriend/girlfriend breakup) and the value of treating the PCA as a flexible document that may need to be tweaked and revisited from time to time becomes clear.

Another area that contributes to the complexity of the PCA and whether its use can lead to success has to do with the people using the PCA—both coach and young person. I've already touched on the young person's role. Is he or she currently coachable—for example, motivated and ready to implement new strategies for success? Do the young person's life circumstances allow him or her to be present for coaching or is the young person distracted by what's going on in his or her world outside of coaching? Is the young person hindered by an untreated coexisting condition such as depression or substance abuse?

As for the coach, a big question regarding the effectiveness of the PCA relates to whether the coach is engaging the young person in a supportive relationship while helping to facilitate the design and implementation of this document. The PCA will mean very little if the coach lacks the ability to create a supportive space in which the client can explore his or her wishes, plans, and goals. Young people will only feel comfortable speaking candidly and taking the kind of mental risks inherent in considering new behaviors if the coach is fostering a safe and nonjudgmental environment in which to explore.

Thus, the PCA is a manageable and concrete tool for bringing about client change that nonetheless needs to be designed with careful attention to a young person's unique goals and situation. It also needs to be delivered in a supportive environment that is client centered, not coach or parent centered. With the structure provided by the PCA—as a framework with concrete plans for change—and the transformative effects that often come from a supportive relationship, the young person can begin to achieve his or her goals, step by step, check-in by check-in, and incentive by incentive.

This chapter provides an in-depth discussion on how to create the PCA with the client through four fundamental steps: setting goals, identifying action steps, creating an accountability plan, and selecting rewards, as touched upon in the previous chapter. The chapter also explores the concepts of support and structure to provide greater insight into how these elements are key to success in coaching and to reveal how they are built into the PCA itself.

Making Change Manageable With the PCA

Let's face it: Change isn't easy. Even for those of us who don't have ADHD or learning issues, it can be extremely hard to try new behaviors, let alone maintain them over the long term. Just think of the countless New Year's resolutions that so many of us set each January, only to have them fizzle within a few weeks or months. Now just imagine that you are a young person with ADHD. You have challenges with prioritization and time management, your self-esteem is low, and you have very little practice at setting goals and working toward them because you are still young and your parents have so far stepped in to help you succeed. You arrive at the coaching intake and are asked by the coach what it is you'd like to get out of coaching, and you feel totally overwhelmed. Where do you begin? Even if you could figure out how to begin, would you stand a chance of finishing what you started?

Enter the PCA, a written document capturing the young person's goals alongside a personalized plan for achieving those goals. Although the actual work of meeting the goals themselves must still be done, the PCA puts the young client on the road to success. By the time the PCA has been formulated, the young person will have spelled out desirable yet realistic goals for him or herself, considered which steps he or she would like to take to achieve those goals, designated incentives that will help motivate him or her to achieve, and specified a clear accountability plan that will have him or her checking in with the coach and/or parents as needed to stay on track. Clearly, there is a lot going on in the PCA. To keep the PCA manageable, the coach becomes the supportive glue that holds it all together by inviting the young person to

- choose what he or she wants the PCA to contain

- discuss the benefits and potential pitfalls of his or her choices

- recognize that the coach will provide support and encouragement as he or she works toward his or her goals.

In this way, the PCA can become a useful tool in a process that could otherwise be daunting or overwhelming.

In sum, the PCA provides a clear, concise, and concrete structural framework for setting goals and taking action steps, using positive reinforcement and coaching support to pull it all together. Whereas parents typically write chores on a list, fill out a calendar denoting their child's schedule, or simply tell the child what to do, the coach asks the client to take responsibility and accountability to a more independent level suitable for the maturing adolescent and beyond. Checklists are replaced by action steps, and reasonable, attainable goals replace the "maybe someday I will" sentiment in order to put reality on the page. The PCA allows the coaching process to be simple, direct, structured, and supported.

PCA: The Cornerstone of Support and Structure

Research has shown time and again that youth with ADHD benefit tremendously from having support and structure in their lives. Thus, as a coach, I asked myself many years back whether there was a tool that I could use to consistently and reliably bring support and structure into the coaching process. In response and after reviewing many materials from behavioral, educational, and life coaching sources, I developed the PCA, a document that doesn't require rocket science to formulate and yet offers incredible value to young people with ADHD and to their coaches, who can use the PCA to guide young clients toward their chosen goals at times when they may become overwhelmed or veer off track. The PCA offers structure to the young person in that it is a tangible document that can be completed, read, discussed, reviewed, and revised. In addition, it spells out the practical aspects of what the client needs to actually do to achieve success, thus turning wishes and goals into real action and progress.

As noted in Chapter 2, *structure* refers to the practical tools one can offer a young person to help the young person stay on track or get back on track on the journey to meeting his or her goals. The PCA is just one of the structures that the client may use during coaching, but it represents one that is foundational. The PCA is a sort of master document—a blueprint or roadmap from which all aspects of coaching work and growth can flow. It is the foundation for all of the work that will be done and includes specific elements to guide the client: realistic goals; small, manageable action steps; a plan for how and when to check in with the coach to report progress and stay committed to change; and rewards that will come with completing the action steps.

The coach, as mentioned earlier, will be the supportive glue that helps the client adhere to and thus get the most out of the PCA. The coach guides the client in the design of the PCA, encouraging the client to return to it when he or she is losing focus or to revisit it when some tweaking may be advisable because of life changes or new personal insights. Ideally, the coach will do all of this within a context that is caring, sincere, and nonjudgmental. That's the support element of the equation.

Support involves things like believing in the young person, championing the young person when he or she tries new things, offering a nonjudgmental presence and perspective, and celebrating successes. The coach provides support during the creation and use of the PCA by encouraging the young person to explore his or her stated goals to ensure that the young person is invested in those goals and has the tools needed to keep the momentum going throughout the coaching process.

Support and structure are beneficial for all young people and essential for youth with ADHD. When a young person knows what is expected of him or her, whether it is to do homework after school or put dinner dishes in the sink, it is much easier for him or her to complete the tasks. When a young person with ADHD is expected to do the same tasks, difficulty arises when there is no concrete structure to support the execution of those tasks.

What time must homework actually begin? How will the youth know what time it is if time management skills and sense of time are not innate? Until you set up support and a structure for completing tasks and how they are to happen, it is difficult to create a plan or develop strategies.

For the young client, once the groundwork of support and structure is in place, the coaching can proceed toward strategies for success and skill building. When coaches provide a structural framework for these clients to use in setting goals, then the client can move through that structure and use it to accomplish coaching goals. The PCA is my tool of choice for providing formalized support and structure for the young people with ADHD whom I partner in coaching.

Josh, the Video Game Designer

Josh was an 18-year-old client who wanted to go into the field of video game design. He loved to play games on his own computer and clearly recognized the need for improvement in his favorite online game. When first discussing his interest in video game design during the coaching intake, Josh became frustrated and agitated. He wanted to get out of school *now* and go to work for the company that designed his favorite game. With the support of his coach, Josh was able to step back from his frustration by creating a structure and a plan, captured in the PCA, through which he would contact the video gaming company with his ideas while staying in school and on task in order to complete his studies and graduate in six months. The coach provided a safe space for Josh to address his present frustrations while simultaneously planning for the future.

Josh's story represents the power of support and structure to help young people make decisions that will facilitate successful completion of their own goals. In particular, Josh was able to work on his goals and dreams within a structure that kept those goals realistic and intact. Because the coach offered nonjudgmental support, Josh was able to clearly see his goals and the steps he agreed to take to reach those goals. The clarity of his PCA afforded Josh the opportunity to follow his dream while focusing on accomplishing the tasks at hand, which, in turn, helped facilitate his long-term goal of becoming a video game designer. Ultimately, the support and structure offered in the coaching experience helped Josh avoid making an impulsive decision to drop out of school, which might have sabotaged his ability to achieve the very goals he was hoping to meet in the first place.

The Nuts and Bolts of the PCA

The creation of the PCA begins at the intake session and may continue for a couple of sessions thereafter while the coach and the client work out the details of the document. The process of creating the PCA may be difficult for some clients. If needed, it is okay to begin the coaching process while continuing to discuss and define goals and actions. Coaches are encouraged to follow their intuition and take more time to develop a plan for success if needed. Rushing a client through the process of creating an acceptable PCA leads to a PCA that may not resonate for the client. That being said, a general timeline for the creation of the PCA is provided below.

Table 1
Typical Time Frame for Creating the PCA for an Adolescent Client*

Time Frame	Step
During intake	Discuss goals with client and parents Decide on preliminary goals and action steps with the client
Within a week after the intake	Client reviews PCA draft and submits changes to the coach Client talks with parents about acceptable rewards Client and coach exchange e-mails to work on the final product Client, coach, and parents receive a copy of the agreement to review
By first or second coaching session (or within 14 days)	PCA is finalized and signed by all parties Action steps begin

*The timetable is the same for young adult clients, but the parents are not a party to the process.

After the PCA has been created, client, coach, and parents of adolescents are asked to sign it. So that no surprises occur and chances of agreement are increased, a good matter of practice is to have the client speak to his or her parents about goals and desired rewards before the final agreement is presented for signature. Doing so confirms that the parents are on board with the PCA and that parents agree to support the client as he or she works the action steps and earns identified rewards.

Now let's look at the four steps involved in the creation of the PCA: setting goals, outlining action steps, creating an accountability plan, and selecting a reward system for completing action steps and achieving goals.

Step 1: Set Goals

Adults often imagine that young people only have a few simple goals for themselves, things like getting good grades and hanging out with friends. Although these certainly may be important goals, young people's goals are often wide and varied, going beyond academic or social life. I've had clients who have wanted to learn how to play guitar, improve communication skills with adults, explore career paths, save money for a new car, or land their first job. They have brought their own unique desires for themselves to coaching, and we have been able to formalize these into written goals through the use of the PCA.

Once we acknowledge that young people are capable of wanting more than good grades or time with friends, we can invite them to share what their ideal goals might be for coaching. Admittedly, some young people are unprepared to answer this question, or they are simply surprised that an adult would give them the choice of doing something that they—not their parents—wanted. For these youth, we want to encourage them to take time to reflect on what their goals might be, not just at school but across all areas of their lives. The power of coaching is that it focuses on a client's whole life: Clients get to attend to all of the important areas of their lives, from physical fitness goals to hopes for their love life to desires for creative outlets to career aspirations. Each client is different, and the goals identified in the PCA will reflect what's most important to the individual client.

Goal-setting begins with gathering the data from the young person. The coach will begin by asking questions like

- What would you like more of in your life?
- How do you like to spend your free time?
- When you think about your future, what comes to mind?
- What are your favorite and least favorite academic subjects?
- What makes you laugh?

- What frustrates you the most?

- What is really important to you?

- How do your goals reflect your values?

The coach then invites the client to examine his or her goals more closely, considering both the satisfaction and the frustration involved in pursuing a specific goal, to ensure that accomplishing the goal is worth the effort to the client and to examine how the client's goals align with his or her values.

If the young person says she wants to get a job, what would the job look like? If the teen says he wants to be happier, what does that mean? If the young adult explains that she wants to choose a career path, what might that entail? When a client states that he values connection with family but sets a goal to spend more time on his own, is the goal contrary to his value of connection to family? The key is to help the client become more focused on goals that truly resonate for him or her. When goals are related to interests, dreams, and values, the likelihood of the client succeeding increases exponentially.

A variety of coaching tools and techniques for goal-setting can be used, such as a life wheel, in which the young person colors in the spokes on the wheel to indicate his or her level of satisfaction in different life areas, such as academic, social, financial, and health. Most wheels are "wobbly," indicating the life areas in which the clients might choose to create change. Other goal-setting tools include visualization (e.g., the coach asks the client to imagine what it would be like to walk across the stage to receive his or her high school diploma and what it will take to get there) or drawing a picture or creating a collage (to put the client's goals and dreams in living color as a reminder of what the future holds). Sir John Whitmore's GROW model also works nicely to guide clients toward realistic, attainable goals:

- GOAL-setting for the session as well as for the short and long term

- REALITY checking to explore the current situation

- OPTIONS and alternative strategies or courses of action

- WHAT is to be done, WHEN, by WHOM, and the WILL to do it.

Whitmore's model is easy to use and draws upon basic coaching principles in a structured manner that is useful for adolescents and young adults. Many young people with ADHD have difficulty connecting consequences to their actions or seeing consequences as being a result of their choices. The GROW model provides a platform for coaches and others to use as a guide for young people as they create new life goals.

For example, if a client sets a goal to be the first-chair violinist in the orchestra but has not been following through with daily practice sessions, the coach can do a reality check with the client as well as help the client consider options toward attaining the stated goal or possibly adjusting the goal to make it more feasible in the short term. The client can certainly choose to create a long-term goal to be the first-chair violinist while working on the short-term goal of improving his or her skill through daily practice.

Although the parent may share some of his or her own goals for the young person during the prescreening or intake sessions, actual goal-setting is done in a private session between coach and client, so that the client takes ownership of the goals identified in the PCA instead of viewing them as the parent's goals. Goal-setting may take place during the portion of the intake when the parent has left the room, and/or it may occur in the first coaching session. During this process, the coach can bridge the gap between parent and client goals by discussing the parent's requests with the client. The coach can help the client see different perspectives on a situation without pressuring the client to choose a parent-centered goal. The client may, in turn, decide that a parental goal is too rigid, whereas a variation on that goal fits just right. The coach is a valuable facilitator of the goal-setting process with adolescents and young adults.

Once the young person has had a chance to brainstorm on his or her goals, it's time to think about how to formulate these in writing. Goals should be clear, simple, and realistic: for example, "learn self-advocacy skills" or ""improve my organizational skills." I suggest selecting no more than five goals, although most of my clients usually identify only three. The reason behind the limits is that for young people with ADHD, even one goal tied to a few daily action steps can seem overwhelming.

I have coached adolescents who came to coaching with a long list of goals created with their parents. When this happens, oftentimes we can divide the goals by priority and agree that one set of goals leads into the next, thus allowing for the PCA to include only the first level of priority, with future revisions including the next level of prioritized goals or the next chunk of a larger goal, and so on. For example, the client may decide that the goal of improving organizational skills trumps the goal of getting on the honor roll because the client needs to be able to find his or her schoolwork before he or she can turn it in for credit. Incremental goals can lead to a broad base of success.

By the end of the intake or first coaching session, the coach and client have ideally written up preliminary goals, which will be added to the growing PCA document. The coach and client decide which party will type up the first draft for the next session. Typically, the coach facilitates the process using a PCA template, shown at the end of this chapter.

In addition to helping clients identify what they hope to get out of coaching, goal-setting can also be a great opportunity for the coach to build rapport with a young person. As the young person discovers that the focus of the goal-setting is on what he or she wants in life, rather than solely what his or her parents want, and as the young person witnesses the coach's nonjudgmental support in exploring the young person's interests, trust in the coach as a support person may begin to grow. Similarly, as the young person experiences the coach's guidance in turning the young person's wishes into realistic goals pegged to a concrete plan, his or her trust in the structure of the PCA—and the process of coaching—may also increase.

Goals are essential to change. A person cannot hit a target without first identifying what that target is and where it exists in time and space. Yet, even with the all-important goals that have been outlined in the PCA, the young person won't be able to get from here to there—from Point A to Point B— without taking some action to get there. As a result, the goal-setting portion of creating the PCA is quickly followed by a discussion of what the young person needs to do to achieve his or her identified goals—in other words, he or she determines the action steps.

Step 2: Outline Action Steps

Action steps are the daily and weekly actions the client agrees to take to achieve the chosen goals. The aim should be to keep action steps clear and simple. Here are a handful of example action steps, with the related goal noted:

- "Set my extra alarm clock before I go to bed" (improve time management skills)

- "Pack myself an after-school snack after I finish dinner each evening" (improve eating habits)

- "Ask my linguistics-group partners one question each at our meetings and listen for 30 seconds before saying anything in response" (improve communication skills)

- "Spend 15 minutes each day cleaning my personal space"(improve organizational skills).

This list offers a cross-section of action steps that might be taken to address goals in a variety of different life areas, from social to academic to personal.

When a young client has a problem with short-term memory and disorganization, the action item for the client (and parent) might be a little longer, such as the following:

> "I will check in with my parents at 8 p.m., Sunday–Thursday, to review my planner and confirm that all of my work has been completed and is in my backpack. This will be a 5-minute check-in with no critique or direct homework review by my parents."

The clarity of this particular action step helps the client feel empowered and alerts the parents to the boundaries around the daily check-in process. Parents are often not accustomed to limitations when their children are involved. The details of the PCA are designed to help the parents work with the coaching plan for the benefit of the client.

How do young people come to decisions on what the action steps will be? This process involves a delicate balancing act in which the coach invites the young person to brainstorm his or her own ideas on desired action steps and come to his or her own conclusions, while the coach respectfully offers extra support and direction as needed. This direction is subtle and often comes in the form of a question. The coach might ask a general, open-ended question, such as "What do you need to do to accomplish your goal?" or something more specific, like "How much time are you willing to spend exercising each day?" This questioning process is individualized, and coaches are encouraged to follow the client's lead as well as to avoid creating the action steps for the client. This is a collaborative process; when the client has the opportunity to take the lead, the feelings of empowerment may begin to flow.

ADHD coaching for youth remains first and foremost a client-centered process, in which the young person is at the helm of the experience, generating his or her own solutions, learning from them, testing out his or her own plan, and tweaking the plan. But the coach nonetheless plays an important role in helping the young person consider all of the available options, inviting the young person to break plans down into the smallest and most manageable of steps. This extra bit of direction is one of the techniques that typically differentiates ADHD coaching from life coaching.

It is difficult, if not impossible, to achieve a goal without engaging in particular action steps. This portion of the PCA provides an opportunity for the client to reflect on which steps will help in the accomplishment of his or her goals, to commit to a plan that suits his or her personality and comfort level, and to try out his or her ideas in the real world. The mere process of selecting goal-driven action steps and then pushing themselves to try them can have a very positive effect on young people. In the process, they learn that they can follow through on commitments and that if they make mistakes or don't achieve the desired outcome, they can adjust the plan or simply try again! For young people with ADHD, this realization can be confidence building as well as life changing.

Step 3: Create a Plan for Accountability

How will the coach know when the client has completed a given step? How will the parent know it's time to provide the young person with his or her reward? The next phase of creating the PCA is to build a plan for accountability into each action step so that the coach (and parents, if appropriate) stays informed during the process. While designing the PCA, clients are asked to select a means of communicating with the coach on a regular basis to give updates on how the action steps are coming along. Parents may also be included in the check-in phase, particularly with young people who are still living at home. Here are some of the ways that a young person may choose to remain accountable:

- send the coach a text message after completing an action item

- send the coach an e-mail to report success or stumbling blocks

- call the coach to give a status update on progress

- set alarms on one's cell phone as a reminder to complete a particular action step

- tell mom each day when one has completed assigned math problems

- have a conversation with dad to share that action steps have been completed every day this week, as planned.

There are a variety of methods by which a check-in can take place; phone, e-mail, and text message are the most common. The key with check-in's is that they need to take place on a regular basis: as often as daily or as infrequently as once or twice a week, between coaching sessions.

In ADHD coaching, coaches hold clients more accountable and usually have a tighter plan with more frequent contact than in general life coaching. This is done as a support to clients who may forget to catch themselves doing something good, who are stuck and would benefit from a coaching nudge, or who are ashamed to admit to not completing action steps on a given day. The frequency and intensity of the check-in's must be spelled out in the agreement and will depend on the needs of the client.

If desired by the young person, parents can also play a role in check-in's. For example, for a high school student, it may be beneficial to have the parent check in with the client at home at a predetermined time each day or each week. For example, Elizabeth has decided that it would be helpful if her mom checks in with her each night at dinner and asks, "What do you have for homework tonight?" to provide Elizabeth with an opportunity to review her assignments with another person and remind herself of the details of the task ahead.

Step 4: Select a Reward

Each step in the creation of the PCA is essential to its success; rewards are no exception. Goals can't be accomplished without action steps, and action steps without accountability often don't take place. Similarly, rewards play an essential role in motivating clients to engage in action steps. We all need incentives to motivate us to act. This is simply human nature, whether the incentives are internal or external, invisible or tangible. Because motivation is often a major problem for youth with ADHD, the rewards portion of the PCA becomes the external motivator often needed to get the young person on board with taking action or trying new behaviors.

Naturally, rewards only work if they are of interest to the young person. Thus, the coach invites the young person to brainstorm ideas for rewards that are desirable to him or her. Once some ideas have been generated, the young person can select the reward that seems most exciting, while also making choices that seem realistic. Young adults will typically choose their own rewards or set up a reward system directly with the coach. For a reward to be effective, it needs to be exclusive (unique) to the PCA. It cannot be made available to the young person at any other time for any other reason.

Oftentimes, especially for younger clients, the parent will be involved in providing the reward. Because of this, before the PCA is finalized, the coach will ask the adolescent to take some time to discuss the desired reward with his or her parents to make sure the reward is considered acceptable. In some cases, even if the reward is not going to involve financial investment from the parent, it might require the parent's time or approval. For example, a reward of driving privileges might not work because a spare car won't be available; extra computer time on school nights may not be an option because a younger sibling can't get to sleep in the next room. Conversations with mom and dad are meant to help eliminate surprises that disappoint the young person when a reward can't be delivered and to avoid angering the parent, whose support is essential to the young person's growth.

Here are some examples of rewards, which vary from weekly to monthly.

Meaningful rewards for adolescents might include

- extra allowance money
- use of the family car on the weekends
- extra time playing video games or watching movies
- buying something new
- choosing the restaurant for a weekly family night out.

Meaningful rewards for young adults might include

- splurging on a specialty coffee
- going to the gym
- an evening out with friends
- buying something new
- sleeping in.

Note that the PCA is designed to offer rewards for effort. This means that the young person receives a reward simply for completing action steps even if the outcome was different than expected or desired. In this way, young people can become more inclined to put effort forth as they see the results of those efforts. This creates a powerful cycle of effort → result → reward → effort → result → reward until the young person finally experiences a success, sees the benefits of working hard, and continues in this vein of putting forth effort to reach goals. Although some parents struggle at first to accept the premise of providing rewards for effort alone, the positive results in terms of a young person's motivation and behavior change often help parents see the value of this approach. Anecdotal reports indicate that over time, as success increases and clients mature, external rewards may become less of a central focus as internal motivation kicks in.

A Snapshot of the PCA

The PCA is designed to be simple and straightforward, with clearly defined goals and action steps. When creating the PCA, the coach invites the client to choose up to five *goals* in a variety of life areas. Goals should be kept very clear and simple.

Next, the client will design *action steps*, with the support of the coach, to help the client move forward, step by step, toward achievement of the chosen goals. For example, if the goal is to improve organizational skills at home, an action step might be to spend 15 minutes each day cleaning up the bedroom or study area.

A *check-in plan* is also designated alongside the action steps, to help clients stay committed, report progress, make adjustments as needed, and receive promised rewards—in short, be accountable.

Last, the client brainstorms on desired and realistic *rewards* and has a conversation with his or her parents to determine whether parents are willing to provide these particular rewards. For example, the client may indicate that she would like to reward herself for a week of completed action steps with a trip to the movie theater on Friday night or a weekly manicure. These rewards could get pricey or may not work with the family schedule, so she will need to make sure mom and dad are in agreement. Young adults will choose their own rewards and review the plan with the coach.

The creation and content of the PCA will vary by client, and every coach will develop his or her own unique style for guiding this part of the coaching process. Some possible questions that the coach may ask the client when helping with the development of the PCA include the following:

- Of all of the goals we have discussed today, which one excites you the most?

- What daily action steps sound reasonable to you?

- How might the plan be structured to meet your needs and address your parent's concerns?

- Are you willing to test drive the agreement for 30 days?

- What might make this agreement more appealing to you?

- What will it take to create a plan that really works for you?

- What might be a fun activity that you could use as a reward?

- How might you connect a personal goal to your reward system?

Regardless of the exact questions used, an open-ended approach that deeply involves the young person can get the coaching process off to a good start and lay the groundwork for coaching success.

Personal Coaching Agreement 1

Jane, 14 years old, would like to spend more time with her friends. Her family moved away from the city, which means she now has to make arrangements to get a ride to see her friends. This takes time: travel time, time away from homework and chores, and time her parents need to invest as her drivers. It also takes planning, a skill which is strong in neither Jane nor her parents. When Jane and I first talked about coaching, she made it clear that her goal was to find a way to use her time wisely for schoolwork and chores so that her free time with friends was unencumbered by the time pressures she and her parents were under. Together, we created the following personal coaching agreement.

Goals:

- Passing grades of C or above
- Less conflict at home about schoolwork
- Be more consistent in my efforts on schoolwork and home chores
- Have more free time with my friends.

Action Steps:

- Use my planner to note daily homework, long-term projects, reading assignments, and test dates and to plan out my after-school activities.
- Meet with my coach weekly at 4 p.m. on Wednesdays. Review all work and progress on my goals and actions.
- E-mail my coach on Sunday, Monday, Tuesday, and Thursday each week. Provide an update on academics and details on the progress of my goals and actions.
- Use coaching strategies to increase my time management skills.
- Use a chore list to keep track of daily and weekly responsibilities.
- Write my activities on the family calendar.
- Review my week with my parents on Saturday mornings. Plan to spend 15–20 minutes talking over successes, struggles, and questions and to review the family calendar for the upcoming week.

Rewards: weekly

- Ten dollars for completion of all action steps
- Five dollars for partial completion/effort
- A sleepover with one of my friends from the city on Saturday — bonus whenever I complete all the action steps!

Signatures:

- Jane   • Mom   • Dad   • Coach

Personal Coaching Agreement 2

The top goal of 17-year-old Steve was to attend college on a sports scholarship. What would it take for Steve to accomplish this goal? He was a star of the football team, responsible for taking the team to the district championship; however, that was not the only requirement for a scholarship to college. We identified the required grade point average (GPA) and extracurricular activities needed to qualify for Steve's desired scholarship. Next, we brainstormed regarding what Steve needed to accomplish to meet the requirements.

Goals:

- Get a college athletic scholarship
- Explore and get involved in extracurricular activities of interest
- Reduce/eliminate missing assignments to improve my GPA
- Begin preliminary college-prep activities.

Action Steps:

- Call my coach weekly at 5 p.m. on Mondays. Review all work and progress on my goals and actions.
- E-mail my coach on Sunday, Tuesday, Wednesday, and Thursday of each week. Provide an update on academics and details on the progress of my goals and actions.
- Write all assignments in my planner—check with teachers as needed.
- Spend two hours each day on homework and studying.
- Visit at least two clubs at school in the next month.
- Spend 15 minutes per day organizing my papers.
- Meet with the college counselor at school to find out more about schools and scholarships.

Rewards: weekly

- One tank of gas for my car when I complete all of the action steps
- Ten dollars cash if I accomplish five of my action steps
- No reward for fewer than five completed action steps.

Signatures:

- Steve   • Mom   • Dad   • Coach

Personal Coaching Agreement 3

Anna, 21 years old, was a junior in college. She was determined to work with her coach to improve her ability to balance her social and academic time to keep up her grades and avoid having to retake any courses. Retaking courses would be very costly because her parents were not willing to pay for them, so Anna would have to work two jobs over summer break to earn the money to pay for the courses herself. Anna admittedly spent much of her time hanging out with friends and taking weekend trips to visit her boyfriend at another college. She barely had time to focus on her studies and, with her learning disabilities, needed to allow extra time to complete her course work.

Goals:

- Maintain a B average in all classes
- Learn to set boundaries on my social time
- Find a better balance in my life.

Action Steps:

- Spend four hours each day on course work (two blocks of time) and 8–10 hours on the weekend.
- Plan ahead for visits to my boyfriend and adjust study hours accordingly.
- Talk with my coach every Monday to review my progress and plan for the upcoming week.
- Text my coach daily by 9 p.m. with an update of progress.
- Look at my plan before saying "yes" to social activities.
- Plan to meet my friends for regularly scheduled meals and break times to stay connected.

Rewards: weekly

- Coffee with a friend
- An extra swim at the campus rec center
- Renewed confidence that I can do this!

Signatures:

- Anna • Coach

A Note for Everyone

The past two decades of research and practice have shown that support and structure are essential to individuals with ADHD who want to lead satisfying and productive lives. Yet for many coaches, parents, and professionals, how to bring that support and structure into the lives of youth with ADHD remains a mystery.

The PCA was designed to capture the support and structure that clients with ADHD need to succeed in their lives and to help personalize the coaching process to them. As a written document containing the client's goals, action steps, plan for accountability, and reward system to help stimulate the coaching process and bring about success, the PCA is a motivational cornerstone of support and structure in the coaching process. Here are a few points to keep in mind to get the most out of the PCA.

First, coaches and parents will want to ensure that the young person is part of the PCA design process. The coaching goals are not the coach's goals, nor are they the parents' goals. The PCA is a client-centered tool requiring the client to land on goals that are reasonable, attainable, and of interest to him or her. There will be input from parents and from the coach based on information gathered in the intake, but the final decision on what the PCA contains will be made by the client.

The PCA is most effective when it is kept simple. Complicated, multilevel goals might look good on paper, but clear, simple, attainable goals tend to lead to success, one step at a time. Another key to success is the rewards that are built into the PCA. Call them what you like—rewards, incentives, or positive reinforcement—but building motivational tools into the PCA will help increase a client's effort, build confidence, and promote success.

Also of note, there are a few differences in the PCA for an adolescent as compared with the PCA for a young adult. For adolescents, parents are asked to sign the PCA after adolescents have shared the document with them and discussed and finalized desired rewards. For young adults, parents are typically not involved in the development or implementation of the PCA. Instead, the coach elicits information from the client and from any data provided at the intake session. Accountability is set up between the coach and the client without the parents, and rewards tend to be self-administered by the young adult clients and occasionally provided by the coach.

The PCA was developed to provide clients with a framework for the coaching process, yet this tool can also be adapted for use by parents, teachers, and allied professionals working with youth with or without ADHD and learning issues. For example, parents can create a PCA for each of their children (including those without ADHD), varying the goals, action steps, and rewards to be age appropriate for each child. Medical and mental health professionals can use a PCA to monitor medication compliance, promote regular journaling of progress and difficulties, or support a daily regime of self-care.

Many of the young people with ADHD who enter into coaching start the process feeling overwhelmed and hopeless because of a lifetime of frustrations, challenges, and setbacks. The PCA—when developed and used with the help of a well-trained, caring coach—can offer the powerful support and structure needed to transform insecurity into confidence, fear into action, and failure into resounding success.

E I G H T

Facilitating Lasting Change: Empowering the Client With Strategies for Success

A room that looks like it's been hit by a tornado. A teen that constantly shows up late for band practice. A young person who can't seem to hold a cohesive conversation. These are just a few of the issues experienced by young people with ADHD that make it difficult for them to be successful. Why is it that young people with ADHD often struggle to engage in actions and accomplish tasks that may seem relatively straightforward or easy to adults or even peers?

Adolescents with ADHD struggle to accomplish tasks and achieve goals for a variety of reasons. One of the most fundamental sources of challenge is their characteristically weak executive functioning skills. Whether it be skills in personal organization; ability to manage time and prioritize tasks, activities, and responsibilities; or the capacity to listen well and communicate in an effective fashion, young people with ADHD are not wired in a way that makes acquiring these skills easy. Because of their brain makeup, these young people often don't have their neurologically based executive functioning skills sharpened or honed to the point where they can actually control day-to-day processes of managing time, getting along with others, prioritizing and scheduling tasks and activities, keeping up with personal hygiene, and so on.

Skill acquisition is difficult for young people with ADHD not only because of executive functioning weaknesses but because the symptoms of ADHD, such as trouble focusing, sometimes disrupt the actual learning process. I often explain to my clients that it's almost as if they blinked and missed the information that others were picking up at that moment. While everyone else their age was learning through modeling and guidance from parents and others, the young person with ADHD did not absorb and integrate important information because of attention difficulties.

When mom was alongside Johnny tidying his room, Johnny wasn't able to pay attention to mom's techniques for keeping things organized because he was distracted by a toy under his bed, unaware that the organizing process was still underway. When Suzy's dad was planning out how they could get to soccer practice at the start of each season, Suzy observed him putting the location of the field into the computer, but because of short-term memory problems and inattentiveness, she forgot that dad always printed out a map to get her to the right field on time. As a result, Johnny didn't learn how to organize his space and Suzy didn't acquire the skills to get somewhere successfully or on time. Young people with ADHD thus often experience a double whammy in which a neurobiology not predisposed to skill acquisition is complicated by learning processes that get interrupted because of ADHD symptoms.

Just imagine the world that can open up to these young people as coaches provide them with a consistent opportunity to build and develop their skills. Coaching often becomes the powerful missing ingredient in a young person's life, which helps to fill in the gap in skills that these young people face and assists them in acquiring the capacities they need to be successful. Suddenly, the young person is going in to talk to the teacher him or herself instead of asking mom to pick up the phone. Or the young person discovers that he or she has everything needed right inside of him or herself to do well on the calculus test. By helping young people with ADHD acquire the skills needed to achieve goals, coaches facilitate the ultimate process of empowerment. No longer do these young people need others to help them achieve things; they now have the ability to accomplish things on their own. Thus, the smooth transition from youth to adulthood begins to take place.

This chapter explores strategies and techniques that can be used to build skills in young people with ADHD. A brief discussion of how the personal coaching agreement (PCA) connects skills and strategies to support and structure is also provided to help readers see how all the coaching pieces fit together. Because every young person is different, there can be no mandates on which strategies and techniques will help a client build skills and reach goals in certain areas. Yet, there are common areas in which young people with ADHD tend to have skill deficits: time management, personal organization, memory, social skills, self-advocacy, and life skills. The chapter walks readers through these different areas, highlighting common outcomes of the young person's weaker skill sets in any given area, to show their importance and to help coaches recognize underlying issues in clients. This particular exploration will also provide insight into a variety of strategies that have been used to help clients build their strengths in these areas.

The Chicken or the Egg?
An Overview of Skills Versus Strategies

As the title of this chapter promises, the discussion in this chapter focuses on helping young people with ADHD attain success through the use of strategies. And yet, the chapter began with a substantial discussion of skills. You may be wondering, then, how do skills relate to strategies? And what's the relevance of strategies to young people's success, now that the value of skills has been made clear?

Let's start with a definition of each. On the one hand, *skill* refers to a person's ability to do something. According to Merriam-Webster OnLine, a skill is "the ability to use one's knowledge effectively and readily in execution or performance" or "a learned power of doing something competently: a developed aptitude or ability." *Strategy*, on the other hand, refers to techniques used to accomplish something, or "the art of devising or employing plans or stratagems toward a goal."

Which comes first: skills or strategies? Does a person need to be skilled at something to acquire a set of strategies for success? Or does a person need to have strategies to become skilled? In the case of young people with ADHD, the latter is typically the case. Because certain skills do not come naturally to adolescents and young adults with ADHD, they need to practice their way toward being skilled at something. In coaching, the client and coach work together to brainstorm personalized techniques or strategies that the client can use to improve a particular skill. So, it is fair to say that

Strategies + Practice = Skill

For example, Jenna sets as a goal for herself in the PCA that she would like to be able to keep her dorm room clean. The *skill* that Jenna needs to develop to achieve this particular goal is personal organization. How does Jenna get better at this skill? She needs to engage in personal organization *strategies* to build and develop her skill in this area. As she enacts strategies, she will essentially be testing out her skill in this area—trying it on, practicing it, and honing it. In the process, Jenna will not only get her room clean, thus achieving her goal, but she will also become more skilled at personal organization.

This does not happen magically; instead, the skill gets built over time, like a muscle, through regular *practice* and workouts. In particular, through the coaching process, Jenna practices her personal organization strategies over and over because her action step for the week is to spend 15 minutes every day organizing her personal space using whatever strategy she has decided might work for her (e.g., picking up one category of items at a time, such as clothes, then books, then trash).

Jenna is also held accountable by the coach, to whom she sends an e-mail at the end of every day to indicate that she has finished her action step. As the personal organization strategies are used, Jenna's skill level is increased. In the process, her personal organization strategies become absorbed and integrated into her daily routine such that she now has the skills necessary to keep her personal space organized. It may take 30 days or three months or even longer for this integration to take place, but eventually, with enough practice, Jenna, like most young people with ADHD, will become adept at using her strategies and incorporating them into a strengthened skill set.

The coaching process recognizes that we can't simply send young people with ADHD out into the world, tell them to do something, and expect them to accomplish it. Success is not a mere matter of helping these young people, like Jenna, see that they need to keep their books, papers, and personal space organized; we need to actually help these young people figure out how they are going to keep their materials organized. Parents can say until they are blue in the face, "You need to keep your desk organized," or "Go study," but a young person with ADHD won't make any progress at all until someone helps the young person discover how to keep the desk organized or how to sit still long enough to study and then gives the young person an opportunity to practice the skill of organization or studying over and over again.

One of the ways that the coaching process can be so effective in helping young people strengthen their skills is that the coach and client work together to identify the unique strategies that the client feels will work best for him or her in relation to a given goal. Whereas well-meaning parents or teachers tend to teach strategies that work for them, based on their own learning styles and experiences, coaches know to bring a blank slate to the session, inviting young people to contemplate whatever strategies they believe will work best for them. Sometimes experimentation is involved and strategies end up being adjusted when they don't seem to be working. In the end, the young client acquires a personalized set of strategies that are tailored to his or her own needs, situation, and learning style. And voila—empowerment occurs! The young person now has the strategies and skills needed to achieve goals, and the strategies are natural for that particular young person.

If a person has difficulty remembering strategies, as is the case for many youth with ADHD, coaches need to find a way for the youth to come up with strategies to learn the skill and then provide opportunities to practice those strategies over and over again until they become habits. By encouraging the use and practice of strategies, coaches provide the young person with a means of developing and building the skills essential to success. The end result is a young person with ADHD who is empowered to take control of his or her life and achieve goals—both small and big.

Strategies for Success: From A to Z

Regardless of the young person's need to build skills, the young person is always starting from somewhere. As a result, I like to begin the skill-building process by tapping into what the young person already brings to the table. "What's working for you now?" I might ask the client. "What has worked for you in the past?" By inviting the young person to identify current strengths, strategies, and skill sets, the coach can help to foster the client's self-confidence. In the process, the client will discover that he or she already has some of the tools needed to make progress toward goals. In addition, this line of open-ended questioning is an effective way to put the client on a road toward identifying strategies personalized to his or her own style, strengths, and comfort zone. By building on what's worked in the past and what's working now, the young person enters the coaching process from a place of strength and comfort.

How does this work, exactly? One way is for the client to identify strategies that are working now in one life area and then replicate them in other life areas and different situations. For example, when a client has experienced success in having a reasonable discussion with his or her parents, the client can examine the communication strategies used in that situation and think about applying them to an identified goal that calls for the use of good communication. The client can look at how the discussion with the parents worked, examine what steps he or she took, and then consider ways to use those same strategies going forward with friends, a teacher, or a boss, as needed for a particular goal.

You may be wondering at what point in coaching the client and coach will focus on identifying strategies for achieving goals. The strategy portion of the discussion flows out of the goals and action steps identified in the PCA. The strategies themselves are not written into the PCA because these are quite specific and the client will need time to test them out. Maybe the client tries a strategy one week only to discover that it is not very effective, it isn't feasible given his or her schedule, or it simply doesn't work with the client's learning style. The client is then free to try a new strategy the following week. The PCA thus remains a flexible document upon which strategies can be applied without them actually being written into it. The PCA states the goals and even action steps for each of those goals, but the strategies themselves come later in week-to-week discussions between client and coach.

For example, the identified goal in the PCA may be "make some friends in my dorm." One of the action steps for that goal could be "sit with at least one acquaintance from the dorm at the dining hall during dinner every night." When it comes time to identify strategies for implementing the action step, the client and coach will brainstorm on what seems like the best approach for the client, for example, asking dorm acquaintances when they usually go to dinner or strolling around the dining hall to identify dorm mates before choosing a seat. Through open-ended questions, the client will identify one or more strategies he or she would like to try.

Although every young person with ADHD is unique in terms of learning style, personality, and goals, the skills these individuals often need to strengthen tend to fall across common domains. For ease of discussion, I have broken these domains into the general categories of time management, personal organization, memory, social skills, self-advocacy, and life skills. The text that follows discusses each of these areas in depth, explaining how challenges with each particular skill set tend to show up in the lives of young people with ADHD. I then share some of the strategies that have been useful in the past for some of my clients. Although coaches will not be making direct suggestions to clients regarding which strategies to try, coaches can bring these strategies to the attention of clients, as appropriate, in supportive and open-ended ways. For example, the coach might say, "Some of my clients have found it useful to audio record their to-do lists and then listen to them when they are ready to execute. Others write their lists in their daily planner, or create a to-do list reminder on their phone. What strategy might work for you?"

Time Management: How Long Will It Really Take to Do That and What Shall I Do First?

Because of their neurobiology and resultant executive functioning challenges, young people with ADHD often struggle to keep a good handle on time. They may not have a natural sense of what time means (what does 15 minutes feel like versus an hour?) or of how much they can realistically accomplish in a given time frame. These young people may lack strategies for managing their time effectively, and they may not have the know-how to make good decisions about which task or activity to work on first in terms of high and low priority. Phone calls to friends may be made before homework is completed. The adolescent may sign up for an overload of after-school activities, thinking that schoolwork can be squeezed in after dinner, when senior-year classes are a top priority that require homework be started directly after school. Time management issues may also result in the young person being chronically late for activities or events, failing to accomplish household chores, not getting sufficient sleep because he or she has to stay up late cramming for exams, or falling behind in schoolwork because of too many extracurricular activities.

Students with ADHD also have a tendency to hyperfocus. This can be beneficial when working on a deadline but detrimental when other priorities are left behind. College students tend to hyperfocus and use the last-minute adrenaline rush as a tool, procrastinating on a regular basis. When they have achieved success by pulling an all-nighter, the pattern repeats itself until burnout sets in or the success turns to failure. Other students procrastinate because they are uncertain of where or how to begin their assignments and wonder how long it will take to complete each task once they get started. At some point, the student will literally run out of time to complete the work and the cycle of uncertainty, prolonged procrastination, and failure continues.

The emotional, social, and academic consequences of poor time management skills are significant. Many young people with ADHD will find it embarrassing or demoralizing that they are always late, even if they don't verbalize their sentiments to anyone. Grades may be low because the adolescent is unable to complete assignments on time; friendships may stall when the young adult misses the departure time for a group ski trip or beach outing. The fallout from poor time management often has a snowball effect, too. What starts out as late arrivals or missed assignments can turn into a reputation with others as the unreliable friend or student, which may cause others to look negatively upon the young person, leading to poor self-esteem and low self-confidence. What starts out as a time management problem can quickly transform into academic, social, or psychological issues.

Coaching helps young people by offering a realistic view of a task or situation. When a client does not have a good sense of time or planning, a coach can ask questions of the client to help determine a more realistic time frame for completion of a project or the time it might take to get up, get dressed, and get to class on time. These are basic time management skills, which, when developed early in life, can provide the client with tools to be a more successful adult.

A variety of strategies can be used to help young people with ADHD increase their time management skills. Here are some sample strategies that have worked for my clients in the past:

- Create a to-do list for the next day every night before bed.

- Write appointment times for doing homework and household chores in a daily planner.

- Check the daily planner every day after school at 4 p.m. to see what needs to be done that afternoon.

- Set phone reminders for scheduled activities and necessary chores, like tennis lessons, youth group meetings, coaching sessions, homework time, or taking out the trash.

- Take a practice drive to a new job or sports location to see how long it will take to get there.

- Set a timer to beep or vibrate every hour to get a sense of what one hour really feels like.

- Install a whiteboard over one's desk and use it to note important work, plan a long assignment, and remember coaching appointments.

As my clients identify and develop strategies personalized to their needs, I also guide them to consider relevant factors. For example, I invite clients who are estimating homework and project time to consider their expected energy level, their degree of boredom with a subject, and the anticipated amount of reading or writing involved. In addition, I might prompt clients to consider how much review time they might need before a test so they can set aside chunks of time in advance, consider how many breaks might be needed, assess whether medication should be taken before sitting down to study, and consider whether snacks should be built into homework time to avoid hunger. For example, a high-school athlete who is focusing on creating a plan for completing daily homework after soccer practice will want to consider things like whether he or she needs to eat dinner before doing homework and which subjects to work on first versus later given anticipated interest and energy level.

When working with clients to set up a system for using a family calendar, coaches can explore the different categories of information and events that will be most helpful to list on the calendar:

- project due dates and long-term assignments

- exam schedule

- sports practice schedule

- plans with friends

- medical appointments

- family events

- laundry day

- other important dates.

Coaches work together with the client to help the client understand that he or she is accountable for his or her time and that it is important to be aware of not just one's own but also one's family members' schedules.

Personal Organization: Where's My Stuff?

Paper-stuffed backpacks, computer files named without regard to retrievability, a bedroom full of dirty dishes and trash, a closet in which a suitable outfit for the day can hardly be found: These are just some of the areas that a young person with ADHD may struggle to keep tidy, clean, user friendly, and organized.

Lack of organizational skills can lead to a variety of problems for the young person. The adolescent may show up late to events, not because of being unaware of the clock or driving time but because of 20 minutes spent looking for shoes or keys. The adolescent may get an incomplete on an academic assignment because he or she can't remember where a document was saved on the computer in order to print it out. The young adult might have trouble making friends with the students in the dorm because others are repelled by the way the young adult keeps his or her living space or the strange outfits the youth pulls out of the messy clothes closet—mismatched or dirty. Poor organizational skills lead to lost homework, missing books, misplaced cell phones, lost articles of clothing, forgotten appointments, frustration, and chaos on a daily basis.

Young people with ADHD often struggle to keep their personal space— whether that is a computer desk, closet, bedroom, bathroom, or simple bag of belongings—organized and clean. Thus, an unkempt room should not automatically be interpreted by parents as willful disobedience; a mess left in the kitchen may have a lot more to do with the young person's challenges with executive functioning than laziness.

In coaching, clients whose goals include improving organizational skills can be given an opportunity to learn and practice organizational strategies in a methodical, nonpressured, and supportive setting. When I work with some of my clients on organization, I literally stay on the phone with the young person as he or she goes through the process of tidying and organizing the room. One of the strategies we sometimes employ is to go through a slow and steady checklist of different categories in the room that need to be addressed: clothes, trash, papers, and so on. I don't actually direct the client to look for each of these items, but I ask the client what he or she sees on the floor.

With the client's first response, I invite him or her to focus in on just that one category. As we progress, it becomes clear to the client that these categories can be used to "chunk down" the oftentimes overwhelming task of organizing to facilitate ease of completion. Clients commonly create steps such as putting dirty clothes in a hamper, hanging clothes that can be worn again in the closet, putting shoes in a designated spot, clearing off the bed, stacking important papers on their desk, putting books back on the shelves, and throwing trash into the bin.

This particular strategy of personal organization involves the young person cleaning his or her room in stages, on the basis of different categories. After that initial session with the coach, the young person will then have an opportunity to practice using this strategy each day as he or she completes the action step to spend 15 minutes every day organizing personal space. The young person may also decide to add another strategy to help him or her become successful, for example, sticking a Post-it note on the mirror with a list of the different categories of items that need to be cleaned up each day (clothes, papers, trash). Below are a few of the other strategies I offer to my clients as we work together to build the clients' skills in the area of personal organization. Keeping a tidy room or desk area is just one of the important facets of personal organization that young people with ADHD need to consider.

- Label everything, from binders to notebooks, from jackets to sports equipment and musical instruments. Include one's name and use color coding or bold print.

- Retrace one's steps through the house and clean up the things left in one's wake.

- Do a daily 15-minute pickup in one's room and study areas. Where do things belong?

- Conduct a daily backpack dumping, emptying the entire backpack upon arrival home, in the same spot every day; then, sort the contents for files, notes for parents, homework to do, and so on.

- Avoid overload—does every piece of paper belong in the notebook or textbook?

- Put important papers in folders labeled *homework, parents*, and *to file*. Have a file box or file drawer for completed papers and tests. Don't throw out work until one is certain it is not needed again for review or regrading.

- Look in one's assignment notebook when packing up at school at the end of day to ensure one brings home necessary papers and books.

- Designate a set place to keep one's assignment notebook/daily calendar.

- Consider using binders with side pockets, accordion file sections, and zippers to keep everything together.

- Color-code notebooks by class or by A and B day when following a rotating class schedule.

With each and every day of practice, a client's strategies will become more and more a part of his or her daily routine. This integration process will take longer for some than for others, but, eventually, practiced strategies turn into learned skills. Personal organization may not ever come naturally for the young person with ADHD, but the young person will nonetheless have reliable strategies that can be used to keep his or her space usable or to tame the chaos if the young person falls off the organization bandwagon for a period of time.

Working Memory Challenges: The Frustration of Forgetting

Difficulty with working memory is a common challenge for young people with ADHD, which can show up in a variety of ways. The adolescent may forget what he or she was supposed to be doing ("What did mom just ask me to do?") or where he or she is supposed to be at a given time ("Was I supposed to go somewhere after school?"), like a doctor's appointment or a planned outing with a friend. Memory challenges may also make it hard for these young people to retain information related to academic subjects: mathematical formulas, lists of dates and events for history class, names of theories, and so on.

Memory problems may be interpreted as the young person not listening, respecting, or caring—when in fact what's really happening is that the information was not retained in the young person's memory. This kind of forgetfulness often has long-term consequences that bring more grief to the young person's life than simply the pain and frustration of the original experience of forgetting something. The forgetful young person may offend a new friend who has been stood up for a get-together and lose out on an opportunity for a meaningful friendship, or the young person may make mom angry when he or she doesn't pick up milk from the store as asked. The young person may miss out on a summer internship in Europe simply because he or she forgot to turn in all of the necessary forms.

Memory challenges may also lead to the client forgetting to contact the ADHD coach for regular check-ins. Although the coach may assume that this is an indicator of lack of commitment to the coaching process, the situation might be a simple matter of the client needing a strategy to aid in remembering to check in with the coach on a regular basis. Clients who forget check-ins may feel frustrated or even embarrassed by this kind of failure. Client and coach can work together to identify a strategy that will help the client remember to do the check-in each day, much in the same way that client and coach brainstorm strategies for effectively completing any of the other action steps in the PCA.

A variety of strategies can be used to compensate for challenges with working memory. These include

- making an audio recording of items that need to be remembered and listening to it when needed

- writing things down and referring back to these written materials as needed; carrying a clipboard or memo pad

- placing bright Post-it note reminders in strategic places to prompt recall

- reviewing academic material in a repetitious manner rather than waiting until the night before a test (e.g., spending 30 minutes a day for five days instead of two hours the night before)

- setting alarm reminders on one's phone with to-do lists or prompts to check one's daily planner

- taking notes as one reads, rather than waiting until finishing the entire book or long chapter

- using Post-it tabs to mark a place in a book or research paper that would be helpful to review or refer to later

- using colors in one's planner as reminders of different types of activities, such as blue for social, yellow for academic, and green for work.

Memory and follow-through in all areas of life tend to be challenges for young people with ADHD. Because of the neurobiology of these young people, they often struggle with recall, whether it relates to what their homework assignment is, the time they are supposed to arrive for class, or where they are to meet friends for dinner. Because it's difficult for these young people to hold on to more than one idea or notion at a time, they need to acquire strategies that help them overcome these challenges. Regular reminders via cell phone alarm, strategically placed colorful sticky notes, or a notebook in which the young person writes everything important down are just some of the many strategies that can be used to compensate for a weak working memory.

Social Skills: Learning How to Fit in

People who don't know much about ADHD and its effects on a young person's life are often surprised to learn that the condition reaches far beyond a young person's academic life and into his or her ability to be successful at getting along in social situations, making and sustaining friendships, or having a relationship with a significant other. Those familiar with ADHD know all too well how a young person's challenges with processing information and maintaining focus can lead to an awkward and painful social life.

Those with ADHD may struggle to carry on a normal conversation, appearing to not be listening one moment, then blurting out a response to something that was said 10 minutes ago. These young people may interrupt, not know how to engage in a discussion, or drift off and miss chunks of a conversation. Young people with ADHD miss social cues and are often viewed as rude or insensitive by others. Many have trouble acting appropriately or getting comfortable in social situations.

Compounding these issues is the problem of impulsivity. Many young people with ADHD engage in risk-taking behaviors: acting before thinking, using drugs, or driving at dangerously high speeds. The young person with ADHD is easily swayed and will be likely to follow the crowd and not consider the consequences, whether they be personal or academic.

As a result of their challenges with social skills, defined as the ability to act appropriately in a given social situation and to communicate effectively, young people with ADHD may develop low self-esteem, have few friends, suffer from loneliness, or hang out with younger children because it's more comfortable than being around peers. They may be labeled the "space cadet," "the bad kid," "the stupid kid," "forgetful," "messy," "disorganized," or the "good-for-nothing" failure! This is a sad reality faced by many young people with ADHD.

While peers are observing and absorbing the social behavior of those around them—taking in when to pause, when to listen, when to ask questions, when to speak, or when to make an empathetic facial gesture—children with ADHD have brains that are racing, making it difficult for them to notice or retain the social cues that are being fed to them by others. As I said earlier, these young people blink and miss the social lessons that the rest of their peers are receiving. The result can be a disrupted social learning process that leaves the young person with ADHD unaware or uncertain of how to act around others.

Many young people with ADHD thus need to go back and learn what they missed. The work of coaching gives them an opportunity to investigate their social world—the cues around them and the reactions of people to this behavior or that—and to practice interacting with their social world. All the while, the young person will have the supportive coach waiting in the wings to help him or her develop social strategies, test them out, handle mistakes, interpret responses to particular behaviors, learn, grow, and cultivate a more fulfilling social experience.

- Strategies for strengthening social skills include

- pause for 10 seconds before speaking or acting on impulse

- ask for permission to interrupt

- practice active listening, being engaged in what the other person is saying

- practice asking questions of other people

- write out conversations in advance

- practice engaging in an important conversation without emotion or yelling

- make eye contact with others

- ask one person to go to the dining hall or join a group of students from your dorm

- consider risks before taking action

when in doubt, talk it out.

Social-skills issues can be widespread, affecting relationships with not only peers but also with siblings, parents, teachers, advisors, coaches, and bosses. And as with other skills, there is often an overlap between social skills and other areas, such as academics. For example, a young person with ADHD who fails to complete his or her portion of a group assignment in history class is likely to experience academic consequences, from a poor grade to a lowered image in the eyes of teacher and classmates. As indicated in Cathi Cohen's book *Raise Your Child's Social IQ*, social skills are just as important as intellectual ability when it comes to success at school, home, and work.

Self-Advocacy: A Big Step Toward Empowerment

For young people with ADHD, self-advocacy skills are commonly under-developed. These are individuals who often require extra support from parents and teachers and who have had accommodations to help them succeed academically. With all of the supports in place and adults stepping up to advocate for these young people, their social skills and their communication skills—which make up, in part, self-advocacy skills—are often weak or lacking. As defined by Wrightslaw, self-advocacy involves

> learning how to speak up for yourself, making your own decisions about your own life, learning how to get information so that you can understand things that are of interest to you, finding out who will support you in your journey, knowing your rights and responsibilities, problem-solving, listening and learning, reaching out to others when you need help and friendship, and learning about self-determination.

In support of adolescents and young adults with ADHD, coaches should help to teach them how to stand up for themselves and communicate effectively to ensure that they get what they need to meet their goals and be successful. Communicating effectively could involve anything from asking for extended time on a test to negotiating a job accommodation, such as wearing noise-cancelling headphones while working.

By helping young people recognize when self-advocacy is required to meet their goals and by encouraging them to practice self-advocacy strategies and build related skills, coaches continue the process of empowering clients. Self-advocacy puts tools in the hands of the young person to ask for what he or she needs and to work to shape the environment so it becomes maximally supportive.

Self-advocacy strategies include

- asking a teacher for a meeting after class
- contacting a local restaurant about a part-time job
- requesting extra time on an exam
- explaining one's attention problems to a new friend or roommate
- e-mailing a professor to get clarification on an assignment
- requesting a raise in one's allowance
- asking to do something oneself, without help
- calling the doctor to change an appointment.

If young people don't learn how to advocate for themselves, they will remain stuck in the chronic dilemma of having someone else always doing something for them. By exercising the muscle of self-advocacy through coaching, clients make strides toward independence and self-confidence. No longer does the young person need someone to jump to the rescue. Instead, he or she has strategies and techniques for addressing challenges and obstacles.

Life Skills: Learning the Basics

Young people with ADHD are often behind the curve in terms of their readiness to handle life on their own. In some cases, parents have unwittingly enabled their children, taking care of the basics of daily life. As young people head off to college or to live and work on their own, it is imperative that they have basic life skills for a smooth transition. As we discussed earlier, it is difficult for many youth with ADHD to pick up on the nuances and the how-to of life skills, including personal hygiene, good nutrition, regular exercise, financial management, laundry, getting enough sleep, and so on.

Life skills are important for many reasons, not the least of which is that ADHD symptoms can be exacerbated by fatigue, poor nutritional habits, or forgetting to take medication. Areas such as diet and sleep habits, exercise programs, and other aspects of self-nurturing need to be examined by clients in an effort to foster health and balance. Add to that the low level of self-awareness often found in young people with ADHD, and this can translate into an inability to see themselves as others do. For example, one of my clients did not like taking showers and honestly did not consider it a problem. When he looked in the mirror, he did not see the greasy hair or notice his overall unkempt appearance. Through coaching conversations and an opportunity to put himself in the place of his peers, he learned that, indeed, a regular routine for showering and shampooing his hair was in order.

Strategies for life skills span a wide spectrum, given the broad nature of this category. Strategies can include

- putting an appointment in one's planner to do laundry once a week

- setting an alarm as a reminder to take a shower every day; when sharing a bathroom with roommates or siblings, plan the time accordingly

- using a Post-it note as a reminder to take medication

- logging expenses daily, from a cup of coffee to gasoline for the car to movie tickets

- finding a fitness buddy and setting a time for regular exercise

- allowing for evening wind-down time to relax one's brain and body before bed

- setting the morning alarm for the same time each day to help establish one's internal body clock

- choosing healthy options for energy and nutrition using a list created on your cell phone.

These techniques represent just a snapshot of the many life-skills strategies available to young people with ADHD.

Once goals and action steps have been identified in the PCA, the coach's role is to invite the client to identify relevant strategies for executing those action steps. Sometimes these will relate to life skills; other times they will relate to time management, personal organization, and so on. Clients can then take the following week to try a strategy out, sharing progress with the coach with regular check-ins by phone, text, or e-mail.

Beware of Reminder Overload!

As you can imagine, too many reminders beeping on a person's phone or a deluge of Post-its could get as overwhelming or become as ineffective for a young person with ADHD as not having enough reminders. The goal is not to have reminder overload but to strategically design a system that prompts the client at important times or that is available to the young person as needed to keep track of where the young person needs to be when and what he or she needs to be doing at any given time to achieve goals. The young person will thus need to make thoughtful decisions about how to set up the reminder system, which items are most important to include in the system, and when and how to feature reminders. The coach can support the young person in this process by asking the young person open-ended questions to help identify his or her learning style, sharing strategies that have worked for other clients in the past, and encouraging the young person to test different strategies until the young person finds one that works.

Some clients keep their reminder system manageable by combining all of their reminders into one pop-up message on their phone rather than having the phone beep over and over again. Others set their reminder to something simple, like "check your to-do list," and allow it to go off every hour after school. Some clients prefer to use a handwritten list of their reminders, on which they have noted their most important tasks, such as "take medicine," "make sure I have all of my papers," and "check in with the coach." Over time, some young people no longer need their reminders as these tasks get incorporated into their daily routines. Others may use the reminder strategy for the rest of their lives to help them stay on track, compensate for challenges with working memory, and reach their goals.

It is up to the client to choose the strategies and to select the area(s) of skill building for focus. The client I mentioned earlier who needed to shower did not come to coaching with personal hygiene goals. Those surfaced over time after basic routines for improving personal organization and time management were underway. The client noticed that although he was able to find his stuff at home and turn in his assignments at school, there was still something missing in his relationships with peers and adults. This led him to take that second look in the mirror and identify the goal of improving personal hygiene. Techniques that may seem simple or intuitive—or even unnecessary—to those without ADHD can make all of the difference in the life of a young person with ADHD.

Facilitating Learning and Results: Avoid Telling Clients What to Do

While helping young people with ADHD generate and identify personalized strategies, coaches will be engaging in a more directive coaching approach (with the coach speaking 35% of the time, compared with the client's 65%) as compared with the life coaching process, in which the coach may say very little (20% to the client's 80%) during a typical coaching session. Coaches will far more frequently be in the "facilitating learning and results" mode, which includes creating awareness, designing actions, planning and goal setting, and managing progress and accountability—as detailed in the International Coach Federation's Professional Coaching Core Competencies —when working with clients with ADHD than is customary in life coaching.

A coach might ask an open-ended question, such as, "What strategy might you be willing to try to improve your relationship with your parents?" but the coach may then follow up with a more directive comment if he or she sees the client flailing to find an answer. For example, the coach might say, "Would you consider requesting a time to sit down and talk with your parents?" Brainstorming is a common skill used in coaching, and I have found it to be especially helpful when coaching young people who just don't have the answer readily available. By volleying ideas with the coach, clients can oftentimes come up with a solution that would have otherwise remained stuck in the recesses of his or her brain for a while longer, leading to frustration or a sense of failure.

Unfortunately, there are times when coaches step over the line and into a realm of teaching and consulting. They tell the client what to do and how to do it rather than eliciting solutions from the client. If we are to stay within the framework of coaching, providing an opportunity for our clients to discover their own brilliance, it is imperative that we refrain from problem-solving. Coaching is not a race, and clients are best served when they have an opportunity to partake in the process of discovering answers to their own questions and feel empowered within the coaching relationship.

Partnering with young people to assist them in the learning process so they are better able to acquire skills and strategies leads to empowerment. The strategies discussed in this chapter just scratch the surface of possibilities. Coaches can encourage clients and their families to investigate resources such as www.additudemag.com, CHADD.org, and www.help4adhd.org. Books for both young people and adults with ADHD offer guidance on ways to manage one's time effectively.

A Note for Everyone

Our tendency as adults is to simply say to young people with ADHD "go study" or "put your nose to the grindstone." We may think that if the young person would just work a little harder or put a little more effort toward something, obstacles would disappear and success would follow. Unfortunately, it's not a case of needing to apply mere effort for these young people. They require strategies that help them compensate for their ADHD-related deficits and to build all of the skills that are essential for success in life: time management, planning, and prioritization; social skills and life skills; effective communication and self-advocacy; and more.

In addition, young people with ADHD need strategies that are personalized to meet their own needs and that fit their own unique situation. Identifying effective strategies is not a one-size-fits-all process. What works for the coach or parent may not work for the client; this is not a coach-driven or parent-driven process, either. Instead, coach and client need to work together to develop strategies, with the coach facilitating but the client in the lead.

Once the groundwork of support and structure has been put into place by creating the PCA, the coaching process can proceed toward developing strategies for success and building skills. Readiness for coaching will be essential for effective skill building; if maturity and coachability are there, success has a good chance of following.

Coaches and clients should take time to explore different options, contemplate what seems right for the client, test strategies out in the real world, and reflect on them in conversation. It can also be useful as coaching progresses to revisit the client's strategies from time to time. Are strategies identified in the past still working? Have new goals emerged that require a retooling of the action plan and subsequent strategies? Has a skill been learned, clearing the way for other skills to be practiced? Coaches and parents should allow time and patience for the young person to test new strategies; this can only happen if coaching is structured to include space for this learning process to occur.

As the skill-building process takes place, coaches and parents can try to keep the process light. Humor often goes a long way to lessen stress for the client; the coach can also let the client know that it's normal for young people with ADHD to benefit from some extra support in learning all of these skills. Coaches can also ask the young person to reflect on his or her strengths when identifying possible strategies. "What's working for you now?" the coach might ask. Drawing strategies from a young person's current strengths or skill set can help to build confidence as well as set the young person up for success over the long term.

N I N E

Roadblocks:
Obstacles and Challenges to Coaching

Whether a coach is interacting with a potential client for the very first time, setting goals with a new client in the first weeks of coaching, or checking in with a client that the coach has been working with for several months, the time may come when progress toward a young person's goals hits a pothole, gets a flat tire, or even gets stuck behind a roadblock.

I know from my own experience coaching young people, as well as from mentoring others who coach young people, that roadblocks to coaching can be frustrating and disheartening. Having a colleague or mentor with whom the coach can speak can help the coach regain perspective and think through a situation. A trusted sounding board can also help a coach brainstorm solutions, boost the coach's energy to tackle the situation, and return to the coaching process with ideas for helpful next steps. Coaches might also find it useful to read or return to this chapter, which explores common coaching obstacles and ideas on how to resolve or move beyond them. With the right approach, coaches can use obstacles as a starting point for helping clients build trust with the coach, learn about themselves through reflection and exploration, and even make breakthroughs that can lead to lasting change.

As this chapter shows, there tend to be two types of obstacles: those that can be overcome through effective communication and those that are like the proverbial brick wall that simply can't be scaled or gotten through, at least at that time. For cases in which the obstacles are manageable, the text in this chapter provides guidance on ways to work through the challenge or issue. For cases that involve the brick wall type of obstacles, this chapter mentions the need for temporarily or permanently ending the coaching relationship: terminating and referring the client elsewhere as needed.

Coaching Obstacles: An Overview

Obstacles and challenges to coaching—defined as issues that complicate, slow, or impede the coaching process—come in all different forms, shapes, and sizes. A client may answer all of the coach's intake questions half-heartedly, or the coach may believe that things are going smoothly with a client until all of a sudden the client stops calling for usual check-ins and misses two appointments in a row. Alternatively, a client may start acting strangely, as if he or she is hiding something, or mom might insist on sitting next to the young person during phone sessions, even when the young person tries to escape to the bedroom or kitchen pantry, thus continually breaching the confidentiality boundary. Unwillingness to participate in coaching discussions, missed appointments, issues related to coexisting conditions, dishonesty, overreaching parents: These are just a few of the obstacles that can interrupt coaching progress or put coach and client at a stalemate.

Obstacles can occur on either side of the table, with both the coach and the client potentially impacting the coaching situation. Coaches may be tempted to blame clients for slow progress, whereas clients may want to blame the coach for mistakes they make along the way. Certainly, challenges can and do stem from one party or the other. For example, a coexisting condition may make it difficult or impossible for a client to participate fully in the coaching process. Yet, oftentimes, the coach and client both play important roles in the obstacles and challenges they are facing.

Possible obstacles to successful coaching include

- personality differences—do coach and client clash?

- learning style differences or learning impairments that may impede coaching

- unwillingness or inability of client or coach to commit to the coaching process

- client financial problems

- time management issues—do the schedules of coach and client conflict?

- too many clients on the coach's plate—an indication of the need to say "no"

- inability to meet the expectations of coaching, either by the coach or by the client

- untreated psychological issues

- chemical dependency issues.

Coaches can aim to spot these potential obstacles early on—during the prescreening call—by attempting to assess whether the client is currently coachable and whether the coach is the right person for the job. Yet, the prescreening experience is relatively short, and obstacles do not always make themselves clear at that point in the process. Only as the process unfolds do some challenges with coaching become clearer.

Communication Is Key

I'm always amazed when coaches who have encountered an obstacle during the coaching process ask, "How can I make the client do this or that?" when I know all too well that we coaches can't *make* clients do anything. Yet, coaches sometimes feel that it is their job to independently fix a particular problem or challenge that is occurring during coaching. These coaches forget that coaching is a joint process and that concerns are often best brought directly to the client. Instead of leaving a challenge unspoken, coaches can bring questions to the attention of the client for a collaborative discussion. If the coach has a concern that the client is unhappy with coaching, for example, the coach should feel free to come right out and ask. "How is this working for you?" "How might we make things better?" and "What is your level of interest in coaching at this time?" are the kinds of questions the coach might use. Open, honest communication is a simple but powerful tool for working through coaching obstacles.

Match or Mismatch: Is This Relationship Meant to Be?

One of the common areas in which coaching obstacles may arise involves situations in which the coach and the client simply don't click. Sometimes that lack of compatibility is sensed by the client; sometimes it's detected by the coach; sometimes both client and coach feel it. When a lack of compatibility is felt on the side of the client, this may manifest in a variety of ways. For example, the young client may

- feel that the coach is pushy and trying to tell the client what to do
- find the coach to be boring or businesslike
- find the coach to be too buddy-buddy
- have difficulty following the pace and processing style of the coach
- be unable or unwilling to trust in the coaching process with a relative stranger.

On the coach's side, an incompatibility may exist when the coach

- feels that he or she is doing all of the work and that there is no effort from the client
- does not make a connection with the client
- senses that the client is very uncomfortable in coaching sessions
- does not relate to the client's style or personality
- dreads the upcoming coaching session with a particular client.

Although obstacles can originate in either the client or the coach, compatibility relates to a dynamic experience between the coach and client. If one of the parties feels uncomfortable, pressured, or misunderstood, the other often senses it, even if only subconsciously.

Imagine for a moment that a teenager comes into the coach's office wearing all black, with nose piercings, tattoos, and a shaved head. Will it make the coach uncomfortable to work with someone whose physical appearance is bold, edgy, or untraditional? Or will the coach be able to conduct coaching effectively? Some coaches find they can't see past the teen's unconventional look. If there is a lack of compatibility for this or any other reason, coaches will do best to recognize the incompatibility and offer a referral to the client.

Some coaches may choose to try to work through their discomfort or sense of incompatibility with a client, and with enough time and trust building, an authentic connection may develop between client and coach. But if a coach continually tries to hide discomfort, all too often the client can sense this and the coaching suffers.

When the coach detects incompatibilities between coach and client, the coach should be honest with the client, letting the young person know that he or she senses that the client may not be totally comfortable in the relationship or that the coach is feeling uncomfortable, and then provide an opportunity to discuss what's really going on. It is counterproductive for coaches to worry in a vacuum without inviting the client, who has valuable insight, into the process. "I get a sense that you are not comfortable talking with me," the coach might say. "What might we do to make this more comfortable for you?" Or, "I am not sure that I am the best coach for you and would like to share my thoughts."

In some cases, it can be helpful for the coach to simply allow more time for coach and client to get to know one another. Building rapport between the coach and young person takes patience and oftentimes requires a few coaching sessions before the relationship seems to click. I encourage coaches and clients to trust their intuition while avoiding jumping to conclusions. It is important to note that when coaches attempt to insert their own agenda into the coaching process, this creates problems for the client and oftentimes sabotages the coaching relationship. Coaches need to check their agenda at the door and practice good self-management skills. Otherwise, the client will not have choices and is likely to feel pressured to follow a coaching plan designed solely by the coach—or to choose to discontinue coaching.

Incompatibility or Something Else?

Occasionally, obstacles that, at first glance, appear to exist as a result of personality differences or issues of compatibility may actually result from another cause altogether. Sometimes an adolescent may come across as rude in the prescreening or intake session such that the coach doesn't really want to work with him or her. The client might bark at the coach or the parent; the client might refuse to answer questions or avoid making eye contact.

Before making snap judgments, coaches are encouraged to consider the possibility that the client may simply be acting defensively under the pressure of an uncomfortable intake session in which the client's parents are present rather than displaying true personality. The early investigative work that is initiated by coaches and conducted in the parents' presence is often very difficult for young people. Young clients may feel embarrassed, angry, or put on the spot by all of the attention, analysis, and seeming criticism. They may act flippantly or rudely as a sort of defense mechanism. Coaches can ease clients' discomfort by acknowledging the difficult nature of the situation, for example, by stating, "I appreciate your decision to get started with coaching and want to acknowledge that it can certainly be difficult to be the focus of the conversation."

When a client decides not to work with a coach, it's possible that the coach will assume the decision was based on personality differences between client and coach. But coaches should also consider whether the issue goes beyond mere differences in personality and points to a coach's unintentionally demeaning or condescending approach to the young person. This occasionally happens with well-meaning coaches: In their attempt to support the young person, they may inadvertently talk down to him or her. Additional training under the support of a mentor coach and more practice may help the coach learn how to adopt an attitude that's more appropriate for working with young people. In some cases, a coach will discover that adolescents and young adults simply aren't the right population for them, given the coach's style, preferences, and approach.

Learning Style Differences and Learning Disabilities

Learning style differences and learning disabilities may also be at the root of coaching challenges. For example, the client may not be completing action steps because he or she has an auditory processing problem and struggles to retain material discussed orally during phone sessions. The coach might jump to the conclusion that the client isn't motivated to work when, in fact, the client is actually struggling because of a learning disability. It will be up to the coach and the client to do some detective work to figure out what's at the root of a particular challenge. Once the learning issue is identified, adjustments can be made, for example, by having the visual-learning client type notes into his or her laptop during the coaching session to help transfer coaching plans from the audio to the visual realm.

Sometimes learning style or learning disabilities are sufficient to indicate that a different coach is needed. That was the case when a family sought out my services for their 16-year-old son. During my in-person prescreening with the teen, his visual learning style showed itself very clearly to me. He was quick to make eye contact and stayed with me visually the whole conversation. He used words like "I see" and explained that it was difficult for him to follow oral class presentations without companion notes.

"I'm noticing that you are a highly visual person," I shared with him. "What would it be like for you to talk with me on the phone for coaching rather than to see me in person?" After some reflection, the young man realized that in-person coaching was what he needed, and because I was located too far from his home for him to come for regular in-person meetings, he decided that he would like to be connected to a different coach in his geographic area. As shown by this example, there are times when coaching obstacles occur and can't be overcome with the current coach.

Working Through the Obstacle Versus Terminating Coaching

Working with the client to overcome coaching obstacles can be a great learning experience. This may lead to a more successful coaching partnership when both parties choose to work together in coaching after addressing the obstacles. Conversely, there will be situations that clearly indicate that successful coaching is not going to occur or that the coaching has stalled out. When the coaching partnership is wandering outside of the ethical boundaries of coaching and/or the coaching agreement, the coach needs to address the issue/s directly with the client. If the coach realizes that the partnership is no longer viable, it is important to discuss options with the client and consider termination.

Unwillingness or Inability: Why Do Some Clients Refuse to Commit to the Coaching Process?

Another reason that the coaching process can break down can be that the client is either unwilling or unable to commit to the coaching process. What does an unwilling client look like? There may be stubbornness or a refusal to participate in conversation. The client may feel forced into meeting with the coach and may be unwilling to share any information. These clients tend to frustrate coaches and other adults and spur coaches to call colleagues for ideas and support. Unwilling clients are those who avoid, through their words, body language, and actions (or lack of actions), getting involved deeply or authentically with coaching. They often won't speak during coaching, won't complete action steps, and/or fail to show up for coaching sessions or to contact the coach regarding progress.

An unwillingness or inability to participate in coaching can happen for a variety of reasons. Perhaps the client isn't mature enough yet for coaching, is too anxious to commit to trying something new, or has too many activities at the moment to fully engage in coaching. Maybe the client's parents struggle with time management and are failing on their part to get the client to sessions on time. Some of the issues that come up regarding lack of commitment to coaching include

- a lack of readiness on the part of the client (immaturity)
- substance abuse or untreated psychological issues
- a lack of understanding of the coaching process
- financial constraints
- schedule conflicts and other time management issues
- realization that coaching is not what the client wants at this time.

The reasons a client might be unwilling or unable to commit to coaching are varied. Let's take an in-depth look at each of these reasons.

A lack of readiness for coaching is often signaled by a client becoming easily frustrated, not being able to take responsibility for his or her actions, and having a tendency to blame others for problems or failures. Instead of seeing the coach as a nonjudgmental partner, the immature client may project the parent onto the coach, expressing complaints like, "You're making me do what my mom and dad want me to do and I don't want to do any of that." The young person may simply not be ready to commit to making a change. The coach can rely on coaching skills to get a handle on whether the young person is ready for coaching or termination is instead indicated.

When prospective clients or their parents request coaching, it is possible that they lack an understanding of coaching. Maybe the parent thinks that coaching is glorified tutoring or the young person imagines that a coach will coerce parents into giving the client whatever he or she wants. The unwillingness or inability to be in or stay in a coaching relationship may be caused by this confusion. Regardless of how the misunderstanding comes to be, if coaching is not what the parents or the client are interested in, then the process will not be able to move forward.

Unfortunately, life events can also get in the way of coaching. Loss of income, change in schedules (client, parent, or coach), drug and alcohol abuse, medical or mental health issues, or a change in the client's priorities that pushes coaching to the bottom of the list can all be obstacles to coaching. Each situation is unique, and it is valuable for the coach to use his or her coaching skills to elicit information to help coach and client decide on next steps.

Let's not forget the parent's potential role in the obstacles to the coaching process. The parents of an adolescent with ADHD may have serious difficulty letting go of the daily monitoring of the young person, thus inadvertently sabotaging the coaching progress. It may help to have the coach revisit with the parents the goals of coaching and the value of creating a safe space for the young person to become more independent and self-sufficient, while guiding the parents toward a less active role in the minute-to-minute activities of the client. Many parents just need a gentle reminder, whereas others choose to stay in the forefront and terminate coaching.

Occasionally, the coaches I teach and mentor will come to me and express concern that they can't figure out how to motivate an unwilling client to engage in coaching. Although there are certainly times that coaches can help increase a client's willingness to engage by discovering the cause of the unwillingness and working through it alongside the client, sometimes there is nothing a coach can do at all (e.g., the case of immaturity or drug abuse).

In such cases, it is best to recommend termination or, at the very least, to put a hold on the coaching for a period of time. Instead of seeing this as failure, I encourage coaches to realize the value of stopping the coaching. Not only is it very difficult to coach an unwilling client (an experience that can cause a coach to waste time and energy and parents to waste money as well), but the client is simply not capable of benefiting from coaching at that time. The client may need the experience of being able to choose to end coaching in order to move his or her life forward in some other way and possibly come back to coaching at a later time.

Note that an inability to commit to coaching can also occur on the part of the coach. Maybe the coach's schedule is too full to adequately handle another client, such that the coach struggles to plan effectively for coaching sessions or is unable to meet the needs of the client in a timely manner. If this is the case, the coaching process may suffer. Occasionally, a coach will agree to drive to a client's home or school only to find that the distance is time and cost prohibitive.

Another potentially challenging situation may occur when a client requests coaching at night and this is not suitable for the coach. I know that my energy decreases in the evenings, so I no longer coach clients after 6 p.m. It is better for the coach to offer only those services that he or she knows can be provided well and to refer the client elsewhere when needed rather than to risk disappointing oneself and the client when coaching doesn't work out. Of course, predictions cannot be made in advance, so the coach simply does his or her best to assess the situation up front and make adjustments later if needed.

Invariably, some clients are unable to meet coaching expectations, whether that means they don't show up on time for sessions, don't engage in action steps, or don't pay for coaching sessions. A young person may express a sincere interest in participating in and committing to coaching during the prescreening and the intake sessions, only for the coach and young person to discover that once the regular work of coaching begins, the young person is unable to meet coaching expectations and cannot continue. When this occurs, the coach can take this as an opportunity to check in with the client to determine whether the obstacles can be overcome or termination is, in fact, the right step.

A failure to meet coaching expectations sometimes relates to resistance to change, a phenomenon not uncommon among young people, particularly adolescents. It is important for parents to understand that for youth with ADHD, learning disabilities, and coexisting conditions, resistance is often a manifestation of unreadiness, emotional immaturity, and unknowing. Oftentimes, adolescents are pushing back against their parents' suggestion of coaching or don't know what they are supposed to change in order to improve and are afraid of yet another failure. I encourage parents and coaches to be patient and open the door to conversation, which may give young people an opportunity to consider what is actually holding them back.

A Note for Everyone

Obstacles may arise in coaching from time to time, whether because of personality incompatibilities, learning style differences, learning disabilities, or behind-the-scenes issues, that lead to a client or a coach's inability or unwillingness to fully participate in the process. In some cases, these obstacles can be addressed by engaging clients in an open and honest dialogue about what's going on and about how things can be adjusted to make the coach or client more comfortable. Other times, a referral to a different coach or professional or a complete termination of coaching will be called for, as in the case of a client who is struggling with drug abuse and may need rehab or a young person who is not yet mature enough to understand and engage in coaching.

When referring or connecting a young person to a coach, it is important to point out that one size does not fit all. As with other professional relationships (e.g., psychiatrists, therapists, tutors), the client has the opportunity to choose which coach is best for him or her. If there are insurmountable obstacles with one coach, another coach may be a better fit. Be open, as well, to this possibility that the young person is not ready for coaching. Maturity lags in adolescents with ADHD, and despite a parent's desire for coaching, the young person may simply need more time to mature before being ready for coaching. When obstacles are identified and the coach and client agree that those obstacles are insurmountable as noted above, a qualified coach will refer the client and the client's family to the appropriate professional. The goal is to serve the needs of the client even if that cannot be accomplished through coaching or by working with the original coach.

Coaching obstacles can occur at the beginning of the coaching process, in the middle, or even at the end. Sometimes obstacles can be resolved with patience and time by allowing the client and coach space to adjust to each other and the process. Other times, coaching with a given coach is simply not feasible, whether because of personality differences, learning style issues, or geographic constraints. A referral may be indicated, or the client may simply need or want to terminate coaching for the time being. Although obstacles that arise in coaching occasionally indicate that a coach could benefit from mentoring or additional training, it can be helpful to think of obstacles in coaching as being neutral rather than personal. By addressing such obstacles through honest communication, redesign of goals to help the client feel more motivated by the process, or termination or referral, coaches treat young people with respect and meet them on their journey, wherever that may lead.

T E N

Wrapping Up the Coaching Process

Completion is the time when coaching ends naturally. Sometimes coaching will end after several months of really powerful progress for the client. Sometimes coaching will terminate abruptly before it has really begun. For some coaches, completion of coaching represents an uncomfortable time. What should be said to the client? If the termination is unexpected, does it mean that the coach has done something wrong? A host of challenges and concerns are sometimes raised for coaches at the time of completion, depending on the circumstances.

Yet, by coming to terms with the reality that the coaching process will not go on indefinitely—that some clients grow wings and become ready to fly solo and that other clients are simply not ready for coaching—coaches can serve the needs of their clients, as well as take care of themselves. Retaining a client who no longer needs or wants the extra support of the coach or staying tied to a client who is unable to commit to the coaching process does not do anyone any good. In such situations, clients may become angry or resentful; coaches may become frustrated, bored, or burned out.

There are two ways in which coaching usually comes to an end: natural completion or unplanned termination. Natural completion occurs when a client has been working with the coach for a period of time, has accomplished the goals he or she set out in the personal coaching agreement (PCA), and feels sufficiently confident in his or her new skills and acquired strategies to stop meeting with the coach. Unplanned termination occurs when coaching comes to an end before the coaching process is complete for any number of reasons, from financial constraints to medical or mental health issues to lack of readiness for coaching on the part of the client. When the obstacles cannot be worked through, termination is often the next step.

Some coaches fear the end of the coaching relationship. When they are about to lose a client—whether at the time of natural completion or with an unplanned termination—they worry about how they will make up the financial income. Some coaches may personalize the experience, worrying that it's a sign that they have done something wrong. Although it's always helpful to solicit feedback from the client and to consider one's role in a situation, most of the time, the reasons that termination occurs are not at all personal. Sometimes a client is simply ready to end coaching; other times, circumstances beyond the coach's or client's control make coaching at the present time an impossibility. It can help to realize that termination represents not just an ending but also a beginning. When one client leaves, the door opens for another client to arrive.

This chapter is designed to provide hands-on guidance for conducting a meaningful completion and discusses how to broach the topic of unplanned termination in conversation, conduct a final coaching session, gather feedback, send exit letters, and solicit survey responses. How to maintain appropriate contact with the client after coaching has ended is also covered, with a goal of helping coaches remain a positive presence in the client's life and keep the door open for re-engaging coaching in the future if needed.

Letting Go Is Hard to Do: Natural Completion as a Sign of Success

Coaches sometimes struggle to end coaching and let their clients go. The reasons can be many, but the result may be the same: a coach–client relationship dangling by a thread; two individuals stagnating rather than growing. A coach may simply fear hurting the client's feelings by bringing up the possibility of ending the coaching partnership. Or the coach may be afraid to call for an unplanned end to coaching because the coach doesn't like conflict, the coach doesn't want to be seen as a quitter or a failure, or the coach feels bad for leaving a client hanging. Yet termination is sometimes exactly what is needed in a coaching situation.

In the case of natural completion—when the client has grown and matured to a point of being ready to go off on his or her own, or the client has simply met his or her goals for the coaching partnership—the end of coaching is a sign of success. The client has been able to benefit from coaching as intended and is ready to go out into the world with a host of new skills and strategies.

In the case of unplanned termination—when coaching ends abruptly before the goals of the client have been achieved—ending may not feel like a success to the coach or to the client. Yet, as uncomfortable, unexpected, or abrupt as the ending to coaching may be, this ending may represent what needs to happen at a given time. Sometimes termination may be a building block for future success; although it's hard to see in the moment, it may set the client up for growth in the future. For example, when a coach terminates coaching with a client who is actively abusing drugs, the coach helps the client by providing real-life consequences for his or her actions rather than enabling. When a coach respects that a client is not yet mature enough for coaching and thus raises the idea of termination, the coach may plant a seed with the client that will sprout in the future. The client may remember the coach at a later time, when needed, and return to the coaching process with readiness and energy.

The common reasons that coaches have trouble letting go of clients range from worries over loss of income to concerns about withdrawing support from a young person in trouble. Table 10.1 provides an overview of the common reasons that it can be hard for coaches to end coaching, along with some guidance on why it can nonetheless be valuable to end coaching.

Table 10.1

Common Reasons for Coach Difficulties in Terminating Coaching

Reason	Perspective to consider
Coach is unsure of how to wrap up the coaching process and so does nothing.	→ When in doubt, ask the client. What does the client want from the coaching at this point? Is the client ready to fly solo? Consider the best next steps for the client.
Coach believes termination is a sign of failure.	→ Coaches need to manage their expectations and learn from every coaching relationship. Termination is often not personal to the coach; sometimes clients are simply not ready for coaching or it was not a good match.
Coach doesn't want to lose business or financial income.	→ It's unethical to continue working with a client simply for financial benefit; working from a place of fear or scarcity does not make for a good coaching partnership. In addition, when one client leaves, a new client is often waiting around the corner.
Coach fears hurting the client's feelings or disappointing the client or parents by mentioning the possibility of termination.	→ When a problem arises that will most likely lead to termination, the coach needs to be honest with the client. Oftentimes, the client is starting to think of termination, too, and the mention of termination does not come as a surprise.
Coach wants client to meet goals on the coach's agenda.	→ This is not about the coach's agenda. The client has a choice of whether to work on new goals or to decide that coaching is over.
Coach is trying to be a backup therapist.	→ Sometimes when a client starts therapy, he or she ends up turning to the coach to talk about emotional issues from the week's therapy session; if coach is unable to steer the client toward coaching-centered issues, it is best to put coaching on hold.

A coach's desire to hold on to a client is often well-intentioned. The coach may want to support the client and not abandon him or her. Even if a referral to a therapist has been made, the coach may fear upsetting a client by suggesting that coaching be put on hold while the client engages in therapy. Yet, in all of the examples listed in Table 10.1, the coach would be doing a disservice to clients by avoiding termination.

Ending a coaching relationship, whether in a natural or an unplanned way, can be a hard thing to do. Coaches may become attached to their clients and want to give them their all regardless of what the client wants to do. Coaches may want to prove that they can handle any coaching case or avoid letting parents down. But sometimes the time is simply right for coaching to end. The client may have reached all of his or her goals for coaching, the client may not have the time and energy to commit to coaching, or the client may lack the resources or capabilities to engage in the process at this time. Whatever the reason, by honoring the client's decision to wrap up or terminate coaching, a coach shows respect for the client, sending a message of support and professionalism that is appreciated by all parties. The coach also opens the door for other wonderful opportunities to help new young people in need of support. In the process, the coach may find renewed inspiration, energy, and fulfillment.

Natural Completion of Coaching

Natural completion of coaching occurs when the client has successfully worked through the coaching process and has acquired the skills and strategies needed to continue working toward goals on his or her own. Although every client and coaching situation is unique, some signs that it is time to wrap up the coaching may include the following:

- a client becomes more independent and less eager for the coaching connection

- the client comes to coaching calls with all of his or her action steps completed

- the client appears to be pulling away from the coaching process

- the client is consistently using the skills and strategies developed in coaching

- the client has very little to say in coaching sessions (this last item can also indicate a lack of commitment to coaching, so it only applies when the other items in the list are also present).

In my experience, I often have a gut feeling that a client is approaching an appropriate time for natural completion. I may find myself having the thought that this is someone who is ready to end coaching; I may see that the individual has accomplished a lot. When I have the sense that the end might be approaching, I will pose a question or two to the client, such as the following:

- "I am sensing that we might be nearing the time to wrap up our coaching. What are your thoughts?"
- "Wow, you have been working consistently on all of your coaching goals these past months. Are you noticing how independent you have become since we started?"
- "We have been working together for a long time now and your progress is fantastic. I am curious—might it be time to complete our coaching?"

I find that the right questions flow when I am in the moment with the client. Trust your instinct and your clients as you raise these questions.

Wrapping up the coaching process with a young person can be handled by scaling coaching back to less frequent sessions—for example, every other week or once a month—until the coaching is completed. In some cases, the client will be ready to wrap up coaching more quickly than that, with only one review session after the subject of ending the coaching is first discussed. Exact plans for scaling back coaching will depend on the needs of a particular client. Those who could use a little more support while building skills and self-confidence might switch to half-time coaching. This type of coaching usually involves meeting or talking every other week and gives the client space to explore the next level of independence and test out the skills developed during full-time coaching. This is a nice way to slowly build self-reliance and self-confidence.

Clients who are eager to go it alone may choose to wrap up coaching more quickly, with the opportunity to continue to have a connection to the coach. This connection leaves room for a refresher session in the future to review progress and gives the client some sense of long-range accountability. Sometimes a client will say, "I'm ready to wrap up, but if I have a question for you, can I call you?" In this case, I let clients know that the door is always open. I will also mention that we can schedule a call for a month from now, if desired. Of those clients who choose to reconnect in a month or so, some will come back from the coaching break realizing that they'd like to continue working with the coach; others will confirm that they are ready to end the coaching. When it comes to designing the completion plan, all of the possibilities are discussed with the client, giving the client the freedom to work out with the coach which timeline seems right for him or her.

Half-Time Coaching: Carmen, the College Student

Carmen was a college student who had been in weekly coaching for four months to help her manage her course load and keep her life organized. By the time winter break approached, she had met her goals of keeping her grades at a B or above and of staying on top of weekly tasks like laundry and grocery shopping. Carmen had been building her skills and seemed to have a handle on which academic and personal organizational strategies worked best for her; as a result, she felt like she didn't need to check in every week. Yet, Carmen was a little afraid to give up coaching completely because she believed it helped her stay on track and follow through on things.

Carmen and her coach decided that she would take two months off from coaching and check back in with a call in February. When they reconnected, Carmen shared that she was having trouble implementing her study strategies even though she knew what they were. Her coach asked her what she would like to do, and Carmen asked if they could resume coaching. The coach mentioned that they could try meeting every other week rather than every week and Carmen liked this idea. She and her coach have been meeting like this for the past two years. The coaching sessions occur just often enough to help Carmen stay focused on her goals and stick to her action plan.

Unplanned Termination

Although it would be nice if every client a coach works with were able to remain in coaching from start to finish—engaging in the full process, complete with PCA, executed action steps, and accomplished goals—there are times when coaching will come to an end before that is the case. Sometimes coaching ends unexpectedly, abruptly, or before all of a client's stated goals have been met. When this situation occurs, it is referred to as *unplanned termination*.

Unplanned termination happens when coaching obstacles occur and make it impossible for the coaching process to continue. As explored in Chapter 9, some coaching obstacles can be overcome. Exploratory discussions between coach and client may help move things forward: Restructuring the PCA, revising action steps, or trying out new strategies may get coaching going again. When coaching gets difficult, the assumption need not automatically be that it's time to terminate. Nonetheless, there are times when coaching is no longer at a point where it can or should proceed.

For example, if a client is struggling with depression and thus unable to engage in the coaching process, the ethical response is to refer the client to a mental health professional. Coaching may resume at a later time if deemed appropriate. Alternatively, if the client is unwilling to meet coaching expectations, holding the client accountable to the coaching process—and terminating coaching, if necessary—may be the kind of real-world response the client needs to experience for personal growth.

Obstacles that may lead to unplanned termination include

- nonpayment issues
- need for therapy
- unmet expectations
- a client's unreasonable expectations of the coach or the coaching process
- unwillingness on the part of the client to fully participate in the coaching process
- lack of motivation to participate in coaching
- chronic lateness
- client stops showing up for coaching sessions
- inappropriate behavior
- drug or alcohol abuse.

The last two obstacles on this list—inappropriate behavior and drug or alcohol abuse—suggest the need for immediate termination and a referral to a doctor or therapist. Inappropriate behavior includes things like stealing, lying, defiance, verbal abuse, physical abuse, or sexual misconduct. Coaching needs to be terminated quickly for the safety of the coach and the client and to send a clear message that inappropriate behavior and drug and alcohol abuse are not to be tolerated by coaches with any client. Conversely, if a coach is acting in an unethical manner, clients and their families are strongly urged to discontinue coaching immediately.

Unplanned Termination:
One Client and Two Enabling Parents

Christopher was a 16-year-old client who had come to me for coaching with the support of his parents. His stated goals were to improve his grades and to become more independent in preparation for college. At the intake, Christopher and his parents shared with me that he had previously been using drugs (smoking pot) but that he was currently in treatment—seeing both a psychiatrist and a therapist—and no longer using drugs. Christopher and I talked weekly and sporadically exchanged e-mails for a period of months, yet, much to my frustration, coaching did not seem to be working. Christopher's engagement in coaching was low and he was still failing at school. Christopher's parents were frustrated with the lack of progress and periodically inquired about what I could do differently to help their son succeed.

When I approached Christopher's parents, with his permission, to discuss possible obstacles to coaching, they admitted that he had still been using pot. They shared that they hadn't told me about the drug use because the frequency of use had decreased from when he first started coaching and they didn't think it mattered because I was just the coach. Unfortunately, drug use is a serious problem that interferes with coaching (among many other things) and requires treatment and stabilization before coaching can be effective. In this case, Christopher and his parents had lied to me earlier when I inquired about how the treatment was progressing, so this added another layer of dysfunction to the coaching experience.

It's never easy for me to tell a family that I am obligated to terminate coaching because of a present circumstance or current obstacle (in this case, active drug use), but this is what I proceeded to do with Christopher and his family because I could no longer enable the addiction or the client. Christopher's parents expressed anger and suggested that I was abandoning him. I truly wanted to help Christopher and I wished that it were within my power to stop his current drug use, but, unfortunately, this was an area beyond my control. Only Christopher could make the choice to stop his drug use. I let the family know that I would be ending coaching immediately and contacting his current therapist to apprise her of the update. Christopher could continue working with his therapist and psychiatrist—or enter a substance abuse treatment program—to address his addiction and, in the future, he could resume coaching when he was truly ready and able.

When I terminate coaching because of substance abuse, as in the case of Christopher, it is not a moral judgment. It relates instead to the reality that coaching cannot be effective while a client is abusing drugs or alcohol. If a client is high during coaching, he or she will be unable to focus on what's going on. If the client is intoxicated every evening, he or she will lack the capacity to execute the strategies and action plan identified in the coaching process. Clients who are abusing substances are often in denial about the consequences of their addiction. By providing the real-world consequence of ending coaching, the coach does what he or she can to provide the client with caring and appropriate feedback. In addition, a coach is not equipped to engage in addictions treatment, nor is this the work the coach and client originally contracted for. As a result, it is the ethical responsibility of the coach to (a) refer the client to someone trained and qualified to do substance abuse counseling and (b) end coaching until a future time when the client may be capable and motivated to engage in the coaching process.

Many of the reasons for unplanned termination relate to a client's unreadiness for coaching or an inability to participate in the coaching process, whether due to immaturity, inappropriate behavior, drug use, or the need for therapy. Occasionally, unplanned termination will occur because of a client's unwillingness or lack of interest in participating in coaching. This can arise for a number of reasons.

Maybe the teen is overscheduled with after-school activities and does not have the time, energy, or desire to engage in coaching. Maybe the college student doesn't feel comfortable with this particular coach because of the coach's approach or differences in personality and learning style. The previous chapter provided insight into how the coaching discussion might be guided to explore a client's concerns or lack of interest and to assess whether coaching can be adjusted to better meet the client's needs. Sometimes tweaks can be made to the coaching experience—from frequency of meetings to strategies used—but at other times, the situation calls for a referral to a different coach or the termination of coaching altogether.

Although unplanned termination may feel uncomfortable to some coaches, sometimes ending the coaching process is the most respectful, appropriate, and/or ethical thing to do. Remembering the broader goal of coaching—to support a young person in meeting his or her goals—can help the coach let go and allow coaching to end when the time is right.

If a client does not have the time or energy to engage in coaching, it is respectful to honor the client's choice to withdraw. If a client is in denial regarding drug addiction, ending coaching and making a referral to an addictions specialist is the ethical and appropriate response. If it becomes clear that the client feels uncomfortable with the coach's approach, helping the client get connected to a different coach may be just the boost the client needs to climb out of an apparent rut. And being willing to say goodbye to a client who is feeling bored in coaching and has developed sufficient independence will help build the client's confidence while freeing the coach up to help another young person in need of support. Ending the coaching—whether through natural completion or unplanned termination—can be easier for the coach if he or she remembers to not take the ending personally but instead to recognize that clients do sometimes falter, move on, or learn to fly solo.

Concluding the Coaching Relationship

Discussing the Next Steps

The completion process begins with a discussion between the coach and the client. In the case of natural completion, the coach might be the one to ask a question of the client, such as, "I've noticed you've really got a handle on things and it makes me wonder when you might be ready to end coaching. Is this something you've given any thought to?" Sometimes, the client might raise the issue: "I've been feeling really good about my progress and wonder if maybe it's time to stop coaching." In these cases, the upcoming end to coaching is usually something that both the coach and the client sense. The conversation then becomes a matter of the coach acknowledging to the client that he or she is making a lot of progress. The coach can then ask, "How do you see this wrapping up?" The coach can also offer all of the options for phasing out or ending coaching, from moving to biweekly or monthly sessions for a period of time to ending coaching immediately.

Unplanned termination will also involve a discussion between coach and client; either individual can initiate the termination. A client uncomfortable with the coach's approach or personality may come right out and express a desire to end coaching, or the client may hedge a bit, saying something like, "I just don't know if coaching is for me." As noted previously, a client who begins a session thinking he or she may want to terminate may simply need support in making adjustments to coaching. In this case, the coach can help this client explore his or her wishes a bit further by asking, "What's got you thinking about ending coaching?" or "What have you considered as your next steps after coaching?" An exploratory discussion can take place between the coach and client to help the client sort through whether now is the right time for termination.

If the coach is initiating an unplanned termination as a result of the client's actions or inaction, the coach will inform the client that because of the situation at hand and in order to stay within the boundaries of proper coaching, it will be necessary to end the coaching. If the client is willing and able, there is time for a brief review of the client's progress thus far and, if deemed appropriate, for the coach to discuss ways for the client to return to coaching at a later time. An example of that might be, "Sarah, I realize that seeing a therapist to address your current problems is the best option for you right now. Please know that as you begin to see progress in therapy and have your medications regulated, I would welcome a call or an e-mail to say 'hello' and, if you are interested, a reconnection for coaching." This serves to support the client's decision and help her be okay with terminating coaching at that time. My clients deeply appreciate my interest in their well-being and my open-door policy for more coaching when appropriate.

After the initial discussion with the client about termination, the client will either talk with his or her parents about the decision or request that the coach make direct contact with the parents. When there is a need for immediate termination, as in the case of Christopher, I initiated a conference call with the parents and the client. If Christopher had not been available, I was prepared to talk with the parents alone, because the drug problem precluded any further coaching sessions with Christopher. Thankfully, that case was not the norm for me. Usually, when unplanned termination arises, I am able to take a week or two to discuss options with the client, work out the plan for talking with parents, and meet for a review and feedback session.

Sometimes parents are the ones to contact the coach to request termination. Just as I would do with a client, I invite the parent to tell me more about what isn't working for the parent in terms of the coaching. What are the parents looking for that I am not currently providing? Are there extenuating circumstances that led to the decision to terminate? If so, would the parents be willing to discuss the issues with me?

Sometimes families are dealing with illnesses, job loss, or divorce, which may lead to financial hardship and difficulty in continuing to pay for coaching. If there is a way for me to continue coaching the young client during this time of difficulty, I want to do so for the sake of the client. For me, money is not always the key to staying in a coaching relationship, and my client families are a valued part of my life. I use this discussion as an opportunity to assess whether the parent is truly set on ending coaching or whether the parent might simply need some reasonable adjustments to the process so that I may continue supporting his or her son or daughter in the venture.

If termination remains the desire of the parent, I always ask that I be given an opportunity to meet with the client a final time so that we can have proper closure. This discussion is an opportunity for me to explain to the client the parent's request to end coaching if the client is unaware of the decision, to applaud the client for the work done to date, and to let the client know that the door is always open if he or she is able and wants to return to coaching in the future. Regardless of the reason for termination, it is important for the coach to remain professional and confident throughout the process.

Wrapping Up: Completing the Coaching Process

Final session. I am pleased to share that most of the young clients I have coached over the years stayed with coaching until their goals were complete and we were mutually ready to part company. Whenever possible, I arrange for a final session to wrap up the coaching process. I provide clients with a few coaching evaluation questions to elicit information that is helpful for both me and the client.

In cases of natural completion, I build celebration into the process. Some coaches will take the client out for ice cream or a cup of coffee to celebrate or offer congratulations. I take time during our final meeting to review the client's successes and to celebrate who the client is and all that the client has already achieved and will accomplish in the future. When appropriate, I offer small parting gifts to my clients as a token of my appreciation for the opportunity to be a part of their lives. I play a supportive role and champion the client for all he or she has done. I invite the client to assess and acknowledge successes as well—to help reinforce what he or she has accomplished.

I might also ask the client how it feels to be moving on. It can be a bittersweet occasion when I watch a young adult go off on his or her own after years of coaching together—one of joy and pride with a smidgeon of sadness at the culmination of a great partnership. Some of my longtime clients feel similarly, and we take time to share our thoughts and be complete.

As mentioned, even when a request for coaching to end is initiated by the parents, who typically pay the coaching fees for the young person, I ask to schedule a wrap-up meeting with the client. If termination is due to financial reasons, I may offer a pro bono session. In the final session, I will take time with the client to review all of the success I've seen in him or her to date and I will invite the client to explore how he or she might continue to use the skills picked up in coaching. I also make a practice of wishing the client well and thanking the client for the opportunity to be his or her coach.

In the case of unplanned termination, the conversation in which termination is broached may be the last conversation between coach and client, for a variety of reasons. For example, a client may report that he or she is stopping coaching and refuse to contact the coach again. Or a case of inappropriate behavior may cause the coach or the parent to sever ties immediately, leaving no place for an additional wrap-up session. I had a parent decide in the middle of a coaching call with her daughter that we were to end our coaching at the end of that session, with no warning and no time for review of what went well or what still needed to change. The coaching plug was pulled! This is certainly not the way any professional wants to end a partnership; if there is an opportunity for even a brief goodbye and thank you, coaches are encouraged to take it.

Tying up loose ends. As coaching comes to a close, the coach will also spend some time wrapping up the logistical aspects of coaching. Because coaching is based on a contractual agreement, the coach should ensure that any outstanding contractual responsibilities are addressed and completed. For example, if the coach has agreed to provide e-mail updates to the client's teachers or therapist, the coach will complete the reports for the month and send them to the appropriate contact/s. The coach will also assess whether any money is still owed for coaching services or, conversely, whether any fees need to be refunded.

The coaching contract guides how these matters are handled, although the coach may choose to bend the contract in favor of the client in certain circumstances. For example, in my own coaching work, if the process is being terminated for financial reasons, such as a parent's job loss, or because I have a health condition and am unable to continue coaching at the time, I might refund the fees for the remainder of the month, even if the contract says no refunds are given. This decision is based on sound judgment and proper ethical conduct.

Referrals are another important part of the wrap-up process. It is helpful to have referral information handy during the final session and/or to promptly e-mail this contact information to the client. If a referral is being made in regard to a pressing issue, such as thoughts of suicide or active substance abuse, the coach should put energy toward making sure that a connection can immediately be made between the client and the new provider.

For example, the coach may call ahead to the psychiatrist to make sure the physician is currently taking on new patients before offering the referral to the client, or the coach may request that the client call the coach to confirm that a connection was indeed made with the new provider. This accountability step has the potential to motivate the client to call the referral source and provides the coach with important feedback for supporting the client as coaching comes to an end.

The coach will also take the wrap-up time to make sure that all of a client's concerns and questions have been addressed. "Is there anything you would like to share as we prepare to end coaching?" the coach might ask. "Are there any problems or concerns that you would like to discuss?" The coach attempts to help the client talk about and settle any concerns, whether financial, medical, or other.

A coach might also take this time to solicit feedback from the client. "Is there anything I could have done to make this a more satisfying experience?" the coach might ask. Coaches who are uncomfortable receiving feedback may feel hesitant to pose this question. In such cases, it can be helpful to remember that the majority of client complaints relate to unmet expectations rather than some fault or error on the part of the coach. It's also nice to know that many clients who are satisfied with the coach's services are happy to provide positive testimonials of their experience in coaching.

Final paperwork. As part of the termination process, it's also recommended that the coach send written communication to the client confirming that coaching has ended. This has the benefit of creating a written record, for legal or other reasons, that coaching was terminated and also makes sure that communication is clear between coach and client. In cases where I've initiated an unplanned termination, particularly in cases related to drug abuse or the law, I will send an official letter of termination of services. In this correspondence, I will thank the client for his or her time and inform the client that our coaching has ended as of the relevant date. I will also offer that the client may contact me if any outstanding questions exist. If money is due back to the client, I will enclose a check with the letter as well. In cases of natural completion of coaching, I will often send an informal thank you note to the client, rather than a formal letter of termination, that touches on similar issues.

Keeping the Connection Alive

The coaches I mentor and teach sometimes ask me whether it's okay to stay in touch with clients after coaching completion or termination. If so, they wonder, "What kind of contact is appropriate?" I make it a matter of practice to stay in touch with former clients, while keeping certain considerations in mind. As a general rule, I keep clients on my mailing list and send them a copy of my monthly e-mail newsletter. I also send an e-card for each former client's birthday, and if I am aware of a big milestone coming up, like a graduation, I will send a card to celebrate the occasion as well. Also, if a client has mentioned to me that he or she might want to return to coaching in the future, I will check in with that client from time to time with a brief "hello" e-mail.

Staying in touch with former clients in a measured fashion has multiple benefits. First, it gives the young clients a sense of belonging and connection. Second, it eases the transition for young people from having a constant partner to having no coaching connection at all. My statement that "the door is always open" is more credible when I occasionally pop up with a hello. And, last, parents and clients appreciate being in the loop about new books, coaching tips, or articles of interest that I might pass along to them. The main guideline I follow when keeping in touch with former clients is to ask their permission to do so at the final coaching session or shortly thereafter.

The coaches I train also sometimes wonder whether a coach will ever re-engage a client in coaching or resume work together. In my experience, this has certainly been the case. Some clients who really believe in the value of coaching will want to return at a future time when they enter a new phase of life, face a new challenge, or develop new goals. Other clients may find themselves falling off the wagon and wanting to return to coaching to brush up on their skills and improve their implementation and follow-through. By sending your clients occasional communications—by way of your newsletter, greeting cards, and so on—you are providing a natural means for the client to reach out to you for support in the future as desired.

A Note for Everyone

Parents and professionals can rest assured that coaching will not go on indefinitely. It is the responsibility of the coach to check in on coaching progress and lack thereof and to determine, with the client, the next course of action. The coach can offer the client an opportunity to scale back coaching over time, moving to less frequent sessions. In other cases, termination may be more immediate, whether because of an unplanned obstacle like substance abuse, financial constraints, or an illness on the part of the coach.

If the client or parent is the one to raise the issue of ending coaching at a time that seems unexpected or premature, coaches will also take time to have a discussion with the client or parent to clarify and come to a greater understanding of the situation. Coaches will provide the client or parent with an opportunity to explain what his or her thoughts are around ending coaching and spend some time assessing whether termination feels like the right choice right now. Sometimes, the client or parent will discover that a few tweaks to coaching will put him or her at ease and allow the coaching process to continue. Other times, the client or parent will simply reaffirm interest in ending coaching at this time.

Once it's deemed the right time for coaching to end, the coach will walk the client through the wrap-up process, addressing any client or parent concerns, soliciting feedback, and settling any contractual responsibilities. Some coaches will send out an official letter of termination or a thank you note to complete coaching. Except in cases of extreme or unacceptable behavior or mismatched personalities, most coaches will leave the door open to resume coaching with the client in the future, if desired. They may ask for permission to keep in occasional contact with the client and the parents through regular newsletters or occasional greetings for birthdays and graduations.

The process of ending the coaching relationship is as important as the initial intake. The coach and client have developed a connection, and there is value for both parties in reviewing and debriefing the successes and lessons learned through coaching. For adults, it is common in professional life to conduct surveys, complete performance reviews, and exchange feedback with others. This may be the first opportunity the young person has had to offer honest feedback to an adult and to receive feedback in return. Parents are strongly encouraged to allow for closure and for the value of the wrap-up experience in and of itself, even if that involves an extra coaching session.

E L E V E N

Building the Business Side of Coaching

Which clients give you the most energy? What drives you as a coach? Where do you envision yourself in 5, 10, or even 20 years? When it comes to designing your coaching business, the canvas is ready and waiting for you to paint. You get to decide the kind of business and clients that will fulfill you and keep you at your best. No one can tell you whom to coach or not to coach, nor can they tell you what would be the best niche/s or best clients for you. It's natural to have some nervousness about the unknown when you are first starting out, but, fears aside, starting a coaching business—or beginning to work with a new type of clientele—can be a very exciting time! As a coach, you get to choose how to create your business, which focus to select, and the kind of client base with which you'd like to work. When you go after what you want and what you enjoy, you are likely to attract the kind of clients in which you are interested. You will have energy and excitement about working with these clients, and your clients will benefit from the match as well.

This chapter covers the fundamentals of building a business for coaching young people with ADHD, from what materials are needed to get up and running to creating a vision for what kind of clients you'd like to coach and the kind of services you'd like to offer these clients. The chapter goes on to explore the variety of methods you can use to build a strong client base and is aimed at helping you think through other business-related topics, such as the importance of having a contract with the client as well as liability insurance. The chapter closes by inviting you to consider how you will continue preparing to work with young people with ADHD and sharpening your skills to be effective practitioners with this population.

Identifying Your Ideal Client Base

Let's start with the fun part—who would your ideal clients be? Although this book is designed, in part, to support readers interested in coaching young people with ADHD and you are likely reading this book because of your interest in this particular group of individuals, no assumptions need to be made. Now that you are at the end of this book, what do you think? Are you still interested in working with young people with ADHD? Sometimes the students who take my training courses discover that they actually would prefer not to coach young people with ADHD, after all. I expect that this might end up being the case for some of my readers, too.

If you do still remain interested in this kind of client base, dig a little deeper. Are you drawn to a particular subset of clients? Maybe you find yourself feeling most excited about working with gifted teenagers with ADHD, or maybe you feel most energized after coaching sessions with college students with ADHD. Perhaps, instead, you like working with student athletes who have ADHD, regardless of age; adolescents struggling with the transition from middle school to high school; or upper-class high school students preparing to go off to college. As you begin to coach young people with ADHD, you will discover that there are a number of subsets within this group and that you may be drawn to working with a particular type of client.

Here are some questions to ask yourself as you work to identify the right client base for you.

- Do you have a passion for a specific niche (or a niche within a niche)?
- What excites you about coaching a certain type of client? What sparks your interest?
- With which kind of client do you tend to develop good rapport?
- How structured or unstructured is your coaching style?
- What frustrates you?
- What drains you or brings you down when coaching?
- What energizes you when coaching?
- Which age group is your favorite?

Identifying the right client base for you may be a gradual rather than an immediate or definitive process. Take time to reflect on what feels or sounds like the right fit for you and then pay attention to how you feel when you prescreen and coach different kinds of clients. Does your stomach knot up when a parent calls regarding her son with oppositional defiant disorder? Do you feel totally drained after a coaching session with an adolescent who barely says anything? Do you feel excited and energized when you work with a young person who is highly creative? Personally, I enjoy coaching all three of the client types mentioned. However, that is a choice I made after years of both great and not so great coaching and learning to follow my intuition.

Noticing how you feel while and after working with certain kinds of clients can provide you with valuable feedback on what client type or types best fit your interests, comfort zone, and/or strengths. Remember, this is your coaching business, your career, and your life: Who you coach is up to you! When you do what you love and coach clients with whom you have a connection, clients will benefit and so will you.

What Will You Offer Your Clients?

The discernment process that you use to identify whom you would like to coach can also be used to pinpoint what kinds of services you'd like to offer to your clients. Although there are core coaching services that are essential to practicing effectively and ethically with young people with ADHD (e.g., regular coaching sessions, periodic check-ins, communication with the client's care team), there is still quite a bit of flexibility in how you deliver those services as well as how you charge for them.

Here are the common areas of service, plus what I call important practicalities to consider when forming or expanding your coaching business:

- coaching sessions
- client check-ins
- communication with client's care team
- length of coaching relationship
- fees.

Thus, questions to consider include, How often will you meet with the client? When and how will the client check in with you to report the status of action items? What role will you play in communicating with the client's other care providers? How long will you have a coaching relationship with the client? and How much will you charge for your services? Each coach will answer these questions differently.

Coaching Sessions

First and foremost, there is the actual coaching session. Practicalities to consider include where you will provide the coaching, how often coaching sessions will take place, what time of day you will schedule coaching sessions, and how long each session will last.

Coaching can take place in a variety of settings: at the coach's office, in the client's home, by phone, or even by videoconference. In the early days of my coaching, I would sometimes travel to clients' homes at the request of parents who wanted coaching to take place in the client's study area. Nowadays, I find traveling to the client's location to be a logistical challenge, and I arrange for coaching sessions to take place either in my office or over the phone.

Coaches have the right to decide which setting works best for them, and clients have the right to choose a coach who can and will meet their needs. Clients who are visual learners may choose to do coaching in person or by videoconference. Other times, prospective clients may want to meet the coach face-to-face, whether in an office or at a coffee shop, before signing on for coaching. In-person meetings can add a level of comfort for parents and adolescents who are wary of phone coaching with a stranger and can be a nice way, when feasible, for the coach to get a visual picture of the young person's readiness for coaching. For example, many of my coaching relationships begin with an in-person meeting and then switch to phone coaching after the parents and the young person feel comfortable with me. If the coach and client have different needs and the coach is unable or unwilling to alter the coaching setting to meet the client's needs, the coach can choose not to work with the client and can make a referral.

As for the frequency of coaching, the most common plan for ADHD coaching is weekly sessions. The consistency of weekly sessions is valuable to clients who need to develop new habits and routines over time. Young people needing more intense support may benefit from two sessions a week, especially when coaching is in its early stages, whereas clients who are phasing coaching out or coming back for a refresher after some time off from coaching may only need to meet once or twice a month. Frequency of coaching will depend on the needs of the young person, with you reserving the right to make a referral if the needs of the young person don't match with your schedule or your preferred type of coaching.

The standard length of each coaching session can be 30 minutes, 45 minutes, or an hour, with the typical duration being 30 minutes. More time tends to be spent at in-person meetings than over the phone, and sessions can be extended at the client's request. This choice is discussed in the coaching prescreening and intake session and is spelled out in the coaching contract.

Another consideration regarding coaching practicalities relates to the time periods during which you will schedule sessions. During the day? In the afternoons? In the evenings? On weekends? If you have a family, are you okay with coaching at the dinner hour or as late as 9 P.M.? The times that you schedule coaching sessions are up to you, and I encourage you to identify what works for you and to build your business around your comfort zone.

When you adopt specific coaching hours, it is possible that you will need to turn clients away solely on that basis, referring them to another coach instead of taking them yourself. For example, if you are only willing to conduct sessions before 3 P.M., the time when your children get home from school, you may need to decline clients who are unavailable for sessions during the daytime hours. Your particular work-schedule preferences may point you toward working with college-aged students who have daytime flexibility. Conversely, if you still have a day job and are only free at night and on weekends, you will only be able to accept clients who can participate in sessions during that particular time frame. Having a defined timeframe during which you will take clients each day or week may also mean creating a waiting list for those clients you can't squeeze into your current work schedule but who are comfortable waiting for a slot to open.

When the potential client's scheduling needs don't match up with your own, you'll need to refer the young person to another coach. This may seem undesirable when you are trying to build your business, but I am a strong believer in the value of coaches identifying what works best for them and making this a priority in how they deliver their coaching. A coach who takes care of him or herself and sets reasonable and comfortable boundaries is an engaged and effective coach, and an engaged and effective coach will make a good name for him or herself. In addition, a coach who makes referrals may also receive referrals back from other coaches as well.

Client Check-Ins

One of the big differentiators between life coaching and ADHD coaching is the frequency of check-ins between client and coach. To help young clients with ADHD accomplish their goals, you will work with clients to set up a personalized plan for them to periodically check in to let you know how things are going in between sessions and to report that action items have been completed. Check-ins may occur once a day or even more for clients who feel most comfortable with or require this degree of structure for success.

For example, some clients need intensive coaching at the beginning. They will have a weekly coaching session plus a 10-minutes-a-day check-in by phone. In this case, the check-in time is scheduled and the coach takes the call rather than letting it go to voice mail. The coach may ask, "What's your plan for today?" and then, "Is there anything that might get in the way?" Then the coach sends the client on his or her way. This kind of intensive check-in protocol might occur only during the first 2–4 weeks of coaching, while the client gets comfortable with coaching and makes a transition from having mom or dad helping to keep him or her on track through frequent check-ins to having the coach provide regular support.

The idea of frequent check-ins sometimes seems overwhelming or undesirable, but even on this issue, I encourage you to design a system that works best for you. Realize that you do not have to be at the beck and call of the client or tied to the desk, sitting and waiting for a phone call or an e-mail. In my case, I am happy to answer client e-mails throughout the day and phone messages at least three times a day; this works fine with my schedule and my approach. But other coaches prefer to set things up differently. For example, some coaches choose to

- check messages and respond to a client's e-mail or phone messages once a day at a specified time

- receive all check-ins via voice mail message or cell phone text, which limits the length of the message and reduces the number of e-mails to review each day

- review voice mail and e-mail for messages from clients at the time the client agreed to check in; this gives clients a high level of support and accountability and can be considered part of the intensive check-in protocol mentioned above.

Although you do have freedom in terms of how you set up the check-in procedure, you may need to make choices about whom to work with on the basis of a client's need for intensive coaching and check-ins. I, for one, am always very careful not to overload my schedule with too many high-maintenance clients so that I can provide the clients I do have with my full time and attention. In cases where parent check-ins are built into the coaching agreement (with client approval), I advise coaches to clearly state the frequency and duration of these check-ins. Whereas some parents simply want to inquire as to the continuation/progress of coaching, other parents provide in-depth data to the coach, which take time to read or listen to as well as to respond to.

It's a good idea for coaches to request that parents of adolescents and young adults keep the check-ins brief, as a general rule. You can also remind parents of the boundaries of the coaching relationship and the importance of confidentiality to keep everyone in sync with the parameters of coaching. When more time and information are required, you have the right to charge for additional time per the coaching contract.

Ultimately, the goal is to design the check-in system to work with both the client's needs and your own needs. For example, if you only have the time or tolerance to view client check-in e-mails once a day but the client prefers or needs to e-mail a few times a day, you can give the client free rein to e-mail whenever he or she wants while letting the client know that he or she will only get a response from you once a day. Discussing and defining the desired check-in method at the intake session and putting it into the coaching contract is a valuable way to communicate clearly with the client on what's expected of him or her and what, in turn, the client can expect from you as the coach.

Communication With the Client's Care Team

Oftentimes, young people with ADHD will have other support people besides a coach in their lives, from psychiatrists to educational specialists, from teachers and tutors to family doctors and neurologists. Although it is not your job as the coach to manage the whole care plan for the client, it is often important to have open lines of communication with one or more of these care providers or allied professionals to make for smooth transitions between types of care and to enhance the multimodal treatment plan.

As a coach, you may want to take some time to think about the degree to which you are willing to communicate with the client's care team and whether this communication is included in your standard fees. In my case, I communicate with the client's care team on an as-needed base, and I include basic, brief communication in my normal fees. This may involve an initial phone call to the client's therapist (with client permission) to let the therapist know I'll be coaching the client and to ask whether there are any important issues I should be made aware of before moving forward with coaching.

Then, as coaching progresses, if I notice the client appears as though he or she might be depressed, for example, I might call the therapist (again with client permission) to share what I am noticing and inquire about the level of support the client may need or to ask if there is any reason to put coaching on hold. Both phone calls will be brief, involving no more than 10–15 minutes of my time, and yet they will provide both parties with information important to the client's well-being. In this way, I am helping to integrate support for the client without making a burdensome investment of time.

I have had situations in which a client's family has requested that I get involved in regular care coordination. I may be asked to write up a weekly progress report and send it to the teacher; I may be asked to attend an individualized education plan meeting at a client's school; or I may be asked to check in with the psychiatrist on a monthly basis before or after a client has a med check to discuss coaching progress and pitfalls in terms of ADHD and related issues. Such requests go beyond what I consider the normal scope of care. If requests fall within the domain of services I am willing to provide, I will work with the client's family to arrange an appropriate fee schedule to cover these additional services.

Brief contact with the client's care team on an as-needed basis is not only ethical, it's helpful and appropriate. For care beyond this degree, you may choose to charge additional fees or to draw boundaries around the exact kind of support you will offer.

How Will You Charge for Your Services?

Many coaches charge a flat fee per month of coaching, which includes weekly coaching sessions and unlimited check-ins. This allows for a seamless process without the need to watch the clock and typically gives the client the support needed during the coaching process. Some coaches charge by the hour, in which case, there may be an additional fee for check-ins between coaching sessions. The fee for coaching varies by geographic location, service being provided, and years of experience. It is best to check out a few coaches' and national coaching organization websites to get a sense of the average fees.

A variety of considerations may go into the way you set up your fee structure. Do you feel most comfortable being compensated for each hour of your time, or do you prefer the simplicity that comes with a flat monthly fee? Will you offer a sliding fee scale or pro bono coaching for those without the means to pay your full fee?

I used to charge for my coaching services by the hour until I realized that it was not only cumbersome to keep track of each and every client check-in (of which there are many with ADHD coaching) but it also had a tendency to make clients' families feel as though we were constantly visiting the issue of fees and finances. As a result, I now prefer the monthly fee approach and recommend to those who charge for coaching on an hourly basis to consider charging a flat fee for check-ins. This can eliminate the hassle of having to track your time for every single check-in and avoid tingeing the coaching experience with a sense that the coach is only concerned with payment.

As for a sliding fee scale, I review each prospective client's paperwork to ascertain both the commitment to coaching and the need for a reduced monthly fee. I build in a few coaching spots for reduced-fee clients and pro bono clients, balancing out my need for an income and my desire to serve the community.

Once you identify your desired payment schedule and fee structure, you are ready to build these items into the contract. What will your monthly fee include: weekly coaching sessions and unlimited check-ins? What kind of communication will you offer to the client's care team at the standard fee? Will the client be charged for missed appointments when 24-hour cancellation notice has not been given? And so on.

By clearly spelling out your fees in the contract and defining the services covered by these fees, you will help set expectations for coaching from the start as well as create a useful guide that can be used to resolve confusion and disputes that may arise in the future. With the fee specifics documented in the contract, the coach may also find it easier to draw boundaries during coaching sessions. A coach might state, "This seems to go beyond the scope of our contract. Would you like to talk about fees for this extra service?" or "I'd be happy to correspond with you via e-mail at no charge or we can schedule a coaching call or meeting for an additional fee." You may find it easier to draw lines around your time and services when the fee structure has been clearly laid out in the contract and discussed with the client and parents during the intake session.

Length of Coaching Relationship

Last, how long will your coaching relationship with any given client last? It's probably no surprise that the answer to that question will depend on the client, but it is a very common question for parents to ask during the prescreening and intake sessions. As a general rule of thumb, coaching that runs its full course (i.e., that does not undergo unplanned termination) usually lasts a minimum of 3–6 months, but it often goes a year or longer. The decision regarding the length of the coaching relationship is made by the client and the client's family. You can provide feedback as to the progress you see being made by the client in the process to assist the client in making the decision about when to end coaching.

Must-Have Items and Managing Expenses

I talk with many coaches who are excited about the prospect of having their own business. Unfortunately, their excitement often gets the best of them, and these new coaches spend much more money getting started as coaches than they will earn during the first months, or even the first year, of coaching. One of the great benefits of being a coach is that once you are trained, you don't have to spend a lot of money. A coaching business can be started with a computer, a phone, low-cost business cards, and some basic supplies.

I recommend that new coaches start by taking on a few clients and using the fees from those clients to support their business. This may involve keeping one's day job in the early stages and accepting coaching clients at night or on weekends. Others may have a spouse or partner who can carry the finances for a while, freeing them to jump into coaching full time from the start. Situations vary. Regardless of your situation, I encourage you to reinvest your initial earnings into your coaching business, then decide on a fixed amount to pay yourself once you get on your feet.

There are specialized marketing coaches who will enroll new coaches in programs to bring business success early on. Yet, after years of coaching, mentoring, and training, I have found that it can be most effective to hire a marketing coach after you have some experience first. Working with a marketing coach too early can be overwhelming and is often cost prohibitive, not simply because of the fees paid to the coach but also as a result of the dollars spent on completing the business-building tasks assigned by the marketing coach. Thus, I recommend that you first find your passion and your niche, even a niche within a niche, while taking on some early clients. Talk with fellow coach trainees or other new coaches to gain perspective and brainstorm ideas. Once you have some money in the bank and are ready to grow, you can get a mentor coach or a marketing coach who can help you promote your coaching services. The gradual approach toward a successful coaching business is often a wise one.

The items that I consider to be must-haves for launching your coaching business are fairly low frills; in fact, you may already have some of these things in place:

- computer and basic software packages
- small backup drive and flash drives
- printer or all-in-one printer (i.e., that prints, faxes, and scans)
- office supplies

- calendar—paper or electronic
- Internet service
- phone—separate line for business use or a separate voice mailbox
- business cards
- business license
- liability insurance
- membership dues for coaching organizations and ADHD organizations
- web hosting fees and domain registration
- desk and chair for coach
- client chair.

As you can see, the essentials for getting your coaching business up and running (post-training) are not financially intensive, especially for those who already have a computer, phone line, and Internet connection.

Meeting space for those who would like to have the option of connecting with clients in person can also be added to the list, although I am a firm believer that the coach does not have to lay out any money to attain that meeting space. For example, during my first year of coaching, I used my living room to meet with clients and slowly transformed the home office space in my house into a usable client meeting space. Coaching was what I wanted to do, so I focused on the clients and not on my office furnishings or slick marketing materials. Other options for meeting space include library conference rooms, coffee shops, clients' homes, and community-center meeting rooms. As your business grows and you have more money to invest, you can consider other solutions, such as renting conference space from local businesses, sharing office space with another small company, or upgrading a space in your home to be an office with a separate entrance.

Now that you have some sense of the materials and resources required to launch your coaching business, let's look a bit closer at managing your expenses. I recommend the following four-step approach.

1. Determine how much cash you will need to start your business, using the list of must-haves as a guide.

2. Make a simple budget.

3. Keep track of your income and expenses.

4. Do what you do best in house and outsource the rest to professionals.

With the mention of managing expenses, I can hear many of the groans out there: Believe me, I understand. For some of us, the thought of keeping track of our business income and expenses seems totally unappealing. But the process doesn't have to be overly complicated or particularly arduous. Just as there is a finite list of must-have items to start a coaching business, there are also a finite number of expenses of which you will need to keep track.

When I first started coaching, I kept things simple and held costs down by listing my income and expenses in a Word document until I was ready to buy accounting software. With 5 or 10 clients, all I needed to track was mileage, costs for a business license, liability insurance, annual professional dues, business meals, postage, copies, and office supplies. I already had a computer and printer and used those for my business until I had the funds for new equipment. Trust me, it was not a hardship!

Of course, I understand that everyone has a preferred way of doing things and his or her own comfort zone. For example, you may choose to buy financial software right away, or you may hire an accountant early in the process. In fact, I advocate for coaches to identify their strengths and weaknesses so they can do what they do best and call in support elsewhere when needed. If you are not good with money, for example, I encourage you to find an accountant to help you figure out how to get your accounting system up and running. Or take advantage of online resources through SCORE ("Counselors to America's Small Business") or the Small Business Administration (SBA). Other people you might call in for additional help could be an attorney for legal consultation on your coaching contract or incorporating your business or a web designer to build a basic website.

Building a Client Base

Now that you've thought through the kind of clients you'd like to coach and the type of services you'd like to provide, the question becomes, how do you start generating clients for your desired niche or client base? Although marketing to an unknown public can seem overwhelming or daunting at first, there are many different ways to get the word out regarding the work you do, which means you have choices and can begin the process wherever it is that you feel most comfortable. Are you most at ease speaking to others one-on-one, or do you enjoy speaking in front of groups? Are you a strong writer, comfortable whipping out newsletters or op-ed pieces for the local newspapers, which can help establish your presence as an expert and drive people to your business? Perhaps you are savvy with technology and capable of driving traffic to your coaching website with search engine optimization (SEO). There are a number of ways to generate leads for your business, and I encourage you to seek out the methods for doing so that get you most excited.

Many great books and resources out there can help you build a personalized marketing plan for your business. To provide you with some ideas and inspiration, I share with you here the marketing techniques that have helped me build a thriving coaching business.

Talk, Talk, Talk: Share Your Passion!

Making small talk. One of the best ways to spread the word about what you do and to find clients is simply to talk to people. Standing in the line at the grocery store, having a cup of coffee at the neighborhood café, sitting on the sidelines at a sporting event for one of your children, or mingling at a dinner party: You never know when a parent, or a friend or relative of a parent, will be excited by the discovery that there is such a thing as a coach who helps young people, with or without ADHD, meet their goals. Did you recently read an interesting article on coaching? Have you just come back from a coach training session that taught you something new or an association meeting that inspired you? This isn't about being pushy or forcing yourself on others but talking naturally about the field of coaching and the work that you do when the occasion is right. You might be surprised at how people seem to come out of the woodwork with an interest in the idea of coaching for young people.

A second support piece to this marketing approach is to make a practice of keeping a supply of your business cards handy in your briefcase, computer bag, purse, or glove box. Some people worry that handing out business cards can seem like too much of a hard sell. Although it's true that each person will have his or her own comfort level with how and when to hand out business cards, there are almost always times when it would be nice to have a business card to share with someone. Remember, you don't always have to give out your card for professional reasons. Think of the many times each month that you meet a new person and want to exchange contact information. Sharing your information via a business card can be an easy way of letting someone else know about the work that you do.

Speak to local groups. On the topic of talking, another targeted and effective way to get the word out about your coaching business is to arrange to speak to groups and organizations relevant to your desired coaching niche. When I first got started in coaching, I spoke everywhere—for free! Social service agencies, my local Children and Adults with Attention Deficit/Hyperactivity Disorder (CHADD) chapter, parent–teacher association meetings, teacher in-service trainings, college counseling centers, student disabilities services departments, chambers of commerce, and company brown bag lunches: You name it, I spoke there. I shook hands, passed out business cards, volunteered, and did everything I possibly could do in my community to get the word out about ADHD coaching for young people. In the process, I learned of many families interested in my services and I became known to those who might refer clients to me as the ADHD coach for adolescents and young adults. Venues and outlets for potential speaking engagements include the following:

- parent support groups, including those for parents of children with ADHD or disabilities
- parent-teacher associations
- parent resource centers
- parent education advocacy training centers
- community centers
- public and private schools
- local community colleges
- colleges and universities
- churches and synagogues
- community mental health centers
- group practices—medical and mental health
- coaching organizations
- nonprofit groups—CHADD, Learning Disabilities Association of America (LDA), Attention Deficit Disorder Association (ADDA)
- business networking groups and chambers of commerce.

There are so many options here that you are limited only by your research skills and imagination. Consider talking to those you know for additional inspiration on what kinds of groups to reach out to. In the process, you may not only expand your list of potential target organizations, but you may also find someone willing to serve as a personal connection or give you an introduction to the identified group.

If you are comfortable speaking in front of groups or if you are willing to push yourself a little out of your comfort zone, speaking to organizations about topics related to ADHD and/or young people can be a wonderful way to generate client leads and get your name out into the community.

Build your own referral network. If speaking in front of a crowd gets you knocking at the knees or sends too many butterflies to your stomach, consider the incredibly valuable technique of building a referral network through conversations and one-on-one meetings. Candidates for your referral network are any of the professionals who may have clients who can benefit from youth or ADHD coaching, such as pediatricians, psychiatrists, neurologists, psychologists, therapists, teachers, school guidance counselors, school psychologists, case workers, occupational therapists, tutors, educational specialists, and advocates. And the list doesn't stop here. You can also reach out to those coaches who do not specialize in coaching young people, as well as anyone else who might be connected to prospective clients and their families, from scout leaders to sports coaches to leaders in local churches and synagogues.

By building your referral network, you will be making a targeted outreach to allied professionals by calling and visiting their offices and then scheduling phone or in-person meetings when possible. In the early days of my coaching business, I made a regular habit of visiting the offices of local professionals whom I thought might have an interest in sharing information with their clients regarding ADHD coaching for young people. I would drop by and say hello to front-desk staff and ask if I could leave my business card or flyers. I would build relationships with the staff, send letters to the professionals themselves, and then follow up by phone, at which point I would introduce myself in a friendly way, briefly describe what I do, and ask if we could schedule a 15-minute phone call so I could provide a little more information on how I might be a helpful referral for patients and clients.

"I'm wondering if you might see a value in this service for your clients?" I would ask. Some professionals declined to talk further, but many were willing and interested in giving me a little bit of their time for the sake of their clients. Through this approach, I have made lasting professional relationships, built my referral network, and helped to bring the value of ADHD coaching for youth into the mainstream. Because ADHD coaching for youth is a relatively new and burgeoning field, there are still many opportunities to build networks in local communities across the country; even as more coaches enter this field, there is room for more than one of us in each locale. It's a very exciting time to be joining the field!

If you are unsure of where to start in building your referral network, consider beginning with the professionals you already know. I can't tell you how many referrals I received in the past simply by reaching out to my son's pediatrician. The doctor knew me as my son's mom, not a stranger off the street, and was really interested in hearing more about the kind of support I was able to offer young people with ADHD. In turn, he allowed me to advertise my services in his office, and all of the pediatricians in the practice eventually became comfortable referring coaching work my way.

Who do you know right now that you could reach out to? A friend who is a school social worker? Your neighbor who is a teacher? Your family doctor, the pediatric dentist or orthodontist who goes to your church or synagogue, or your children's teachers? If you begin with those you know and then build from there, you may be surprised at how quickly you are able to cultivate your referral network and the way in which this web of contacts can drive qualified business your way.

Marketing Virtually

Although I don't believe there's any replacement for telephone conversations, face-to-face meetings, or in-person speaking engagements, the Internet can offer a nice complement to the other marketing work that you do. In this realm are any of the following:

- your own professional website
- paid professional listings on ADHD and coaching websites, such as those for CHADD, ADDA, the International Coaching Federation, the ADHD Coaches Organization, and the Institute for the Advancement of ADHD Coaching
- e-newsletters, e-zines, and blogs
- social networking through postings and comments on LinkedIn, Facebook, other people's blogs, and so on.

Websites. A basic website is a good place to start, not only to add a sense of credibility to your business, as many people these days like investigate people and businesses online before engaging their services, but also to serve as a second tier to your marketing plan. For example, you may meet someone in the waiting room of your doctor's office or while picking up kids from school who shows some interest in coaching for youth. There may not be enough time to explain what you do during your initial conversation, but by handing the person a business card with your website address on it, you provide a realistic follow-up opportunity for someone to learn about the work that you do. This also allows for some privacy and confidentiality when a person would rather move the discussion from a public place to the comfort of his or her own home. People enjoy seeing your photo and reading a short overview of your credentials, experience, and coaching style. Start small and build your site over time as you continue to define and solidify your coaching niche and your preferred client base.

Websites can cost thousands of dollars, but they don't have to. You can build a basic brochure site (simple, with only a few pages advertising your services and providing contact information) for a reasonable cost these days, whether you find an inexpensive website designer or you build the site yourself through one of many online services. As always, I recommend that new coaches use patience and care when laying out up-front funds for website marketing costs. A simple, affordable site may be all you need to create an effective web presence; over time, as your business grows, you can make revisions and upgrades to your site that match your expanding budget and clientele. For example, you may choose to hire a consultant to help you optimize the programming on your site so that web traffic naturally gets driven your way (i.e., SEO), or you may choose to place paid ads on search-engine sites or other targeted websites.

To set up your website, you will need a domain name (i.e., the words that make up your website address). Deciding which domain name will be most reflective of your coaching business and then making sure you've chosen a domain name that is not yet in use by another entity can take some time. Once again, I encourage brainstorming with colleagues, friends, and family to help move this process forward. Surf the net to review other coaching sites and to quickly cross off the names that are already taken. The basic fees for registering a domain name and setting up a web hosting account are minimal and the options are plentiful.

Blogs and E-Newsletters

Other ideas for online marketing include writing a regular blog, which you can share with your personal and professional networks to help generate readership, advertise on your business cards, and capture traffic through SEO and effective use of trackbacks and pingbacks. Blog entries are a great way to create a professional identity for yourself that helps solidify you as a potential referral source for your readers and also provides you with an opportunity to get "eyeballs" by sharing fresh content on a regular basis.

The same goes for e-newsletters and e-zines. As with websites, many services are available today with free or low-cost solutions for creating online content. Note that e-newsletters can be very simple, too. I send one out on a monthly basis and keep my comments to a simple theme with just a few paragraphs of text, plus announcements. This keeps me from spending hours upon hours crafting my message and also recognizes and respects the limited time and attention of today's busy readers.

Social Networking

A whole world of social networking is out there to be explored! Many coaches, and I include myself in this group, are just beginning to understand the ways in which these tools and forums can be leveraged to market our businesses and services. For some, building a network or a following on LinkedIn, Facebook, or Twitter is a natural fit for their style, personality, and approach. These networks and microblogging services can be a powerful way to grow one's network, build an identity in the virtual world, and maintain a presence in front of potential clients. Posting comments on other people's blogs and including a link to your website as part of your identity can drive traffic your way as well. You can also build credibility by posting a link on Facebook or LinkedIn to an online article you've written or recent newspaper coverage of your work. Or you can simply reach out to acquaintances in a friendly way by inviting them to join you as a friend or fan on a given social network. If people enjoy your posts and comments, they may invite their friends and contacts to join your social network as well.

There are many schools of thought on how best to use these social networks and platforms. If you are intrigued by the virtual possibilities here, take some time to learn more by experimenting online and reading about the social media buzz in the news. As with anything, a slow and steady approach can be one way to get your feet wet and discover whether social networking is the right marketing platform for you.

Print Media

For those of us who enjoy reading the printed page and writing for print media, the opportunity to create and publish articles and books is certainly an inviting option. The array of outlets available for getting your work into print is wide and varied, from the newspaper column and standard glossy magazine to professional association newsletters and communications. Success in the publishing arena often comes by starting locally and zeroing in on specialized outlets. Editors of the neighborhood association newsletter, the small-town newspaper, or the local CHADD or LDA chapters are often hungry for content and happy to connect your article with their local or specialized readers.

Take time (and get support if needed) to craft meaningful, well-written pieces, and you can then use these clips to build a writing portfolio that has the potential to help you land bigger assignments at more well-known or national outlets. As you read in your daily life, pay attention, too, to those columns or sections within national magazines and newspapers that seem open to average citizens who aren't journalists. These spots provide opportunities for new writers to break into bigger name publications. As with the other marketing possibilities for your coaching business, many resources are available to help you sharpen your writing skills and learn more about the publishing industry, including writing classes, books, online resources, associations, and networking groups.

Staying Connected to Former Clients

I make a regular practice of staying in touch with my former clients and clients' parents to help them feel supported after the coaching has ended and to let them know that the door is always open should they want to resume coaching in the future. This approach has the added benefit of serving as a good marketing practice as well, as it keeps my name alive in clients' minds, whether they should realize they want to return to coaching or refer my name to someone they know. Sometimes former clients decide they want to resume coaching as they move into a new life phase, or parents realize that it's time to connect one of their other children to coaching. In the process of staying in touch with former clients and their parents, I am able to show that I still remember them and care.

Follow-up strategies with former clients can come in the form of

- check-ins at milestone times—graduation, new school, birthdays
- newsletters
- notes about new offerings in your coaching
- announcements of your recent training or certification in coaching
- updates on ADHD or other topics of interest
- timely articles you'd like to share.

When you choose to stay in touch with former clients, it's essential to start by getting permission from the client to stay in touch. Also, it may sound obvious, but when building your mailing list, think about whether a particular former client really belongs on the list. Would you like to work with the client again? Did the client and client family feel satisfied with the coaching when it ended? Did you check the exit interview notes? Next, as you craft your message, bear in mind the value of not getting too personal and avoiding a tone or approach that is "salesy." Sincere efforts to stay connected to your former clients are likely to have a greater impact than will a barrage of marketing letters.

Slow and Steady Wins the Race:
Expanding Your Marketing Incrementally

As you can see, there are countless ways to market your business and to expand your client base. From speaking to groups on topics related to coaching and ADHD; to building a referral network among allied professionals in your community; to developing a web presence and generating regular online content through outlets such as blogs, newsletters, e-zines, social networking sites, and print media, the possibilities for how, when, and where to market yourself are limited only by your time and imagination. With so many choices available, you have the freedom to focus on those marketing techniques that feel most comfortable to you, fit with your knowledge and expertise, and match your budget.

Over time, as your coaching profits increase and you refine your vision of the kind of clients you'd like to serve, you can adjust and augment your marketing strategy. You can also move from a local to a regional to a national approach to get maximum return on your marketing plan and to continue to expand your client base. Although some kinds of coaching lend themselves well to a nationally based marketing campaign from the start, beginning with local outlets and then working your way up the hierarchy can be a great way to go. For example, it is often easier to break into a local marketplace, whether in the realm of writing advice columns for the community newspaper, getting air time on the local TV news, or securing a speaking audience from a local group, than it is to get time, commitments, and opportunities from national entities. When people ask me how I built my own business, I often share that I began with a lot of hard work at the local level and slowly moved to the regional and then national levels as my contacts, reputation, and expertise grew.

When designing your marketing plan, you can also select strategies that fit best with your desired target market or coaching niche. For example, if you want to coach college students, you would aim to build a referral network at colleges or maybe career centers at high schools. If you pitch articles, you'd aim to get published in outlets read by the college set. In contrast, if you'd like to work with adolescents, you would focus on building your referral network at a local level because this age group often requires in-person intakes and/or coaching and would thus need to come from the community in which you live and the surrounding areas.

Regardless of the marketing plan you put into place, take some time to think through and design your strategy. A shotgun approach of printing up a thousand glossy brochures or building an expensive website with no clear goal on what to do with these items is a potential waste of time, energy, and money. A thoughtful, low-cost approach can be incredibly effective in building your client base when applied strategically and focused to meet the needs of your desired niche.

Protecting Yourself and Your Business: Contracts, Incorporation, and Liability Insurance

Last but not least, I discuss here those less flashy and exciting aspects of running a business that are nonetheless essential to setting you up for a successful working relationship with your clients and protecting your assets—things like contracts, legal business status, and insurance.

Why Have a Contract?

When one hears talk of contracts, it's easy to make assumptions about too much legalese, stringent requirements, or binding agreements. Although the coaching contract is a legal document enforceable by law, the goal in creating a contract between the coach and the client or the client's family is not to create a situation that is potentially combative or skewed in the coach's favor. The coaching contract is designed to help set out clear expectations among all parties involved in coaching, to provide a useful document for guiding the process when questions emerge or new situations and needs arise, and to safeguard both coach and client.

The coaching contract, which is initiated and signed during the intake, clearly defines the terms to which the coach, client, and parents (if client is a minor) agree. The contract specifies the material terms that are necessary to create a legally valid agreement, such as fees per hour or month; number of hours and check-ins included in the monthly fee, if relevant; and the term of the agreement. The contract also spells out the coaching boundaries, such as confidentiality and the limits of coaching (e.g., it is not therapy).

Further, the contract outlines the conditions under which the coach might contact the parents directly. On the basis of ethical standards of the profession, these conditions should include risk-taking behavior that endangers the life of the client or others as well as urgent medical or mental-health-related issues that have not been reported to the parents by the client when requested by the coach. It is helpful, too, if the contract specifies when and how the coach should contact a client's parent if the client misses coaching sessions. Instead of leaving this decision to the coach's intuition or guesswork, the coach can refer to the contract for guidance and proceed in a manner that was agreed upon by both the client and the parent at the start of coaching. I encourage you to consult with an attorney to ensure that you have a contract that is accurate and legally binding.

Providing a clearly written coaching contract is critical to minimizing miscommunication and misunderstanding among coach, client, and parents. Remember that in your client base of young people with ADHD, it is often the case that one or both parents have ADHD and possibly coexisting conditions as well, all of which may combine to make the terms of coaching discussed during the intake difficult to remember. By providing written documentation of the agreement (i.e., the contract), you are offering an additional means of helping clients and their parents understand exactly what they are getting with coaching as well as what coaching is not.

Should You Incorporate?

Incorporation is a good means of protecting your personal assets. As a result, many coaches form a limited liability company (LLC) to protect their personal assets. I advise you to talk with other coaches, a business advisor, the SBA, SCORE, and an attorney as you determine the appropriate legal status for your coaching business and identify the necessary steps and protocols to set up such a status. Yes, you can set up an LLC on your own, but if you have questions, it's always a good idea to ask the experts first. All of this being said, please note that setting up your business as an LLC does not protect you from liability. As a result, it is advisable to carry liability insurance.

The Importance of Liability Insurance

You start a coaching business, maybe on a shoestring. Do you want to risk your personal assets? Of course not! The cost of annual group liability insurance can be paid for after one month of coaching with one client. Liability insurance is for your peace of mind, your family, and your clients, and it is a smart business decision. Need I say more?

Conclusion:
Where Will You Go From Here With Your Coaching?

The exciting world of coaching is completely open to you! With some strategic decision making, a dose of creativity and optimism, a measure of financial discipline, and some thoughtful planning, you will be well on your way to building the coaching business of your dreams. Presumably, your coaching career—or your specialization in working with young people with ADHD—will not end with your reading of this book but rather will continue to evolve into the very business you envision for yourself tomorrow, next year, even 5 or 10 years from now. I continue to remain in awe of the many coaches I see in my training classes each year and delight in watching their successes unfold as they venture into this rewarding and meaningful profession.

As you move forward in building your business, I recommend you add the following three practices to your professional arsenal:

- continue learning
- collaborate with others
- maintain a positive outlook.

Continue Learning

Although this book is intended to be a robust reference for individuals interested in becoming an ADHD coach for young people, think of it as a starting point and a useful reference for your foray into this new coaching arena rather than a be-all, end-all guide. No one book or even one training course can serve that purpose. The field of coaching, the arena of ADHD, and the domain of supporting young people are three overlapping areas that require hours of reading, observation, and hands-on practice to fully master. In my training course for ADHD coaching for youth, I have my students read numerous outside texts to supplement the work we do. When the term of the course is complete, I also invite my students to continue seeking knowledge from the world around them through continuing education courses, association publications, academic research articles, new books, and ADHD and coaching discussion boards.

Continuing to increase or maintain your knowledge base and skill set shouldn't be a bore. Instead, seek out opportunities that excite you; keep you engaged in the work that you do; and best fit your learning style, personality, and approach. Educational opportunities range from in-person seminars to online or telecourses to speaking panels and forums with other practitioners. On your learning journey, also take time to reevaluate your goals and strategies and make sure you are still heading in the direction you truly want to go. On the whole, coaching should be energizing and rewarding. If you are overly stressed or find yourself feeling bored with your work, it may be time to revamp some things or to reconsider the kind of work you are doing.

Collaborate With Others

I also strongly encourage you to reach out to others when pursuing and building your coaching business. Other people can support you as well as help you to keep perspective, move past obstacles, learn about new resources and information, and think of new ideas and strategies regarding your business.

One aspect of collaborating with others involves reaching out to peer coaches—those who are new, those who have experience, and those somewhere in between. Every coach has unique wisdom to share and an interesting perspective to offer. Find those with whom you feel most energized or excited and make staying connected a priority. Different ways to build and maintain your network of peer coaches include

- joining networks of local coaches or online groups
- setting up a regular time to have coffee or lunch with your peers
- sharing office space to decrease your alone time and reduce costs
- attending local, regional, and national workshops and conferences related to coaching and/or ADHD.

Another way to collaborate is to find your own coach. As someone who works in the field of coaching or is about to begin work as a coach, you probably understand more than most people do how valuable it can be to work in partnership with someone else to define and work toward your goals. A coach can do for you what you do for others, including help you gain clarity around your next steps for the business, your goals, and your aspirations. A coach can also support you and nudge you during times when you are unsure about taking on a new venture, whether it is a challenging speaking engagement, a new type of client, or a foray into the sometimes mysterious world of online marketing.

Maintain a Positive Outlook

Last, I encourage you to maintain a positive attitude and keep your mind open to all of the opportunities that await you. In the hard moments, try to avoid the temptation to see the glass as half empty and focus instead on all of the potential that exists for growth, success, and fulfillment in your coaching business.

Although the uncertainty of starting a new business or making inroads into a new niche of coaching can feel a bit nerve-wracking or daunting at times, I am here to tell you that there are many, many opportunities out there to connect to young people in need and to serve them well. I've seen the blossoming of many a career as new coaches whom I know envisioned the type of work they wanted to do, created a viable plan, and developed a thriving business that excites and energizes them.

Results are not always immediate and it may take time and patience to build your clientele, but rest assured that there are many, many young people out there whose lives you have the potential to touch. If you continue to be drawn to working with this particular group of individuals, stick with your plan, work your marketing strategy, take breaks, reach out to others to reenergize and stay focused, and watch as your clientele grows! You can be successful in coaching young people with ADHD!

T W E L V E

A Vision for the Future

What will your role be in supporting young people with ADHD? The canvas is blank; the sky's the limit!

Are you ready to get trained as an ADHD coach and start building your business? Do you find yourself feeling inspired to go volunteer in your child's classroom or to dedicate some time to raising awareness of coaching in the schools? Perhaps you are a medical or mental health professional who has moved from intrigue to interest and you find yourself ready to begin building a referral network of ADHD coaches that you can share with your patients. Maybe you are a parent who now understands how valuable coaching can be for young people or even your child specifically. If you have been inspired by this book or your own investigations into ADHD coaching for youth, I hope that you will take your new knowledge and excitement and invest it back into the community in a way that can create a brighter future for all young people with ADHD.

Each small action we take can multiply to make a significant difference. What begins as a mother hiring a coach for her child can turn into a referral to another parent for a coach a few months down the line, which then leads to more awareness and additional referrals, until the whole neighborhood or community is talking about and aware of the power of coaching. What starts as one doctor's decision to provide coach referrals to patients with ADHD or learning disabilities can turn into a whole practice of physicians informing their patients with ADHD of this complementary treatment. What originates as one father sharing with his son's teacher that the family has hired a coach can transform into that teacher sharing coaching referrals with the parents of students with ADHD, not just this year but in years to come.

One by one, those of us who believe in the power of ADHD coaching can reach out into the world in our own way and bring coaching to the forefront of people's minds and lives. Through small gestures, we can bring the idea of ADHD coaching into the mainstream and connect others—directly or indirectly—to this life-changing opportunity. Here are some ideas on how coaches, parents, and professionals can build on the knowledge gained in this book and continue moving forward in a way that supports young people with ADHD.

Coaches:

- Stretch yourselves and explore this exciting and rewarding coaching niche.

- Get properly trained—life coach training and ADHD-specific training are the best blend.

- Network with coaches and allied professionals to learn more, gain a support community, and open up opportunities for referrals.

- Talk, talk, talk—share your passion for coaching youth with ADHD with everyone you meet to help increase awareness and spread the word.

- Volunteer with local and national organizations focusing on improving the lives of young people with ADHD and learning disabilities to have a positive impact on the community and get the word out regarding your services.

- Join local and national coaching organizations to broaden your network and to share the joy of youth coaching with fellow coaches.

Parents:

- Ask for help. You are not alone! Resources and support are within reach.

- Practice letting go; consider the value of giving your child a support team that extends beyond you.

- Talk to others about your experiences as a parent of a young person with ADHD.

- Join a support group.

- Attend conferences and workshops on ADHD, learning disabilities, and parenting.

- Let your teen know about the powerful tool of coaching and ask if he or she would like to learn more. Discuss the concept of coaching with your teen.

- Consider becoming trained as a coach for other parents' children.

Professionals:

- Learn more about coaching and get to know the trained coaches in your community.

- Build a collaborative relationship with coaches—we are all part of the same team.

- Know when to refer out and help coaches to know when to refer to you.

- Join local organizations that support youth with ADHD and learning disabilities.

- Start a professional networking group that brings together allied professionals who share a common knowledge of and interest in ADHD.

Although this book has focused mainly on coaching for young people with ADHD and this is the area of coaching I've chosen as my life's work, I believe in the power of coaching for each and every one of us. Coaching has changed my life, allowing me to accomplish things I once would not have dreamed possible, and I have watched coaching improve the lives of many others as well. As you go out into the world, you may choose to embrace an area of coaching other than the one that was the subject of this book, or you may become a proponent of life coaching as a whole. You may choose to dedicate yourself to helping young people in some other capacity altogether. As I have discovered over the years while helping others work toward their coaching goals and in my own life's work, there are a 1,001 ways to accomplish something and just as many ways to make a positive difference in the lives of others.

What's your angle? Where does your dream lie? If you are inspired to enrich the lives of young people with ADHD through coaching, I hope you will join me in this movement to make a difference in the lives of many!

Resources

I have included a small cross-section of resources to help you on your journey. For recommended readings and additional, up-to-date resources, I invite you to visit my website, www.jstcoach.com.

ADHD Organizations

Visit these websites to find local chapters and support groups in your area and for listings of regional and national conferences.

Attention Deficit Disorder Association (ADDA)	www.add.org
Children and Adults with Attention Deficit Disorder (CHADD)	www.chadd.org
Learning Disabilities Association of America (LDA)	www.ldaamerica.org

Additional ADHD Websites

National Resource Center on AD/HD (a program of CHADD)	www.help4adhd.org
ADDitude Magazine	www.additudemag.com
ADDvance	www.addvance.com
ADD/ADHD Guide	add.about.com
ADD WareHouse	www.addwarehouse.com

Learning Disabilities

Association on Higher Education and Disability (AHEAD)	www.ahead.org
International Dyslexia Association (IDA)	www.interdys.org
Learning Disabilities Association of America (LDA)	www.ldaamerica.org
National Center for Learning Disabilities (NCLD)	www.ld.org

Gifted and Talented

Council for Exceptional Children (CEC)	www.cec.sped.org National
Association for Gifted Children (NAGC)	www.nagc.org

Advocacy

Wrightslaw	www.wrightslaw.com

Information on Coaching and Coach Certification

International Coach Federation	www.coachfederation.org
International Association of Coaching	www.certifiedcoach.org
The Coaching Commons	www.coachingcommons.org
Institute for the Advancement of AD/HD Coaching	www.adhdcoachinstitute.org
ADHD Coaches Organization	www.adhdcoaches.org
American Coaching Association	www.americoach.org

Find a Coach

International Coach Federation (not limited to ADHD)	www.coachfederation.org
American Coaching Association	www.americoach.org
Children and Adults with Attention Deficit Disorder	www.chadd.org
Attention Deficit Disorder Association	www.add.org
ADHD Coaches Organization	www.adhdcoaches.org
Institute for the Advancement of ADHD Coaching	www.adhdcoachinstitute.org
The Edge Foundation	www.edgefoundation.org
ADD Consults	www.addconsults.com
ADDitude Magazine	www.additudemag.com

Business Resources

SCORE "Counselors to America's Small Business"	www.score.org
U.S. Small Business Administration	www.sba.gov

Professional Organizers

National Association of Professional Organizers (NAPO)	www.napo.net

National Study Group on Chronic Disorganization (NSGCD)
www.nsgcd.org

References

Chapter 1

Institute for the Advancement of ADHD Coaching. (2009). Our philosophy. Retrieved January 6, 2010, from http://www.adhdcoachinstitute.org/joom2/content/blogsection/10/145/

The quote from the Institute for the Advancement of ADHD Coaching in this chapter is found in the first paragraph of the Core Competencies section on the Our Philosophy web page.

International Coach Federation. (2009). International Coach Federation website. Retrieved June 10, 2010, from http://www.coachfederation.org/

The quote from the International Coach Federation in this chapter is found in the first paragraph under the heading "What is coaching?" on the home page of the website.

Whitmore, J. (2009). *Coaching for performance: Growing human potential and performance* (4th ed.). Boston, MA: Brealey.

Whitmore's GROW model can be found on page 54 of his book.

The quote from David R. Parker, Ph.D., came from a personal communication on December 5, 2009.

Chapter 2

Helicopter parent. (n.d.). In *Wikipedia*. Retrieved June 22, 2010, http://en.wikipedia.org/wiki/Helicopter_parents

Jensen, P. S., Hinshaw, S. P., Swanson, J. M., Greenhill, L. L., Conners, C. K., Arnold, L. E., ... Wigal, T. (2001). Findings from the NIMH Multimodal Treatment Study of ADHD (MTA): Implications and applications for primary care providers. *Journal of Developmental & Behavioral Pediatrics, 22*, 60–73.

Chapter 3

American Academy of Pediatrics, Subcommittee on Attention-Deficit/Hyperactivity Disorder and Committee on Quality Improvement. (2001). Clinical practice guideline: Treatment of the school-aged child with attention-deficit/hyperactivity disorder. *Pediatrics, 108*, 1033–1044.

American Psychiatric Association. (1994). *Diagnostic and statistical manual of mental health disorders* (4th ed.). Washington, DC: Author.

Barkley, R. A. (1995). *Taking charge of ADHD: The complete authoritative guide for parents.* New York, NY: Guilford Press.

The first quote from Barkley in this chapter is found on page 105.
The second quote from Barkley in this chapter is found on page 90.

Biederman, J., Faraone, S. V., Keenan, K., Knee, D., & Tsuang, M. T. (1990). Family-genetic and psychosocial risk factors in DSM–III attention deficit disorder. *Journal of the American Academy of Child Adolescent Psychiatry, 29,* 526-533.

Brown, T. (2006). *Attention deficit disorder: The unfocused mind in children and adults.* New Haven, CT: Yale University Press.

Brown's labels for executive functioning skills can be found on page 22; the quote from Brown in this chapter can be found on page 200.

Cooper-Kahn, J., & Dietzel, L. (2008). *Late, lost, and unprepared: A parents' guide to helping children with executive functioning.* Bethesda, MD: Woodbine House.

The quote from Cooper-Kahn and Dietzel in this chapter came from page 10.

Council for Exceptional Children, Division for Learning Disabilities. (2008). *Understanding learning disabilities.* Retrieved from http://www.teachingld.org/understanding/default.htm

The quote from the Council for Exceptional Children, Division of Learning Disabilities, in this chapter is found in the fourth paragraph under the heading What are learning disabilities?

Cramond, B. (1995). *The coincidence of attention deficit hyperactivity disorder and creativity.* Retrieved from http://borntoexplore.org/adhd.htm

DuPaul, G. J., & Volpe, R. J. (2009). ADHD and learning disabilities: Research findings and clinical implications. *Current Attention Disorders Reports, 1,* 152-155.

Handleman, K. (2010). Hyperfocus [Web log message]. Retrieved from http://www.addadhdblog.com/hyperfocus/#c5f23

The quote from Handleman in this chapter is found in the fourth paragraph of the blog post.

Kaufmann, F., Kalbfleisch, M. L., & Castellanos, F. X. (2000). *Attention deficit disorders and gifted students: What do we really know?* (Monograph RM00146). Storrs, CT: University of Connecticut, National Research Center on the Gifted and Talented.

LD Online. (2008). *ADHD basics: Other disorders that sometimes accompany ADHD.* Retrieved from http://www.ldonline.org/adhdbasics/other

The quote from LD Online in this chapter comes from the first paragraph under the heading Learning disabilities.

Lorenzo, D. (2009). The unique brain: The link between ADHD and creativity is turning a problem into a gift [Web log message]. Retrieved from http://designmind.frogdesign.com/articles/motion/the-unique-brain.html

The quote from Lorenzo in this chapter appears in the eighth paragraph of the blog post.

Ma, L. (2007, March 28). ADHD: Always on the go. *Psychology Today.* Retrieved from http://www.psychologytoday.com/articles/200703/adhd-always-the-go

National Institute of Mental Health. (2009). *Attention deficit hyperactivity disorder (ADHD): Medications.* Retrieved from http://www.nimh.nih.gov/health/publications/attention-deficit-hyperactivity-disorder/medications.shtml

The quote from the National Institute of Mental Health in this chapter can be found in the first paragraph of the Medications web page.

National Institutes of Health. (2008). *Attention deficit hyperactivity disorder* (NIH Publication No. 08-3572). Retrieved from http://www.nimh.nih.gov/health/publications/attention-deficit-hyperactivity-disorder/complete-index.shtml#pub10

Neihart, M. (2004). *Gifted children with attention deficit hyperactivity disorder.* Retrieved from http://www.ldonline.org/article/Gifted_Children_with_Attention_Deficit_Hyperactivity_Disorder

Thapar, A., Harrington, R., & Mcguffin, P. (2001). Examining the comorbidity of ADHD-related behaviours and conduct problems using a twin study design. *The British Journal of Psychiatry, 179,* 224–229.

Chapter 5

Mayes, S., Calhoun, S., & Crowell, E. (2000). Learning disabilities and ADHD. Overlapping spectrum disorders. *Journal of Learning Disabilities, 33,* 417–424. doi:10.1177/002221940003300502

Whitmore, J., & Maker, J. (1985). *Intellectual giftedness among disabled persons.* Rockville, MD: Aspen Press.

Whitworth, L., Kimsey-House, K., Kimsey-House, H., & Sandahl, P. (2007). *Co-active coaching: New skills for coaching people toward success in work and life* (2nd ed.). Mountain View, CA: Davies-Black.

The quote from Whitworth, Kimsey-House, Kimsey-House, and Sandahl in this chapter is from page 207.

Chapter 6

Barkley, R. (1995). *Taking charge of ADHD*. New York, NY: Guilford Press.

Brown, T. (2005). *Attention deficit disorder*. New Haven, CT: Yale University Press.

The citation of Erikson, 1968, in this chapter comes from its citation Brown's book.

Carlson, C., & Tamm, L. (2000). Responsiveness of children with ADHD to reward and response cost: Differential impact on performance and motivation. *Journal of Consulting and Clinical Psychology, 68,* 73–83.

Dendy, C. (2006). *Teenagers with ADD and ADHD*. Bethesda, MD: Woodbine House.

Mather, N., & Goldstein, S. (2001). Behavior modification in the classroom. In N. Mather & S. Goldstein, Learning disabilities and challenging behaviors: A guide to intervention and classroom management (pp. 96–117). Baltimore, MD: Brookes. Retrieved from http://www.ldonline.org/article/6030

The quote from Mather and Goldstein in this chapter comes from paragraph 1 of the Positive reinforcement section.

Chapter 7

Murphy, K. (2005). Psychosocial treatments for ADHD in teens and adults: A practice-friendly review. *Journal of Clinical Psychology: In Session, 61,* 607–619.

Whitmore, J. (2009). *Coaching for performance: Growing human potential and performance* (4th ed.). Boston, MA: Brealey.

Whitmore's GROW model can be found on page 54 of his book.

Chapter 8

Cohen, C. (2000). *Raise your child's social IQ: Stepping stones to people skills for kids*. Silver Spring, MD: Advantage Books.

International Coach Federation. (2010). *Core competencies*. Retrieved June 22, 2010, from http://www.coachfederation.org/research-education/icf-credentials/core-competencies

Wrightslaw. (2010, February 24). *Self-advocacy.* Retrieved June 17, 2010, from http://www.wrightslaw.com/info/self.advocacy.htm

The quote from Wrightslaw in this chapter came from the first paragraph of the web page.

About the Author

Jodi Sleeper-Triplett, Master Certified Coach and Senior Certified ADHD Coach, is the founder of the movement for ADHD coaching for youth and has been working with young people for nearly 35 years. As cofounder of the Institute for the Advancement of ADHD Coaching and director of coach training for the Edge Foundation, Sleeper-Triplett is seen by many of her peers as the foremost expert in the field of ADHD coaching for youth.

Through hours of hands-on coaching, Sleeper-Triplett has developed a unique and powerful system for coaching youth with ADHD, from working directly with the young person rather than the parent, to coaching the whole child rather than focusing only on academics, to using the personal coaching agreement—an extensive tool for accountability praised by clients, parents, and coaches alike. Sleeper-Triplett's approach is captured in her popular training course for individuals interested in coaching young people with ADHD, the only International Coach Federation–accredited program of its kind.

From the time she began her work in 1975 at the Walter E. Fernald State School in Waltham, Massachusetts, Sleeper-Triplett has worked tirelessly to support the needs and advocate for the rights of children with ADHD, learning disabilities, and developmental disabilities. She is a long-standing volunteer for Children and Adults With ADHD (CHADD) at the national, regional, and local levels.

Sleeper-Triplett completed her coach training with the Coaches Training Institute, Success Unlimited Network, and the American Coaching Association and graduated from the unique BDIC (Bachelors Degree With Individual Concentration) Program at the University of Massachusetts, Amherst, with a B.A. in human services/mental health. She has professional memberships with CHADD, the Attention Deficit Disorder Association, the Learning Disabilities Association of America, the International Coach Federation, the ADHD Coaches Organization, the Institute for the Advancement of AD/HD Coaching, and the American Counseling Association. She resides in Northern Virginia with her husband and son.

Index